Conflict, Community, in Late Imperial Sichu

Exploring local practices of dispute resolution and laying bare the routine role of violence in the late-Qing dynasty, *Conflict, Community, and the State in Late Imperial Sichuan* demonstrates the significance of everyday violence in ordering, disciplining, and building communities.

The book examines over 350 legal cases that comprise the "cases of unnatural death" archival file from 1890 to 1900 in Ba County, Sichuan province. The archive presents an untidy array of death, including homicides, suicides, and found bodies. An analysis of the muddled and often petty disputes found in these records reveals the existence of a local system of authority that disciplined and maintained daily life. Often relying on violence, this local justice system occasionally intersected with the state's justice system, but was not dependent on it. This study demonstrates the importance of informal, local authority to our understanding of justice in the late Qing era.

Providing a non-elite perspective on Qing power, law, justice, and the role of the state, this book will be of great interest to students and scholars of Chinese and Asian history, as well as legal history and comparative studies of violence.

Quinn Javers is Assistant Professor of History at the University of California, Davis.

Routledge Studies in the Modern History of Asia

For a full list of available titles, please visit: https://www.routledge.com/
Routledge-Studies-in-the-Modern-History-of-Asia/book-series/
MODHISTASIA

Conflict, Community, and the State in Late Imperial Sichuan
Making Local Justice

Quinn Javers

Routledge
Taylor & Francis Group

LONDON AND NEW YORK

First published 2019
by Routledge
2 Park Square, Milton Park, Abingdon, Oxon OX14 4RN

and by Routledge
52 Vanderbilt Avenue, New York, NY 10017

First issued in paperback 2020

Routledge is an imprint of the Taylor & Francis Group, an informa business

British Library Cataloguing-in-Publication Data
A catalogue record for this book is available from the British Library

Library of Congress Cataloging-in-Publication Data
A catalog record has been requested for this book

ISBN 13: 978-0-367-66089-5 (pbk)
ISBN 13: 978-0-367-14080-9 (hbk)

Typeset in Times New Roman
by codeMantra

For Sophie, of course

Contents

List of maps and figures

Maps

Figures

Acknowledgments

I have racked up many debts over many years, and I thank everyone for their help and apologize for remaining errors. Foremost among these debts is to Matt Sommer, who encouraged me into, through, and out of graduate school. His intelligence and kindness are a rare gift. Kären Wigen was inspirational, and I benefited deeply from Christian Henriot's many visits to Northern California. Philip Thai and Dan Asen intervened at a crucial moment in the project, and I am deeply grateful for their help.

At UC Davis, I have been fortunate to work on a campus filled with generous colleagues and friends. Ian Campbell, Marian Schlotterbeck, and Matthew Vernon made my first years here much more fun. Beverly Bossler has been a wonderful senior colleague, and would I also thank David Biale, Corrie Decker, Ed Dickinson, Greg Downs, Katie Harris, Sally McKee, Kathy Olmsted, Rachel St. John, and Louie Warren for their support.

Many others have commented on my work along the way, and I thank Chiu Pengsheng, Joe Esherick, Andrea Goldman, Bryna Goodman, Gail Hershatter, Chris Isett, Melissa Macauley, Brad Reed, Janet Theiss, and Matti Zelin for their comments. I would also like to thank Wes Cheney and Maura Dykstra for conversation and camaraderie.

In Sichuan, I thank Li Zan and Zhao Weini at Sichuan University Law School for being such wonderful hosts, guides, and mentors. Also at Sichuan University, I thank Zhou Haifeng and Ning Kai for all their help. I also thank the staff at the Sichuan Provincial Archive. The owners of the now-defunct *yibin ranmian* shop behind the archive have my best wishes and deep thanks.

The years spent researching and writing this project were supported by a number of institutions, including Stanford's Weter Dissertation Fellowships, a Mellon Dissertation Fellowship from the Stanford Humanities Center, Fulbright IIE fellowship, and a Dissertation Grant in Chinese Studies from Freeman Spogli Institute for International Studies at Stanford. I would also like to thank the Stanford University's Center for East Asian Studies at Stanford for a number of small grants as well as for Department of Education Foreign Language and Area Studies fellowships. A Taiwan Ministry of Education fellowship as well as a small scholarship from National

Taiwan University's International Chinese Language Program helped fund a fruitful year in Taiwan.

My thanks also to Stephanie Rogers and Georgina Bishop at Routledge. Parts of this manuscript appeared as "The Logic of Lies: False Accusation and Legal Culture in Late Imperial Sichuan," *Late Imperial China*, 35, no. 2 (December 2014): 27–55.

Further thanks go to Alex Bay, Stephen Whiteman, Pierre Fuller, Josh Chin, and David Winning.

Finally, I would like to thank my family, particularly Ron and Eileen Javers, as well as Mick and Joanne Pateman, for their love and support. My two boys, Cullen and Cormac, are a complete joy. The boundless pleasure of their company made this book much harder to complete, but I didn't mind. To Sophie, what can I say: I remain "looped in the loops of her hair." Always.

Note on conversions and conventions

Length: 10 *fen* = 1 *cun*; 10 *cun* = 1 *chi* (12.5 inches)
Capacity: 10 *ge* = *sheng* (32 fl oz); 10 *sheng* = 1 *dou*; 10 *dou* = 1 *shi/dan*
Weight: 16 *liang* = 1 *jin* (20.9 oz); 120 *jin* = 1 *dan/shi*
Area and Distance: 1 *mu* = 1/6 acre; 1 *li* = 1/3 mile

Monetary units: 1 *liang* = 1 "tael," a unit of silver currency used in large transactions; 1 *wen* = 1 "cash," a unit of currency in copper coin (the nominal exchange rate was 1 tael = 1,000 cash, but the actual market rate in nineteenth-century Sichuan varied from 800–1,800 cash); and 1 *chuan* = 1 "string" of cash conventionally = 1,000 cash, although the actual number of coins per string varied in practice.

Qing documents rarely mention women by their given names and instead identify woman by her husband's surname followed by her surname followed by the term *shi*. So, Liu Mou Shi is Mrs. Liu née Mou.

During the Qing, age was counted in *sui*. An individual was one *sui* at birth and aged a *sui* every year at New Year. The difference between *sui* and Western "years old" was one to two years.

Introduction

In 1896, Zhou Ma Shi, aged 50 *sui*, reported that her son, Zhou Xuexiang (aged 18 *sui*), had killed himself by ingesting a lethal amount of opium after being raped.[1] Ma Shi explained that Zhou, an apprentice in the cotton trade, had returned home to change his clothes and then had headed out with a group of friends. In her testimony to the Ba County court, she chronicled her son's final hours out with three men. One of the men, Zeng Hengqing, had recognized Zhou as "naïve and young" and "forced" him to get drunk. Zhou, who was so inebriated that the others had to help him walk, then went with his companions to the opium bar of Zeng's employer to smoke opium.[2] That night, while he was sleeping off the effects of his indulgences, Zhou was raped and robbed by Zeng Hengqing. The next day, awakening from his stupor, Zhou ate a lethal dose of opium and killed himself. The legal case that followed his death fit Zhou into a larger social world that existed among non-elites in Ba County and provides insight into persistently local contours of authority and their interactions with state power.

Community leaders described how the opium bar's owner, He Hou Shi, erected a series of sheds and shacks in a temporary encampment outside the city walls as part of a seasonal migration among Chongqing's poor.[3] When the rivers' waters were low, vast mudflats were exposed and large shanty-towns sprouted annually as the city's poor migrated into this seasonal real estate. When the waters rose, these settlements migrated to a high-water "campground," and this was where Hou Shi had located her opium bar. This mean and temporary settlement was a known center of vice and economic opportunity, sustaining its own marginal population of petty urbanites and rural transplants: the barber who shaved heads in the camp; Zhou himself, coming to drink and be merry; opium bars and their customers; and myriad other figures populated this muddy world. This short description in the legal record conjures a world of people, relationships, meanings, and power, dragging the reader down to the muddy banks of the river.

The shifting assemblages of power laid bare in the case's mixture of sexuality, work, play, family, and state authority reveal the sweaty reality of life in the late-Qing dynasty (1644–1912), and are the focus of this book. In particular, acts of everyday violence and the court cases that followed them expose social tensions, the workings of local power, and the role of the state in local life. Rather than focusing on a single aspect of local power – lineage, family, economy, state power – this book takes these several key forms of authority and considers them jointly to construct a composite picture of conflict and resolution that was the local process of justice making. By adopting an almost ethnographic approach to the past, I recover the social and moral landscapes of local life in the late-Qing period, particularly for non-elites, and chart the contours of everyday justice as it was negotiated in local communities and in the courts. Indeed, much of the local justice system was generated by the complex interplay of these two sites.

This study focuses on the over 350 legal cases that comprise the "cases of unnatural death" [*ming'an*] file from 1890 to 1900 in the Ba County, Sichuan province, archives.[4] This file presents an untidy array of death, including homicides, suicides, found bodies, and other corpses requiring explanation. The muddled and often petty disputes found in this file grant access to aspects of life – and particularly those of non-elites – that are otherwise difficult to see. Indeed, local legal cases, as opposed to those at the central level, tend to exhibit a messiness that is often lost at higher levels. The bureaucracy shaped cases to conform to institutional expectations and interests. The formal order that seems to exist in Beijing's records is absent at the local level.

Instead, the local legal record makes clear the existence of a local system of authority that disciplined and maintained life for the majority of people in Ba County. This local justice system, which often relied on violence, occasionally intersected with the state's justice system but was not dependent on it. Indeed, the self-regulating power of the local system worked even when the state did not. Consequently, an exclusive focus on the state's justice system, as represented by the county court, misses the fundamental power of informal, local authority. Many people in the late-Qing period would never meet an agent of the state. Instead, their lives were lived in the thrall of a local system of authority and power.

Philip Huang has characterized Qing rule as "centralized minimalism," meaning that the state and its agents accepted the key role the unofficial and local authorities played while delivering the state's demands.[5] Yet, this insight continues to view local power from the perspective of the state. My study inverts this view and considers it from the generative sites of power in county-level communities. Power was not simply granted by the state, but actively constructed at the local level. The particular structures of local authority were produced at the local level. Huang's understanding of Qing authority is powerful, yet it still places too much emphasis on state-directed efforts.

Even his "third realm" of politics, where formal and informal authority met and negotiated dispute settlements, puts the state, and particularly the country magistrate, in command.[6] This book argues that locals were central players in the construction of local authority, and that these efforts were made by a diverse range of individuals, and not simply local elites.[7] Power was largely constructed and contested outside state authority, and even when the state engaged in local disputes, it did so only after the conflict had been shaped by local politics and on the basis of local informants and understandings. In Ba County, the state and its authority were another avenue for the pursuit of local politics. This was true even in cases beyond "minor matters" [*xishi*], including acts of grave violence. Consequently, the scope of local politics, the arena for locals to direct dispute resolution, was much larger than has been previously considered. This book, in turn, explores the strategies late-Qing subjects deployed to achieve favorable outcomes in conflicts with others, and focuses on the control of information, competing venues for the pursuit justice, kinship networks and justice, and the economy and justice.

Norms and expectations had to be asserted (sometimes with deception) and fought over (sometimes violently).[8] Consequently, local justice was a political project that involved conflict, and often violence. These clashes were not simply debates concerning abstract principles, but were conflicts over specific everyday problems, and, in this study, frequently involved a dead body. Each incident had a local context and a particular potential for justice. The blood-and-sweat assertions of justice detailed in this study expose the politics of justice in local communities, and the thoughtful use of state authority to reach these ends. I argue that justice was fundamentally a *practice* rather than a *system*, and it had to be made again and again.

As this book takes justice as a central theme, I will spend a moment on definitions. "Justice" is the purview of both law and philosophy, and what John Rawls has called the "first virtue of social institutions."[9] This book largely leaves philosophy aside and pursues Rawls' assertion of the centrality of the social to the concept. In Ba County, justice was not fixed to either law or philosophy (though both addressed it). Instead, justice was an essentially contested virtue, made and remade in each conflict by appeal to law, philosophy, and custom (a lived philosophy not written by scholars alone but by members of communities as well). "Making justice" refers to this process (not the result), and stresses the work required to produce an outcome. "Community justice" was made by locals alone (I consider this "rough justice" if violence was used), while "local justice" refers to outcomes produced in the county, often by the interaction of the state and community.

In the end, I argue that justice making was a form of everyday politics that saw individuals mobilize resources (human, cultural, institutional, economic) to further their goals. The local justice system was constantly contested and ceaselessly under construction. These struggles all employed forms of everyday politics, which "involves people embracing, complying with, adjusting, and contesting norms and rules regarding authority over, production of, or allocation of resources and doing so in quiet, mundane, and subtle expressions and acts that are rarely organized or direct."[10] Michael Szonyi has argued that for Ming subjects, the dynamic relationship between the state and its subjects was constantly reformed as individuals sought to further their interests.[11] This is equally true for the late-Qing subjects, and I examine these contestations by exploring the making of local justice.

The centrality of non-elites is key to my understanding of these processes. Many scholars have noted the power of local elites, but this study furthers the scope of local authority to consider the essential ways in which non-elites participated in the production of "social institutions." They worked in creative and adaptive ways to achieve their ends. In my conception, justice functioned across categories. Formal/informal, high/low, official/unofficial were all permeated with claims of justice. This reveals a shifting sphere of authority that bound society together and gave peoples' actions meanings.

Everyday politics tried to reconcile competing visions of order from diverse sources of power. The examination of justice produced by these interaction forces us to abandon simple notions of state and society and to envision a locally embedded and deeply social Qing state, and forms of local state authority that were mediated through various socially contested expressions of power. The magistrate had his orders from above, but he also needed to reproduce his (and the bureaucracy's) standing through local interventions and extractions. As he attempted to walk this narrow path, the magistrate was confronted by powerful forms of local authority, the local elite, who worked to further their own interest and power. My study focuses on a third, key actor in this churning admixture of authority: the petty commoners who came into conflict and sought to exploit all these forms of authority to further their particular interests, whether it was control over land, others, or cultural prestige. These three sets of various actors constituted the system of local power, yet they were all trapped within it as well. I use *justice making* to delineate the process through which these manifold needs were ordered, validated, and empowered through expressions of official and unofficial power. Through this process, communities were built.

Given the multiple forms of authority present in local communities, the expressions of order and power found in everyday conflicts differentiated and individualized unique claims to particular forms of justice even as they drew on shared social scripts to make these demands. Consequently, the fundamental modes of ruling power were not systematically challenged. Indeed, these conflicts often worked to reinforce extant forms of power at work in Qing society. The Qing state, even at the end of the dynasty, functioned as a key local arbiter of authority. This was not a flat, shared system of power, and the state could indeed be dominant if it chose to be so. In the main, however, the magistrate was hesitant to overturn local expressions of justice when they were presented in a unified voice. However, when locals' understanding of the social meaning of a particular conflict was mixed, the state was much more likely to intervene. Despite this dominant hand, locals' control over information – local knowledge – could shape the interventionist impulses of the state. The state acted on the basis of local intelligence, which was never disinterested or objective.

Two final terms require introduction. First, throughout this work I use "local truth" to describe locals' attempts to interpret the meaning of a conflict through shared norms and values.[12] This was often a contest of competing understandings of events and their significance. Frequently, local authorities – kin, landowners, security heads, and others – used the weight of their local power to produce a generally accepted, community-based rendering of the dispute, which was presented in court as "what happened." Clearly, other members of the community could resist this assertation, and individuals used the county court to do so, but dominant forms of local authority were quite powerful in this construction of local reality.

Second, and following from my notion of local truth, I use "legal truth" to consider the magistrate's own construction of an authoritative interpretation of the conflict. In this project, he routinely built on the local truth brought into court by community informants, and, in this way, official justice was deeply shaped at the outset by local truths. Bradly Reed has considered the magistrate's construction of a "judicial truth," noting that he was manufacturing "a narrative that set forth a single judicially relevant truth in such a way as to make the linkage between event, statute, and punishment transparent, seamless, and irrefutable."[13] In my conception, legal truth focuses on the interplay of the state and the society, while Reed's concern is primarily between the magistrate and the superior bureaucracy. Although related, these two truths stress different moments in the legal process and focus on separate fields of authority. The magistrate could not pass judicial truth on to his superiors until he had first created legal truth, which had already been deeply shaped by local truth.[14]

This local system of authority that rested on the interplay of state, local, and non-elite participation would outlive the Qing. The demise of the imperial state did not undo local justice making, which lived on in a complex and negotiated interplay of state, elite, and local interest and authority. As the Qing empire struggled toward collapse, this local system endured, and, indeed, outlived the imperial system. James Scott notes that in periods of "collapse," more durable, elementary units endure.[15] The local justice system in Ba County was such a unit. Indeed, multiple Chinese states, down to today's People's Republic of China, have contested local systems of authority. Yet, despite these successive tides of state exertion, local life has remained resistant.

The local setting

By the 1890s, Sichuan and Ba County in particular were heavily populated and well integrated into the broader economy. Two related trends deeply shaped Ba County. First, the agricultural economy was transformed over the course of the Qing. By the eighteenth century, the province's booming population and attendant economic changes were working to drive down average land holdings. This agricultural pressure was acute in Sichuan, considering the amount of land given over to opium production, with the province eventually becoming the Qing's largest producer of the drug. This alteration in rural production had more than just economic consequences.

For example, ingesting opium became the leading form of suicide by the late nineteenth century. Moreover, the intense filling-in of the population after the considerable bloodshed during the Ming-Qing transition brought abundant social conflict to the region.[16] These two trends, alterations in the peasant economy and social pressures stemming from population growth, are central to the Qing's nineteenth century.

At the same time, Ba County is key because it fell outside the direct orbit of Western colonization and its attendant legal, social, and economic ruptures. Although Chongqing was opened as a treaty port in 1891, the city had a limited foreign presence.[17] In particular, the city's lack of regular, direct steamship service until 1908 further impeded Western encroachments. This arms-length engagement with Western powers positions Ba County as a leading site to consider the Qing's interior.

Ba County is hilly and lush, and the rivers, the Yangzi and Jialing, play major roles in locals' lives. Madeline Zelin has described a strict division between the county seat, Chongqing, and its hinterlands in the nineteenth century, with the former being dominated by extra-provincial guilds and the latter characterized by widespread peasant poverty and tight control exercised by landlords who squeezed the peasants as much as they could.[18] The county was a major producer of dry grains, including wheat, barley, and corn, as well as cash crops such as cotton and hemp, in addition to the widespread trade in opium and salt. Zelin argues that a pattern of widespread rural poverty and limited commercial development was not broken until Chongqing was opened as a treaty port in 1891.[19] Her stark depiction of rural life is echoed in Wei Yingtao's calculation that, due to steady population growth, by 1875, the amount of arable land per person had fallen to just 1.7 *mu*, far below the 4 *mu* that was the minimum required for a sustainable livelihood.[20] All of these factors contributed to social conflict in the county.

The county seat, Chongqing, is situated along an east-west trade route that led through Wuhan and onward down the Yangzi.[21] The network flourished, and by the early nineteenth century, the county court listed 109 extra provincial native-place associations and merchant guilds.[22] In the second half of the nineteenth century, commerce – especially of salt, opium, and foreign goods – continued to expand along this riparian road.[23] The opium trade in particular repositioned Sichuan within the empire's economy and secured the rivers' vital centrality to this trade. By 1900, the drug accounted for almost half of Sichuan's exports to other provinces, and by 1906, the province produced 40 percent of the empire's total supply.[24] The state's engagement with the riverine economy can be seen in its incorporation and expansion of the so-called "Red Boats" [*hongchuan*], a system of lifeboats that patrolled sections of the river. The Red Boats were an innovation first backed by local elites, but the lifeboats were soon taken over by the state, and then expanded to secure the growing trade on the river.[25]

Lifted by trade, by 1900, Ba County had an estimated population of 990,474.[26] The population of Chongqing alone is difficult to determine earlier than the late nineteenth century, but an increase in the city's wards [*fang*] from 8 to 29 between the Ming and mid-Kangxi period suggests sustained growth.[27] The earliest population figures available are from 1824 when the population was thought to be 65,286 people in 17,750 households. In 1897, the US consulate in the city estimated the population had reached 250,000–300,000.[28] Yingtao Wei, however, has suggested a slightly more conservative estimate of only 214,000 by 1900.[29] The city continued to grow rapidly, with the Municipal Police Department estimating Chongqing's 1937 population at 475,968.[30] In the period covered by my study, Chongqing was a fairly large and dynamic city.[31]

Beyond the sheer number of people living in Chongqing, its geography limited the city's options for growth and resulted in the cramped living conditions that characterized the city. Situated on a neck of land between the Yangzi and Jialing rivers, an expanding Chongqing had nowhere to go. The narrow streets were 5–15-feet wide, while the business streets ranged from 8 to 20 feet in width.[32] This, along with the city's rocky and hilly disposition, gave the city a unique feel: "probably few other cities in China have been so densely built over."[33] One can imagine the crush of humanity on Chongqing's spit of land. This density resulted in a narrow warren of streets:

> many so-called streets were only slits between high walls; often a street was nothing more than a narrow flight of stone steps, many of them cut from the living rock. On these confined thoroughfares the open shop fronts displayed every sort of activity and occupation.[34]

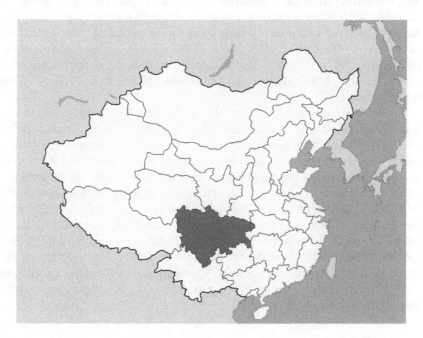

Map 0.1 Sichuan province in the Qing dynasty.

The city was further divided into the Lower City and Upper City, roughly along the ridge that bisected the city. The Upper settlement, where much of the modernizing would occur in the 1920s, was dominated by the well-to-do people. The Lower City, in contrast, was packed with tenements along with a crush of temples, warehouses, shops, and a busy waterfront. Seasonal fluctuations in the water levels of the rivers offered the poor additional space at times. In the winter, when water levels were at their lowest, many of the most desperate would construct temporary houses on the exposed riverbed. They had to be on guard for the spring runoff, which could appear suddenly and claim the lives of those not quick enough to abandon these meager homes. These were the settings for the conflicts that populate this study – city and countryside.

The local state and local powers

This study deploys a specific and limited vision of the state that I call "the local state." This concept is a useful corrective to overly broad visions of the state that fail to capture its diverse expressions across the empire as well as the embedded nature of its authority in a particular locale. Simply put, there was no unitary Qing state. Instead, there were many competing forms of state authority. An image of a monolithic state simply reproduces the state's own imagined position, and is better replaced with a vision of the state as constituted by a series of actors, sometimes working together and sometimes at odds, that moves through various processes while interacting with other local power holders. From this perspective, the vastness of the Qing bureaucracy falls away and is replaced with a local set of concerns. The local state was not autonomous – it still had to answer to its superiors – but it was also driven by smaller, more contingent concerns that may have clashed with the stated policies and ideology of the imperial center.

The local state was strongest in the county seat, Chongqing, which was a site of administrative control and home to the Ba County court, administered by the country magistrate. This position was officially recognized as an "important post" [*yaoque*] by the central government, and the county qualified for three of the four criteria used to rate counties throughout the empire: "frequented" [*chong*], a center of communication and commerce; "difficult" [*fan*], with a great deal of official business; and "troublesome" [*nan*], with a violent and crime-prone population.[35] The city was also home to the Chongqing Prefect and the East Sichuan Circuit intendant. These two superior courts, housed next door to the Ba County magistrate, ensured an added degree of oversight. Consequently, only experienced officials were appointed as magistrate, a position officially held by nine men during the period of this study.[36]

Even as the county magistrate represented the local state, his authority was shaped by both the multiple demands of superior state officials (governors and governors-general, for example) and local non-state authorities (such as lineage heads and wealthy landowners). As Joel Migdal has suggested:

> While state leaders may seek to represent themselves as distinct from society and as standing above it, the state is, in fact, yet another organization in society. And, as one organization among many, it is subject to the pushes and pulls in society's arenas that can change the line between it and other social forces.[37]

The local state was made as the magistrate navigated these forces, as he worked to enact his own understanding of his obligations. He could be quite powerful, but his authority was limited by his knowledge of local happenings, his other responsibilities, the interventions of other authorities, and the active manipulation of those seeking to bend his power to their own causes. More, the local state's penetration into the countryside was not uniform. Indeed, imperial power was a patchwork laid over the Sichuan countryside.[38] In Ba County, the Qing was held together locally by the matrix of power formed by the intersection of state and informal local authority. A map illustrating actual state power cannot be drawn with neat, straight lines. Instead, this map would bend and twist with the social and physical contours of the landscape, and the strength of local authority. A view from the totalizing heights of Beijing erases the uneven presence of the state and the particularistic expression of state power in the actual landscape.

"Local powers" formed a sea of counter-authority that surrounded, interacted with, and helped to shape the local state. Indeed, local life in the Qing was organized around several often-overlapping systems of power. The forms of local control have been a steady theme in the study of Chinese history, but just as the local state suggests the complexity of local state authority, unofficial local power was also quite complex. Earlier conceptions of local power in the historiography stressed the divide between the state and the local elites who controlled land and the gentry, and were connected to the state through participation in the civil service exams.[39] These men and their families played a central role in local life, often taking up work that now falls to modern states, such as dispute resolution and tax collection. These families could also organize themselves into corporate structures, or lineages, which sought to maintain their position and navigate state authority.[40]

In addition to gentry and lineage authority, various religious organizations played key roles in local life. Beyond orthodox religious authorities, various associational communities created forms of authority that were based on shared faith, which could also cut against state and family power, and occasionally erupted into mass outbreaks of anti-dynastic violence.[41] Religion was a powerful tool in the construction of local identity, both through specific local cults and through intra-village religious performances.[42] These forms of voluntary association and authority were mirrored in a range of mutual aid practices that ranged from simple brotherhood associations up through full-formed secret societies.[43]

Broadly, these forces constitute what Prasenjit Duara has called the "cultural nexus of power," in which popular culture, expressed through religious groups, merchant organizations, and cultural and symbolic structures, came together to legitimate Qing authority through the late nineteenth century.[44] To Duara's organizational perspective, this study adds the legal system, and the broader legal culture that surrounded it, to our conception of local authority. As I consider social conflict and its resolution, this book drags the analysis of the law out of the courtroom and into local communities to explore local forms of justice and their relationships with state authority.

I reorient our perspective on law away from the magistrate and toward the locals who populated the legal system. Consequently, this work places the courtroom within the larger context of dispute resolution practices available in late-Qing society and draws thick connections between an active local state and the myriad communities it oversaw. My study joins a body of work that explores the social life of the law.[45] Within this scholarship, this study focuses on county-level legal cases to make clear the daily work of the courtroom rather than its institutional and ideological imperatives. These cases also allow historians to view the attempts, cunning and otherwise, by individuals to bring state power to bear on their conflicts. From this perspective, the process is much more untidy and opaque, and authority less unidirectional and concentrated.

This story is not simply one of local resistance to state authority. Indeed, locals sought to draw state power into the conflicts in communities as much as they sometimes attempted to resist expanded state authority. Individuals exploited the institutions, ideals, and ideologies of the state to further their own ends. The relationship between the state and society was not statically oppositional. Instead, while there were acts of "rightful resistance," in the main, practices of conflict resolution expose the workings of unofficial systems of power and their interactions with state authority.[46] The *ming'an* cases make clear both the limits to state authority and expanded opportunities for state engagement in local communities. The myriad quotidian and catastrophic conflicts found in the county records demonstrate that the local state was deeply imbricated in the needs, wants, and desires of local communities. On the eve of dynastic collapse, the people of Ba County came into conflict over many things, often money and family. In this Qing twilight, how was local justice made, and who made it?

Everyday violence

Although it is a well-studied phenomenon in late imperial China, most studies of violence in the Qing have focused on episodic occurrences and have passed over everyday violence, such as homicide, assault, and suicide.[47] William Rowe has described "a local culture that was persistently and systematically violent" in central China.[48] Ba County had its own "culture of violence," where it worked to enforce debts, protect land, and police sexuality.[49] Everyday violence was an in-group tool that actively constructed and maintained local communities by reaffirming connections and responsibilities. It split communities apart and, perhaps more importantly, sutured them together by strengthening connections between individuals. Violence was often an opportunity as well as a tragedy. Loss could be converted to gain through dispute-resolution processes – dead bodies had value. Family members called on those responsible for the death of a relative and demanded compensation. Their claims exposed the ongoing relationships between the two parties, and, at times, also worked as form of extortion, drawing connections where none existed.

Interpersonal violence usually occurred within the confines of normal, archetypal relationships. The late-Qing paranoia of roving gangs of rootless young men unsettling peaceful communities was largely out of touch with local reality. There were, of course, anonymous murders. An unknown man was found hacked to death.[50] A nameless thief was beaten to death.[51] And there was a shadow reservoir of unreported deaths, many of which might have fit the above profile. However, for legal cases to develop, reported deaths required someone in the community to care about the corpse. Without this, it could be just another body by the road. Consequently, the acts of violence found in the *ming'an* file demonstrate the work violence did within local communities.

While court cases tended to overrepresent violence and the role of the state, I focus on practices at work in the larger communities that can be seen in the backgrounds of these cases – ongoing brawling, didactic violence, and so forth – and the various social structures visible in these moments of crisis, and not just the violent act that was the cause of adjudication. The disruptive quality of violence forces into stark relief the common understandings that animated everyday life that often remain unspoken in the historical record.[52] As the magistrate brought various locals to court to explain dead bodies, these men and women, in their testimonies, articulated local visions of order, as well as quotidian forms of daily life. Violence also generated paperwork at court and consequently produced fine-grained details of life where the everyday can be found in the exceptional. Violence exposed the local face of power. In these acts, the tensions within family, lineage, and local community, and with the state, appear.

Legal cases

Legal records present historians with a vast opportunity to consider life in the Qing. In these documents, the illiterate, non-elite enter the record as individuals to make their case, explain their lives, and defend themselves. This is one of the strengths of legal records, and the Ba County collection held in the Sichuan Provincial Archives is the largest and most complete historical record of any Qing dynasty county in China outside Beijing.[53] Madeline Zelin and Philip Huang first introduced these resources to Western scholars in the 1980s, and a number of scholarly works based on them have since been published.[54]

The county [*xian*]-level government office [*yamen*] was the court of first instance in the Qing judiciary. County-level case files typically include plaints and counter-plaints, magistrates' responses, summons and warrants, runners' reports, coroners' reports, transcripts of court hearings, contracts, and other documents submitted by litigants, as well as magistrates' final decisions. Legal records do not offer direct access to the late-Qing subject. While testimony was recorded using the first-person voice, a scribe massaged commoners' speech into formal testimony.[55] Legal cases offer a wealth of insight into the pitfalls and possibilities of life under the Qing during the nineteenth century.

More broadly, the Qing legal system as a whole was formally governed by the *Great Qing Code* [*Da Qing lü li*].[56] The Qing Code's official priorities were protecting status and gender divisions along Confucian lines, and clearly defining the crime so as to leave little room for independent action or misinterpretation by the magistrate.[57] The Code was brought to life by the state agents who carried out its vision of order, with the local magistrate as the primary local enforcer of law. The local magistrate was kept in check by a robust system of review and appeal in which local cases of a more serious nature were continually kicked up to a higher authority for evaluation. In death penalty cases, the emperor himself would theoretically review the evidence before making the ultimate decision. This system of oversight ensured that the local magistrate pursued with vigor cases that would be reviewed by his superiors as a matter of course. This was coupled with a performance-based system of reward and punishment: a magistrate's record was reviewed each year by his superiors, and he was awarded merits or demerits affecting his career prospects based on his performance.

Despite the clear importance of maintaining law and order, magistrates faced enormous obstacles in carrying out this mandate. Classically educated magistrates were often adrift in the particularities of the vast Qing Code, and law enforcement was only one of many assignments that troubled the magistrate. Further, the rule of avoidance, under which a magistrate could not serve in his home province, ensured that magistrates frequently could not speak or understand the local dialect, and were often ignorant of local conditions. Many magistrates were unwilling to spend the time required in developing an understanding of the law, and consequently relied on private secretaries for legal expertise.[58]

This dependence in the court was mirrored by the magistrate's dependence on his runners outside of the court. This essential but much-maligned segment of local government has often been negatively portrayed by historians who have uncritically absorbed the biases of their official sources.[59] Bradly Reed's work rejects these excoriations of "yamen vermin" [*yadu*], and sees them as essential rather than parasitic, moving away from the ideals of local administration into actual practice. In doing so, Reed finds that

> although they operated outside of the statutory system, and often in direct violation of the legal code, yamen clerks and runners exhibited a remarkably consistent degree of organization and rationalization in the form of internally formulated and regulated rules and procedures.[60]

These runners were tasked with the detection and apprehension of suspected criminals, as well as with parts of the criminal investigation and ensuring security for the yamen and in the surrounding community. The magistrate also relied on a local "coroner" [*wuzuo*] to examine corpses.[61]

The aforementioned system describes only the formal, official system of justice, an arrangement that was paralleled by an informal system in which local elites, religious leaders, lineage elders, guild leaders, and others took the lead in dispute resolution and the production of justice. All subjects in the provinces of China proper were supposed to be further organized into *baojia* units of mutual security and surveillance. This system, which was frequently in disarray and often the subject of reformers' exhortations, was based on household registration records. While the *baojia* scheme may have needed propping up, even the system's notional existence suggests the state's ideal of outsourced local rule.[62]

Most scholarship on Chinese legal history focuses on the eighteenth century, the period of the Qing's supposed golden age. By considering the nineteenth century, this study captures legal and social realities beyond this imagined zenith. The problems and potentials of the Qing legal system are not confined to the eighteenth century. My snapshot of local life on the eve of collapse complicates declensionist narratives, as I find the system still engaged and working to produce local justice. Further, a focus on the 1890s also complements the existing scholarship on late-Qing and early-Republican governance, much of which is focused on the late-Qing "new policies" (*xinzheng*) that began to unravel the old order.[63] My study examines the final moments before these momentous changes. Indeed, this period can be seen as an inflection point between these two bodies of scholarship. The 1890s sits between the high point and dynastic collapse, and just before the renunciation and disassembly of the old legal order.

The records of this entire system present historians with overwhelming possibilities for studying the Qing. Yet, while county-level court records provide insight into local life and legal practice, their fragmentary nature often frustrates the interested historian. Many of the case files are unfinished, ending abruptly and without conclusion. Frequently, the magistrate's decision (if there was one) is lost, and the same case reappears in multiple, non-consecutive files. Pages are sometimes torn diagonally in half, or there is a hole in a crucial section. The fractured nature of the archive is reproduced in many of my narratives. I cannot always say who did it, or what the punishment was. Often, there is no beginning, middle, and end. Sometimes it is all middle!

Yet, the fragmentary legal narratives make clear the state's partial view (and understanding) of the world beyond its courtroom. The local archive demonstrates the gap between the state's formal authority and the complex world that its subjects inhabited. The archive is a testament to a process of simplification that rendered local realities legible to the state. The Qing's shaping of this abridged reality in part obscures the vast domain of local justice that regulated most people in the late-Qing period.

An overview

The rest of this book is organized to slowly move the reader out of the courtroom and into the county. Chapter 1 begins, as does the archive, in the county courtroom, and considers how local conflicts made their way into the formal legal system and demonstrates the enduring role locals had in shaping the information that the court used as the basis of its decisions. More broadly, this chapter describes how locals engaged with state power and sought to bend it to their justice claims. In particular, individuals attempted to control the information that made its way to the magistrate. Two forms of information presented to the county court – false accusations and "vernacular" maps drawn by litigants – expose the sophisticated strategies the Qing subjects employed to advance their interests in court. False accusations often granted individuals access to state authority in cases that might otherwise not attract the magistrate's attention. And litigants used vernacular maps to present argumentative depictions of local realities.

Chapter 2 attempts to leave the courtroom behind to examine forms of everyday justice outside the courtroom – local justice forged without state intervention. Indeed, most justice in the Qing was of this extra-judicial type. This chapter examines two forms of rough justice: kidnapping (or private detainment) and violence surrounding sexual impropriety. The chapter concludes with a consideration of the importance of *simultaneity* for our understanding of conflict and community in the late-Qing period. Disputes emerged from local communities, and, once in front of the magistrate, many of these clashes continued to play out at the local level. Together, Chapters 1 and 2 describe the interactions between state and local justice, charting the interplay between these two forms of authority.

Chapters 3 and 4 consider two key areas for the production of local justice, family matters and economic exchanges, to expose the workings of local authority. Specifically, Chapter 3 explores the family as a force in the making of local justice. Kinship networks were a form of oversight that surveilled social relations and could make demands, both locally and in court, for justice. This power is visible when natal families reached across and made demands on their married daughters and their new families, clamoring for justice and restitution for the mistreatment of their kin. Sojourning or otherwise distant family members could use the power of the local state to demand justice for their dead kin.

Chapter 4 considers economic conflicts and the production of local justice. In these clashes, local norms policed market transactions and enforced social expectations for fair treatment. Informal power shaped these transactions, bending market logic to local needs. Moreover, the local state's intervention in these disputes demonstrates the magistrate's support for this local reasoning. The scope of the local justice system included the market, and subsumed these exchanges within the larger social dynamics that shaped relationships.

Woven through these brief reports from local life are a series of key relationships, those found in local communities, between individuals and the Qing state, within kinship networks, and those forged in economic exchange. This study focuses on these relationships to examine disputes and their resolutions – the making of local justice – in a single county at the end of the Qing dynasty. Justice was largely made by locals, as communities disciplined themselves first, and only later considered state intervention. In this way, the late-Qing local state remained engaged on the ground. Yet, the state's involvement was predicated on an invitation from locals to intervene. State power, in the form of the local magistrate, was yet another tool to resolve conflict, and was often used simultaneously with available local systems. The state was reactive, while individuals, including non-elites, were active, strategic manipulators of state authority and power. Chapter 1 takes up this issue, and considers specific strategies individuals deployed to shape the magistrate's justice.

Notes

1 *Baxian Dang'an* [BXDA] 7881, *Sichuan sheng dang'an, Chengdu* [Ba County Archive, file 7881, Sichuan Provincial Archive, Chengdu].
2 "Opium den" as a translation for *yanguan*, although widely used, is loaded with associations of a "sick" China and Oriental squalor, and it fails to accurately portray opium and its use in the Qing. It is perhaps best to think of an "opium bar." Although one can safely assume that people are consuming alcohol at a bar, the term is value-neutral in that it encompasses a wide range of establishments. While there are dank, seedy bars, there are also expensive, chic bars. "Bar" implies the activity occurring in the establishment, but does not suggest

the character of the patrons. For these reasons, I have translated *yanguan* as "opium bar."

3 I use the term "community leaders" generically to refer to the shifting amalgam of local authorities who spoke to the court. These could include lineage leaders, village headmen, as well as the heads of local security and tax organizations.

4 As the broader context of this project, I also examined several hundred Ba County cases from other periods of Qing rule, central-level cases, and cases from Nanbu (Sichuan), Danshui/Xinzhu (Taiwan), and Baodi (part of the capital prefecture of Shuntian) counties.

5 Philip Huang, "Centralized Minimalism: Semiformal Governance by Quasi Officials and Dispute Resolution in China," *Modern China* 34, no. 1 (2008): 24–25.

6 Philip Huang, "Public Sphere/Civil Society in China? The Third Realm between State and Society," *Modern China* 19, no. 2 (April 1993): 216–240. Symposium: "Public Sphere/Civil Society" in China? Paradigmatic Issues in Chinese Studies.

7 Di Wang makes a related point in his study of the *paoge* and this secret brotherhood's informal power in Sichuan during the early twentieth century. In fact, the non-elite forms of local authority wielded by the *paoge* have clear resonances with my understanding of local authority. Di Wang, *Violence and Order on the Chengdu Plain* (Stanford: Stanford University Press, 2018), 93.

8 I'd like to thank Chris Isett for this formulation.

9 John Rawls, *A Theory of Justice, revised edition* (Cambridge: The Belknap Press of Harvard University Press, 1999), 3.

10 Benedict Kerkvliet, "Everyday Politics in Peasant Societies (and ours)," *The Journal of Peasant Studies* 36, no. 1 (2009): 232.

11 Michael Szonyi, *The Art of Being Governed* (Princeton: Princeton University Press, 2017), 245.

12 In thinking about these two terms, I follow Mark Granovetter's distinction that "'values' are broader concepts about what the good life and good society consist of, from which the more specific and situationally oriented norms may, in principle, be inferred." Mark Granovetter, *Society and Economy: Framework and Principles* (Cambridge: The Belknap Press of Harvard University Press, 2017), 27.

13 Bradly Reed, "Bureaucracy and Judicial Truth in Qing Dynasty Homicide Cases," *Late Imperial China* 39, no. 1 (2018): 79.

14 Reed correctly notes that Qing court did not recognize a distinction between absolute and adjudicated truth. Ibid., 78.

15 James C. Scott, *Against the Grain: A Deep History of the Earliest States* (New Haven: Yale University Press, 2017), 187.

16 Perhaps the majority of the province's population died in this cataclysm, leaving only about one million inhabitants in the province by 1680, with most of these living on the harsh and unproductive periphery. In response to this cataclysm, the newly sovereign Qing actively promoted the resettlement of Sichuan with incentives in the form of tax benefits, land, and even oxen – a course of action that not only helped to stabilize the province but also served to release pressures in more densely populated regions. Sichuan's population may have fully recovered by the 1730s, bringing increased stability to the region and the Qing as well as broadening the new dynasty's tax base. By the end of the eighteenth century, the pressures facing the province had reversed. No longer underpopulated and able to serve as a release for pressures in other parts of the empire, Sichuan itself began to experience intense demands for land as well as concomitant social stresses. As the frontier began to close and even less desirable land was settled, weak administrative control and a growing population without skills or farmland led to a dramatic increase in salt smuggling, counterfeiting, and banditry. For a description of these changes, see Robert Eric Entenmann,

"Migration and Settlement in Sichuan, 1644–1796" (PhD Dissertation, Harvard University, 1982).

17 Chongqing was opened to foreign residence and trade incrementally from the late nineteenth century into the early twentieth.

18 Madeline Zelin, "The Rights of Tenants in Mid-Qing Sichuan: A Study of Land Related Lawsuits in the Baxian Archives," *Journal of Asian Studies* 45, no. 3 (May 1986).

19 Ibid.

20 Yingtao Wei, *Jindai Chongqing chengshi shi* [*Modern Urban History of Chongqing*] (Chengdu: Sichuan daxue chubanshe, 1991), 397.

21 The name Chongqing dates to 1188 CE during the Song, but the first references to the region reach back to around 2200 BCE and Chongqing would eventually, around 375 BCE, become part of the Kingdom of Ba. During the Ming (1368–1644) and again in the early Qing, the city walls were rebuilt and extended. The city walls had taken their final form, more or less, by 1760–1761. For a general history of Chongqing, see Wei, *Jindai Chongqing chengshi shi*. Also see, Maura Dykstra, *Complicated Matters: Commercial Dispute Resolution in Qing Chongqing from 1750 to 1911* (PhD Dissertation, UCLA 2014), 2–72.

22 Wei, *Jindai Chongqing chengshi shi*, 409.

23 Chongqing's prominence in the late nineteenth century came at the expense of Chengdu, the provincial capital. More than simply competing centers of political, economic, and cultural power, these cities also represented central nodes in different trade and transport networks. Chengdu was part of a north-south axis along the imperial highway that extended through Xi'an all the way to Beijing. For histories of Chengdu, see Kristin Stapleton's *Civilizing Chengdu: Chinese Urban Reform, 1895–1937* (Cambridge: Harvard University Asia Center, 2000) and Di Wang's *Street Culture in Chengdu: Public Space, Urban Commoners and Local Politics, 1870–1930* (Stanford: Stanford University Press, 2003).

24 The growing dominance of opium and the importance of export trade resulted in increased government oversight, particularly as the drug became a key tax base for the provincial government. The state's position regarding the substance changed over time. The Qing's resistance to opium was severely weakened by the series of "unequal treaties" imposed by Western imperialists, which legalized the importation of opium. Once this barrier to the international trade was removed, the Qing had less interest in suppressing domestic production, and by 1859, Sichuan provincial authorities leveled taxes on the drug. Consequently, between 1859 and the Qing's 1906 edict prohibiting opium, it played a major economic, social and political role in the province. Chongqing in particular benefited from opium's growth, as it was the upstream center of this export economy. Judith Wyman, "Opium and the State in Late Imperial Sichuan," in *Opium Regimes: China, Britain, and Japan, 1839–1952*, eds. Timothy Brook and Bob Tadashi Wakabayahi (Berkeley: University of California Press, 2000), 213–214, and Xiaoxiong Li, *Poppies and Politics in China: Sichuan Province, 1840s to 1940s* (Newark: University of Delaware Press, 2009), 28.

25 Igor Iwo Chabrowski, *Singing the River: Sichuan Boatmen and Their Work Songs, 1880s–1930s* (Leiden: Brill, 2015), 65–66.

26 Di Wang, *"Chengshi renkou yu chengshi jingji, shehui zuzhi* [Urban Population and the City's Economic and Social Organization]", in *Chongqing Chengshi Yanjiu* [Studies of Urban History of Chongqing], ed. Yingtao Wei (Chengdu: Sichuan Daxue chubanshe, 1989), 319. Yingtao Wei, however, puts the population at only 904,100. Wei, *Jindai Chongqing Chengshi shi*, 395.

27 Mary Lee McIsaac, *The Limits of Chinese Nationalism: Workers in Wartime Chongqing, 1937–1945* (PhD Thesis, Yale University, 1994), 32.

28 United States. *Dispatches from the US Consulate in Chungking, 1896–1906*. The consulate opened on July 1, 1896, but closed on March 20, 1901 due to the

outbreak of the Boxer Uprising, and reopened in early 1905. This, not surprisingly, produced many gaps in the US government records.

29 Wei, *Jindai Chongqing Chengshi shi*, 396.

30 He Yaozu, *Chongqing yaolan* (Chongqing, 1945), 19.

31 For comparison, according to William Rowe, Hankow's population in 1890 could have been 800,000, and Lu Hanchao puts all of Shanghai County's population in the mid-nineteenth century at 540,000, though this would rise incredibly quickly. William Rowe, *Hankow: Commerce and Society in a Chinese City, 1796–1889* (Stanford: Stanford University Press, 1984), 40; Lu Hanchao, *Beyond the Neon Lights: Everyday Shanghai in the Early Twentieth Century* (Berkeley: University of California Press, 1999), 26.

32 Later, as part of the city's modernization drive, the select streets were widened to 40–60 feet and were equipped with sidewalks as well as topped by electric and telephone cables. These changes also saw traditional stores that opened directly onto the street replaced by "modern" ones close to the street, though "open-faced" shops prevailed on the smaller streets. J.E. Spencer, "Changing Chungking: The Rebuilding of an Old China City," *Geographical Review* 29, no. 1 (1939): 56–57.

33 China. *Imperial Maritime Customs, I. Statistical Series: no. 6. Decennial Reports on the Trade, Industries, etc. of the Ports Open to Foreign Commerce, and on Conditions and the Development of the Treaty Port Provinces, 1882–1891*, 109.

34 Grace Service, *Golden Inches: The China Memoir of Grace Service* (Berkeley: University of California Press, 1989), 35.

35 The remaining criterion that Ba County did not carry was that of "wearisome" [*pi*], which indicated a large amount of overdue taxes. Xun Zhou, *Shu Hai Cong Tan* (Wenhai chubanshe, 1966), 82.

36 *Baxian zhi minguo* [Ba County Gazetteer, Republican Period], reprinted in *Zhongguo Difangzhi Jicheng: Sichuan Fu Xian Zhi Ji* [Compendium of China's Local Gazetteers: Volume for Sichuan's Prefectures and Counties] (Chengdu: Bashu shushe, 1992), 231.

37 Joel Migdal, *State in Society: Studying How States and Societies Transform and Constitute One Another* (Cambridge: Cambridge University Press, 2001), 128.

38 In a somewhat parallel fashion, Lauren Benton has argued that European empires "did not cover spaces evenly but composed a fabric that was full of holes, stitched together out of pieces, a tangle of strings." Lauren Benton, *A Search for Sovereignty: Law and Geography in European Empires, 1400–1900* (Cambridge: Cambridge University Press, 2009), 2.

39 For classic scholarship on the gentry, see, Philip Kuhn, *Rebellion and Its Enemies in Late Imperial China: Militarization and Social Structure, 1796–1864* (Cambridge: Harvard University Press, 1970); Chung-li Chang, *The Chinese Gentry* (Seattle: University of Washington Press, 1955); T'ung-tsu Ch'u, *Local Government in China Under the Ch'ing* (Cambridge: The Council on East Asian Studies, Harvard University, 1988); Ping-ti Ho, *The Ladder of Success in Imperial China: Aspects of Social Mobility, 1868–1911* (New York: Columbia University Press, 1962); Kung-chüan Hsiao, *Rural China: Imperial Control in the Nineteenth Century* (Seattle: University of Washington Press, 1960).

40 See, David Faure, *Emperor and Ancestor: State and Lineage in South China* (Stanford: Stanford University Press, 2004); and Michael Szonyi, *Practicing Kinship: Lineage and Descent in Late Imperial China* (Stanford: Stanford University Press, 2002).

41 For an example of this tradition, see Susan Naquin, *Millenarian Rebellion in China: The Eight Trigrams Uprising of 1813* (New Haven: Yale University Press, 1992).

42 For the former, see Eugenio Menegon, *Ancestors, Virgins, and Friars: Christianity as a Local Religion in Late Imperial China* (Cambridge: Harvard University Asia Center, 2009), and for the latter, see David Johnson, *Spectacle and Sacrifice: The Ritual Foundations of Village Life* (Cambridge: Harvard University Asia Center, 2009).

43 For general practices, see David Ownby, *Brotherhoods and Secret Societies in Early and Mid-Qing China* (Stanford: Stanford University Press, 1996), and for a Sichuan-specific expression, see Wang's *Violence and Order.*

44 Prasenjit Duara, *Culture, Power, and the State: Rural North China, 1900–1942* (Stanford: Stanford University Press, 1988), 1–6.

45 For examples, see Melissa Macauley, *Social Power and Legal Culture: Litigation Masters in Late Imperial China* (Stanford: Stanford University Press, 1998); Bradly Reed, *Talons and Teeth: County Clerks and Runners in the Qing Dynasty* (Stanford: Stanford University Press, 2000); Tom Buoye, *Manslaughter, Markets, and Moral Economy: Violent Disputes over Property Rights in Eighteenth-Century China* (Cambridge: Cambridge University Press, 2000); Janet Theiss, *Disgraceful Matters: The Politics of Chastity in Eighteenth-Century China* (Berkeley: University of California Press, 2004); Matthew H. Sommer, *Polyandry and Wife-Selling in Qing Dynasty China* (Berkeley: University of California Press, 2014).

46 I borrow "rightful resistance" from Kevin O'Brian's work on contemporary disputes in China. O'Brian uses the term to describe citizens' appeals to shared, official norms and morality to press their demands. See Kevin O'Brian, *Rightful Resistance in Rural China* (Cambridge: Cambridge University Press, 2006); and Neil Diamant, Stanley Lubman, and Kevin O'Brian, eds., *Engaging the Law in China: State, Society, and Possibilities for Justice* (Stanford: Stanford University Press, 2005).

47 For studies of these forms of violence, see Elizabeth Perry, *Rebels and Revolutionaries in North China, 1845–1945* (Stanford: Stanford University Press, 1980); Joseph Esherick, *Origins of the Boxer Uprising* (Berkeley: University of California Press, 1987); Tobie Meyer-Fong, *What Remains: Coming to Terms with Civil War in 19th Century China* (Stanford: Stanford University Press, 2013).

48 William Rowe, *Crimson Rain: Seven Centuries of Violence in a Chinese County* (Stanford: Stanford University Press, 2007), 326.

49 Ibid., 2–11.

50 BXDA 7649.

51 BXDA 7880.

52 As EP. Thompson writes: "one way to discover unspoken norms is often to examine the *un*typical episode or situation." EP. Thompson, "History and Anthropology," in *Making History: Writings on History and Culture* (New York: New Press, 1994), 205.

53 These records were largely forgotten after they were moved to a temple outside Ya'an to escape Japanese bombing during the Pacific War. While the archive was rediscovered in 1953 and moved to Sichuan University, work on the collection's 113,000 files [*juan*] did not begin in earnest until the 1980s. Catalogued according to dynastic reign period, the Ba County materials are further subdivided into six sections: administration, economy, military, culture and education, foreign relations, and law. This last category, law, is by far the largest, with over 99,600 files comprising roughly 88 percent of the archive's entire collection. While the archive's holdings for earlier reign periods are relatively fragmentary, records from the nineteenth century are substantially more complete. For a general introduction to the archive, see Ma Xiaobin and Liu Jun, "*Sichuan Qingdai dang'an pingshu*," in *Sichuan Qingdai dang'an yanjiu* [The Study of Qing Archives in Sichuan], ed. Li Shigen (Chengdu: Xinan jiaotong daxue, 2004), 23–34; and

Yasuhiko Karasawa, Matthew Harvey Sommer, and Bradly Ward Reed, "Qing County Archives in Sichuan: An Update from the Field," *Late Imperial China* 26, no. 2 (2005): 114–128.

54 See Zelin, "The Rights of Tenants in Mid-Qing Sichuan" and Philip Huang, *Civil Justice in China: Representation and Practice in the Qing* (Stanford: Stanford University Press, 1998). For other examples of scholarship employing Ba County legal cases, see Mark Allee, "The Status of Contracts in Nineteenth-Century Chinese Court," in *Contracts and Property in Early Modern China*, eds. Madeline Zelin, Jonathan K. Ocko, and Robert Gardella (Stanford: Stanford University Press, 2004); Matthew H. Sommer, *Sex, Law and Society in Late Imperial China* (Stanford: Stanford University Press, 2000); and Reed, *Talons and Teeth*.

55 An exception to this mediation can be found in cases of "fighting words." In these cases, cursing or other provocative speech was seen as leading directly to violence, so language itself was of central importance to the court and one finds direct transcription of local (and often colorful) language.

56 The Qing Code owes much to the Ming Code, which was carried over almost in its entirety, as well as to earlier iterations of dynastic law. The Code is composed of statutes [*lü*] and sub-statutes [*li*]. While the former were infrequently amended or abolished, the sub-statutes continued to evolve and instruct the magistrate in the administering of justice. The seeming consistency in the statutes has given past observers a false sense of an unchanging code; the sub-statutes reveal the dynamism of the system.

57 The second theme is a result of Legalist philosophy's interest in developing a universal system free from the corrupting influence of personal interest and connections. Derk Bodde and Clarence Morris, *Law in Imperial China: Exemplified by 190 Ch'ing Dynasty Cases (Translated from the Hsing-an Hui-lan), With Historical, Social, and Juridical Commentaries* (Cambridge: Harvard University Press, 1967), 23.

58 See Li Chen, "Legal Specialists and Judicial Administration in Late Imperial China, 1651–1911," *Late Imperial China* 33, no. 1 (2012): 1–54.

59 For examples of this, see Tongzu Qu, *Local Government in China under the Ch'ing* (Cambridge: Harvard University Press, 1988) and John Watt, *The District Magistrate in Late Imperial China* (New York: Columbia University Press, 1972).

60 Reed, 5.

61 For more on medical examiners, see Dan Asen, *Death in Beijing: Murder and Forensic Science in Republican China* (Cambridge: Cambridge University Press, 2016).

62 For more on this system see, Qu, *Local Government*, 150. For Ba County's system of collective responsibility, see Dykstra, *Complicated Matters*, 80–93.

63 For example, Xiaoqun Xue, *Trial of Modernity: Judicial Reform in Early Twentieth-Century China, 1901–1937* (Stanford: Stanford University Press, 2008); and Asen, *Death in Beijing*.

Part I
Practices of conflict

1 False accusation and vernacular maps

Local tools for shaping justice

In Ba County, justice did not simply emanate from the court into the county. Indeed, as locals exerted influence on the state, they bent this authority to their needs. Local power could even extend into the courtroom, and, as locals engaged the state's authority, they deployed various strategies to bend that power to their ends. In particular, when navigating state power, individuals attempted to control the information that made its way to the magistrate. By doing so, locals profoundly shaped the reality that was presented to the sojourning official in order to direct the outcome of the state's intervention. They attempted to use local truths to fabricate legal truths. Rather than simply reacting to state power, these stratagems lay bare the very real ways in which locals – including the poor – drove disputation even as it entered the court. While moving from informal processes of dispute resolution to the courtroom altered the possibilities for a successful outcome, individuals continued to be key participants in the legal process. Locals brought their everyday politics and local truths into court, and continued contributing to the making of justice.

Two forms of information presented to the county court, false accusations and maps drawn by litigants, expose the sophisticated strategies Qing subjects employed to advance their interests in court, as well as the limits local intelligence could impose on the county court. The joint consideration of these two techniques highlights the driving role that members of local communities played in drawing state authority into their disputes, and stresses the enduring influence Qing subjects had on the making of justice.

The first of these techniques, false accusation [*wugao*], provided access to state authority, and the legal record is rife with this practice.[1] In particular, with false accusations of homicide, a seemingly daring act in which the litigant formally risked her or his life, individuals resorted to bold and potentially dangerous accusations to further their claims, suggesting that locals had a reasonable expectation that their falsehoods would succeed in gaining the magistrate's ear without provoking severe punishment.[2] Strikingly, a wide range of individuals engaged in this behavior, including the rural poor.

A second strategy to influence state authority was the use of maps. These were often drawn by litigants themselves, yet even when sketched by court clerks, they relied on local information, and must be seen as expressions of local power. I call these disputative depictions of local realities "vernacular maps" in order to stress local and narrow goals of these cartographic projects, as opposed to those drafted by the central state. Vernacular maps are clear depictions of the shaping hand of local influence on state power, and make clear the enduring presence of everyday politics in the court.

Profiting from death: false accusation as legal strategy

Common people used false accusation to force the court to consider disputes it might have otherwise ignored. In many instances, individuals deployed explicitly illegal means to bring their grievances to court. Not only did the court *not* punish these transgressions, the magistrate commonly ruled on the underlying conflict, frequently economic, that was the root of the dispute. These cases demonstrate the degree to which ordinary people were able to work the system by exploiting illegal but common strategies of deception. These practices are especially surprising given the formal risks of lying at court.[3] The Qing Code states:

> In the case of anyone who falsely accuses another of an offense punishable with strokes of the light bamboo, sentence him to the penalty of the offense of which he falsely accused [the other], increased by two degrees. If the penalty is exile, penal servitude, or strokes of the heavy bamboo (regardless of whether it has been executed and the accused has gone to the place of punishment or not), add three degrees to the penalty for the offense falsely complained of. Each penalty is limited to 100 strokes of the heavy bamboo and exile to 930 miles. (Do not increase to the extent of strangulation.)[4]

Yet, despite the threat of these punishments, false accusation constituted a common legal strategy deployed by a range of litigants.

By design, the court was not interested in hearing petty economic disputes. Philosophically, litigation was seen as a sign of poor governance and unruliness. And practically, late-Qing magistrates were overwhelmed with legal cases.[5] A false accusation of homicide, however, provided entry into the court as a site of mediation. Consequently, locals resorted to formally dangerous tactics to pursue their interests. False accusations of murder posed an even risker proposition for their tellers since homicide was a capital crime and the Code mandated even more severe penalties for these falsehoods: "If the offense which was the subject of the false accusation is punishable with death, and the sentence has already been executed (then, according to whether the original law imposes strangulation or beheading), sentence [the accuser] to death."[6] With these claims, individuals legally put their lives on the line. Yet, individuals continued to resort to this tactic.

As a consequence, these legal strategies reveal a broader legal culture surrounding the court, and evoke a social world in which legal knowledge was generally present or at least widely available for purchase.[7] Moreover, this legal culture was broadly dispersed both geographically and in terms of social standing. Rural residents, for example, are well represented in the following cases. With both "litigation masters" [*songshi*] selling their talents and inns catering to petitioners, the concentration of legal knowledge and culture would have been densest near the court. However, that peasants from as far away as 43 miles brought their claims to Chongqing suggests that legal culture was not the exclusive domain of the county seat. Moreover, the geographic pervasiveness of this legal culture was mirrored in the range of social classes engaged in legal combat. It may have been true in the nineteenth century (as it is today) that the rich and powerful had greater access to legal remedies. Yet, the host of lowly tenant farmers and barbers in the legal records shows that the manipulation of the legal system was not beyond their imagination or reach.

In many of these legal cases, the goal of the false accusation was financial gain. Death could be an unexpected opportunity for an economic windfall.[8] By agitating at court, many litigants hoped to secure a payoff from the death of a relative. In other instances, plaintiffs used the death of a relative to draw the court into ongoing contractual disputes, and we see the magistrate arbitrating the underlying dispute even after the false accusation has been exposed. At the very end of the nineteenth century, individuals in Ba County still wanted the state's authority brought to bear on their conflicts, and found ways to compel this intervention. One such individual was the tenant farmer Chen Bingtang.

In a plaint filed in 1895, Chen, 38 *sui*, described how he had fallen behind on his rent, in part, due to flooding.[9] As a result of the disaster, he wanted his rent deposit returned. There was no accusation of violence in this initial plaint – this was a tenancy dispute pure and simple. In 1894, Chen had sublet land from Wang Fengshan, but flooding wiped out his crop, leaving him in debt. Chen filed a plaint stating:

> This summer at flood season the water rose. The seedlings were wiped out. The entire large field was soaked. You can still find the piles of mud now. During the autumn harvest, [Wang's] workers [took my grain as my final rent payment]. I wasn't left with a single grain. Relying on local leaders, Li Juefu, Yang Jingqi and others, my rent was dismissed. The community discussed it: if you don't have grain, then you don't pay rent. At that time, [Wang] delivered [some of my deposit]. [But] there remained 40 [*liang*] from my original [cash] deposit. I have repeatedly demanded [this money], [but he] delays to this day.... This has forced me to move house. Farming is cruel and bitter to me.[10]

The magistrate wrote on this initial plaint that Chen should have his deposit returned but that he did not want the case heard in court. Chen's second plaint, filed almost three months later, complained that his deposit had still not been returned as ordered by the magistrate's rescript. He then further accused his landlord, Wang, of coming with a gang of family members to intimidate him into signing a statement releasing his claim on the deposit. Finally, in addition to all these economic grievances, Chen added that an employee of Wang's had killed his infant son during the clash at his home. Chen reported:

> Qiu Biaoting [Wang's employee] led over twenty people to my house. They for some reason cooked up this statement. They forced me to sign [this statement saying] that my deposit was not valid. They [then] crowded into my house and threw all my furniture and other household items outside. You can go and see the damage. They tied up my wife, Guo Shi, and caused my one-*sui* child to be thrown to the ground. His face and eyes received serious injuries. He bled and [then] died.[11]

Now there was an alleged homicide, although the accusation (later proven false when Chen admitted that his son had died of illness) came only after the magistrate had explicitly said that he did not want to hold a formal hearing about what seemed a purely economic dispute. Chen's desire for a court hearing was heightened by local mediation's failure to resolve the dispute. An accusation of homicide guaranteed that Chen's case would be heard at court.

To counter these allegations, Wang filed his own plaint. In this document, he detailed the economic dispute, but made no mention of the death of Chen's child – an incident that, if true, would certainly seem to require some explanation, refutation, or at least obfuscation. Further, He Xingfa, who had initially assisted Chen in renting Wang's land, also filed a plaint in which he stated that Chen's young son had, in fact, "died from some illness."[12] This document again paints the dispute in purely economic terms, clearly laying out the terms of the rental and the consequences of Chen's inability to recover his initial deposit on the land. As Chen himself reported: "I rely on the deposit to pay a deposit"[13] – meaning that he first had to recover the monies deposited on Wang's land before he could move and put down a deposit on a new piece of farmland, leaving him trapped in his dispute with Wang.

Chen was unable to extract himself from this economic relationship despite concerted local attempts at mediation. In his first plaint, Chen had indeed reported that the community had intervened on his behalf, but that Wang had still not returned his deposit. Chen again stressed the failure of community mediation in his second plaint, but it was not simply that this process could not help him. Now, the community actively worked against him by witnessing the public pledge in which Chen (apparently against his will) had renounced his right to the deposit.[14] With this act, the local authority moved to block Chen's claim.

In their own report to the court, local community leaders related the basic contours of the quarrel, highlighting their own engagement as the conflict intensified from a simple rent dispute into something more protracted. In fact, the local warden, security chief, and village head had visited Chen's home following his accusation of trouble caused by Wang's men and the death of his son. They reported that Chen's things were strewn about outside his house and that his son had indeed exhibited injuries on his "face, eyes, upper arms and hands."[15] They also stated that the boy had died the next morning.

Local leaders noted that even before this visit to Chen's home, they had attempted to mediate the conflict a total of four times. They had interceded on Chen's behalf, arguing that the flood constituted what contemporary insurance companies might call "an act of God," which entitled Chen to relief. The failure of their interventions to produce an amicable settlement led to the legal case, which had been driven into the court by Chen's false homicide accusation, despite the magistrate's explicit attempt to avoid hearing the case. Chen was able to continue to push his case by injecting violence into the dispute that caught the court's attention, although he quickly dropped the murder charge once he no longer needed it.

This strategizing suggests both a fairly wide scope of judicial engagement and a keen understanding of how to use the court to one's advantage. The magistrate continued to bring his official authority to bear on this relatively petty economic dispute. And it was Chen's successful manipulation of the court that brought state power to bear in his conflict, and shockingly, despite the dire dictates of the Qing Code, Chen was not punished for his misrepresentations.

In fact, Chen was rewarded for his stubborn and illegal litigiousness because, in the end, Wang appeased Chen by giving him silver. The first reference to this assistance comes during testimony in which Wang states that he had "helped" Chen by giving him ten ounces of silver. In testimony from the same hearing, Chen also reported that he was given this money as a result of local mediation. But this is clearly not what had happened. Chen was able to secure a cash payment by drawing state power into his dispute by means of false accusation. Finally, in signed settlements, both Chen and Wang noted that the local leaders had "clearly calculated" the monies owed, and that Chen was given the ten ounces of silver in addition to this amount. Again, this "help" came only as a direct result of Chen forcing a court hearing by making a false homicide accusation, despite written assurances of the efficacy of local mediation.

Community leaders mediated this settlement, but it was the court's intervention that was crucial in motivating the agreement. The parties were not simply "bargaining in the shadow of the law"[16] because the dispute was already in court, but the prospect of a formal court settlement compelled Wang to agree to an informal financial settlement out of court. Chen's false accusation of homicide both drove the case into court and allowed for its resolution. By deploying this strategy, Chen was able to engage the authority of the state to resolve a conflict that was proving intractable at the community level. In this one case, there was an almost complete reversal of the court's stated policies. Instead of discouraging litigation, particularly over small matters, by severely punishing tricksters who attempted to manipulate the court through false accusation, the opposite occurred. Moreover, Chen was hardly a savvy urbanite. He was a relatively poor tenant farmer whose home registration was 43 miles from the county seat. Chen, a country bumpkin, made his way to the big city and successfully worked the system. Moreover, this case also illuminates the limits to local efforts to diffuse the conflict. Because he was unsatisfied with the results of village-level mediation, Chen chose to opt out and appeal to a higher authority. His false accusation was a rejection of routine systems of resolution. This overturning of normal networks of authority makes the court's decision to hear the case even more odd.

The dynamic between local power structures, false accusation, and state authority is also clear in a case from 1895 in which Li Yuting, 35 *sui*, claimed his mother had been beaten to death by his landlord's son.[17] Li testified:

> I rent Zhou Xuansan's house and land to live [on] and farm. In my spare time, I work for other people as a manual laborer. I only leave behind my mother and my younger brother to protect the house when I am working elsewhere. This month on the fifteenth, my landlord's... wife, Zuo Shi, asked my mother, Long Shi, to her house to wash the mosquito net.[18]

Li then stated that his landlord's son, Zhou Ziyuan, had beaten his mother for not cleaning the net thoroughly, and that his mother had died from her injuries.

This account of a brutal and petty attack on an elderly woman was countered four days later by a plaint from Zhou Xuansan that was also signed by community leaders. This account dismissed Li's story, saying that his mother had died in an accident: the wall near where Long Shi had been working was old and had collapsed on her, a sad accident that was widely known in the community. Community leaders added a second plaint of their own in which they supported Zhou's account. Finally, an official coroner's examination concluded that Long Shi had indeed been crushed to death.

In the testimony delivered at a hearing four days after his initial plaint, Li stated that his mother "stepped on a stone collapsing [the wall and] crushing her."[19] After backpedaling from his earlier accusation, he furthered testified that Zhou, whose son he had just accused of beating his mother to death, had "helped" him with 24,000 *wen* to pay for burial expenses. Although both Zhou and community leaders openly questioned Li's honesty, the court did not punish him for his falsehoods. Instead, it endorsed Zhou's gift, noting that Li was quite poor. Whatever the motivations behind Zhou's gift, it is clear that by involving the court Li was able to extract 24,000 *wen* from his landlord. Instead of punishing Li for his scheming, the court sanctioned it. Li was another rural non-elite who showed surprising agility in working the system. His home village was 37 miles from Chongqing, and he was a tenant farmer who also had to hire himself out as a laborer in order to make ends meet. Despite his lowly standing, Li must have known enough to suspect that he would not be punished for his lies, at least not to the full extent mandated by the law.

Perhaps Zhou's "help" was an expression of paternalistic obligation from a superior to an inferior, a bond that often dictated compensation to the weaker party even for a no-fault death. These ties are also seen in suicide and homicide cases, and between employer/employee as well landlord/tenant, and suggest that these economic relations imbricated one in a more complex, ongoing social relationship rather than a simple economic exchange.[20] But Li's case complicates our understanding of paternalistic obligations in local society in that it was Li's obstinate, daring, and technically illegal litigation strategy that opened Zhou's wallet. The landlord's "help" was evidently a contingent paternalism that depended on the involvement of the court, which Li had sought out and activated with his accusation. In this case, Confucian-style paternalism was set in motion by the willful machinations of a tenant farmer. Perhaps surprisingly, agency here seems to reside with the weaker member of the dyad.

This expression of moralism appears less like a guiding principle then a defensive strategy deployed by Zhou to stave off greater intervention by the state into local disputes. His "help" was an attempt to return to the authority of the local community by means of both a financial settlement and an appeal to shared normative values. This again may not quite constitute "bargaining in the shadow of the law" given that the court was already involved, but the mere possibility for further court intervention evidently produced an out-of-court settlement. Payment was a strategy that minimized the court's formal role – a strategy that dovetailed with both the court's abstract notions of good governance and its immediate concerns with getting out from under mountains of litigation. This encounter suggests an alternate way in which the dominant moral system could be deployed, one that was in the interests of the weaker members of local communities.[21] The poor could exploit normative values just as chaste widows of commoner heads of households did to support their positions.[22] Supposedly shared values could bind the powerful as well as the weak.

Li's exploitation of shared values is slightly different from Philip Huang's "third realm" of Qing justice.[23] In Huang's formulation, the third realm resided in a specific moment in a case when the formal system, represented by the magistrate, and the informal system, formed of overlapping layers of local power holders, came together to produce informal solutions to disputes. The third realm then was where state and society "met and collaborated."[24] While Huang envisions the magistrate as the prime driver of this third-realm mediation, arguing that it hinged on the "expression of opinion from a magistrate,"[25] my discussion of Li's case, however, finds agency with the plaintiff, who kick-started the formal process with a plaint made to the court, suggesting a slightly different dynamic at work. So, while Huang sees the magistrate dictating the process, I find Li in the driver's seat. Some of this difference in emphasis might be attributed to our differing moments of entry into the case. Huang explicitly defines the third realm temporally, locating it in the middle stage of the lawsuit,[26] but I begin my consideration of court strategies with the first step in the process: the filing of the plaint. This orientation diminishes the magistrate's centrality and emphasizes legal disputes' position as just one moment in a larger, ongoing, local conflict.

Returning to the case at hand, Li's actions appear to have been driven by a desire for financial compensation, but it was not only the weaker party in land relations who could resort to false accusations in order to secure payment. Landlords too could use lies to force their disputes into court. This again cautions against an overly sanguine view of the leveling potential of false accusation. The following clash between a landlord and his tenant, which lasted nearly four years, is one instance of such legal manipulation.[27] In this case, false accusation was again instrumental in getting the dispute into court.

This protracted case had two phases. The first began in 1887, when Sun Guofeng, age 40 *sui*, filed a plaint accusing his mother's tenant, Chen Rong'an, 50 *sui*, of falling behind in his rent and "allowing" his son to beat Sun's mother. The feud escalated until finally, according to the plaintiff, the Sun family's cook was beaten to death in an affray. So, the case at first appears of a landlord, Sun, accusing a tenant, Chen, of violence. The events seem clear: poor man attacked his landlord's household members; landlords sought out state authority for redress. However, the day after he filed his initial plaint, Sun signed a document renouncing his previous statement and claiming that the cook had in fact died of illness. In this new document, he confessed that he should not "fabricate" plaints submitted to the court.

This swift reversal was followed by signed statements from others involved in the case, including community leaders, and the following day, Chen filed his own plaint detailing the dispute from his perspective. He claimed that there had been no problem in paying the rent and that the deceased cook, Tang Xingfa, had committed suicide for unrelated reasons. Chen, however, alleged that Sun was of dubious moral quality and that Tang had been stealing his grain. Finally, after this brief bit of character assassination, Chen accused Sun of bilking his family of money and causing trouble, and reported that community leaders had already been involved. The power dynamics had shifted: it was now the landlord who was accused of sundry malfeasances. Chen moved from the accused (of both acts of violence and status transgressions against his landlord) to the victim (with Sun now painted as violating social expectations by exploiting his social and economic position to extort his tenant).

At this point, the legal records end, only to resume roughly three years later, with Chen back in court. This time he claimed that his landlord was still harassing him, and that Sun had even changed his name in order to continue his false accusations. Most egregiously, Sun had kidnapped Chen's son and demanded a ransom of 30 *liang* of silver for his release.[28] Neighbors, witnesses, and community leaders all supported Chen's account. They admitted that the local community had been unable to broker a resolution to this enduring conflict, and they further explained that this had driven Chen to court. Unfortunately, the records do not contain the case's conclusion (if there was one), but the documents that do survive make clear that the homicide accusation fell away almost immediately, whereas the economic dispute – and the larger court case – continued. Sun's bald accusation of murder served to get the dispute into court. His lie was instrumental.

Sun's actions suggest that he was engaged in a profiteering form of false accusation. The cook's death was an opportunity and excuse to increase the pressure on Chen to submit to Sun's machinations. The rapidity with which the murder accusation was dropped – within a single day – is telling. The dispute no longer contained an accusation of violence, yet the case continued. Once involved, the court continued to hear the economic complaint. Since there is no conclusion in the records, I do not know if Sun was punished, rewarded, or simply dismissed. But, the duration of the case shows that Sun's false accusation at least succeeded in having the court hear the dispute.

When considering the use of false accusation as a legal strategy, the relationship that ensnared the two sides of the dispute and the relative power available to each contestant are keys. This case was a dispute between a landlord and a tenant, and it was the landlord who first pressed the case. However, once the dispute reached the court, it was the tenant, Chen, who turned to the court for relief. In this particular case, local power structures had not scuttled his chances for a favorable outcome – indeed, the community leaders seemed to support him – instead, a single, relatively powerful individual[29] obstinately pressed his demands locally, apparently even resorting to kidnapping Chen's son.

In her foundational work on false accusation, Melissa Macauley has noted that: "one does not encounter many cases of tenants taking on their landlords. The presumption of an ongoing economic relationship would have militated against tenants routinely resorting to litigious attack."[30] But, as this chapter makes clear, there were exceptions. Moreover, once a dispute came before the magistrate, the court's power was available to both sides, making false accusation a potentially volatile strategy. Macauley's observation is predicated on the existence of stable and ongoing economic relations. In Chen's dispute (and in many cases), the ongoing clash had upset any sense of harmony in the relationship. Yet, surprisingly, Chen and Sun remained locked in this economic relationship for at least four years. Clearly their entanglements were not easy to shake off. This relationship was fraught with tension, yet neither party cut ties. Land may have been largely commodified by the late nineteenth century, but extra-economic constraints continued to shape economic relationships. Why didn't Chen rent a different field and release himself from Sun's torments? It is unclear and unknowable, but clearly their economic relationship, even when damaged, was not easily discarded.

It was typically the weaker party in an economic relationship that brought the dispute to court. In the single instance in which a landlord brought his tenant to court, the tenant farmer was able to make use of the court to seek redress from the harassment he experienced at the hands of his landlord. In this case, the tenant appeared to have the backing of the community leaders. These cases suggest that false accusation was primarily a "weapon of the weak"[31] that sought to force compliance with customary norms and, perhaps more importantly, financial compensation for perceived wrongs or damages – it was a tool for making justice.

Macauley describes false accusation as an "integral part of late imperial legal culture."[32] In her eye, false accusation functioned primarily as a means of entry into the court, and as a means to escape the hermetic power structures of local mediation. In this way, she considers false accusation a tool of social empowerment. The general thrust of all the cases from Ba County that I have examined, however, suggests a less sanguine understanding of the social leveling potential of the court, but false accusation cases do show how this tactic could work to alter local power dynamics.[33] In some cases, the court acted to support the weaker party even in situations that were explicitly no-fault deaths. I am hesitant to declare this civil justice, but this practice does stress the expanded scope and flexibility these practices offered magistrates. But first one had to get the dispute before a magistrate, and false accusation could be the price of admission.

However, while I see false accusation as forming an expanded sphere of engagement between the magistrate and local communities, other scholars have argued that false accusation was handled within the formal confines of the legal system. Linxia Liang notes that the law included several provisions that allowed magistrates to overlook or dismiss cases based on false accusation, and further suggests that this accounts for the relative infrequency of punishment for false accusation.[34] While she also acknowledges the frequent successful use of false accusation to gain access to the court, her discussion of specific sub-statutes that allowed plaintiffs or the magistrate to walk back on untruths does not explain the frequent absence of the lesser penalties required by the Code in these instances.

For example, sub-statute 336.09 allows for the withdrawing of an accusation of homicide if the accuser discovers that he has been misled by gossip or slander.[35] The sub-statute provides a limited window for this action and also requires accusers to acknowledge their misdeeds and – most importantly – then to be punished under the article for "doing what ought not to be done (in a serious matter)," which carried a formal punishment of 80 strokes of the heavy bamboo.[36] So, while the sub-statute does provide a nimble exit strategy for plaintiffs, the Code still requires that false accusation be punished with blows of the heavy bamboo. In cases from Ba County, the Code was not applied. Instead, cases continued – sometimes to the great benefit of the accuser. Cases found in the county archive make clear the magistrate's active interventions in local society. In spite of the Code, locals continued to make false accusations, and the court magistrate continued to mediate their disputes.

In the cases I have examined, a conflict usually only reached the court after several failed attempts at local mediation, which are referenced in the case record. Individuals unhappy with the outcome of local interventions could employ false accusations to push their disputes into court. False accusation could be a means of appealing to a higher authority, and of escaping the confines and constraints of local society. Palimpsests of local mediation stress the chronology of these disputes – they originated and often lingered in local communities before making their way to court. The county court, when it engaged with local disputes, often did so well into the lifespan of the clash. False accusations were often key in making this jump from local dispute to court case.

Negotiated space: vernacular maps and the court

Maps are often discussed as tools of hegemonic state power. The center names and knows its lands. Clearly, Beijing possessed enormous power when it chose to focus on it, although this power usually remained diffused at the local level. Local actors in the Qing actively sought to tie their interests to that power, creating an exchange of power and meanings that drew state authority into local communities. Maps found in local court records expose the relationship between the county court and the local communities it oversaw. Previous studies of maps in imperial China did not have to consider the instrumental use of argumentative maps in local courts.[37] In *The History of Cartography*, Cordell Yee discusses maps in political culture, mapping as government measurement for managing and controlling space, artistic aspects of maps (particularly representation, style, and production), and the Westernization of mapping, while, in the same volume, John Henderson contributes a chapter on traditional Chinese cosmological thought.[38] This encyclopedic work does not consider the role of vernacular maps produced for use at court.

Yee stresses that "maps studied [in his chapters] were generally products of a highly educated elite."[39] These elites, and Yee's study, focus on the aesthetic, religious, and political aspects of mapmaking, leaving the role of maps in legal disputes unexplored. Yet the sheer number of maps in the archives proposes that court suggest another, popular form of cartographic usage in late-Qing China.[40] Indeed, this practice seems to have had a wider impact. While only a handful of people ever saw the beautiful Jesuit maps produced for Qing emperors, in the late nineteenth century, rougher sketch maps seem to have been produced regularly even for relatively petty disputes, revealing a hidden, popular social life for maps.

Vernacular cartography also illustrates the give and take between the court and locals, laying bare individuals' attempts to exploit state power by shaping the local circumstances known to the state. This translation project served specific needs – the state's backing of legal claims – and the maps in these cases illuminate the process by which local actors invited the state into their communities. Having drawn this connection to state power, locals then tried to shape the outcome of this encounter, and the court's production of legal justice. Through the power of the court, abstractions of land and social circumstance gained reality and force.

A case from 1897, for instance, introduced a map as part of a long-running feud over property borders.[41] The dispute pitted Wu Youheng, 45 *sui*, against Zhou Yuanqi, 48 *sui*, and dated to a land sale during the reign of the Jiaqing Emperor (r.1760–1820), which eventually led to Zhou and Wu sharing a common property line. An argument over the felling of bamboo was the immediate cause of the court case, and the magistrate dispatched a court clerk to fix the borders with the help of the community leaders. The magistrate ordered the disputed site mapped so that he could "see" it and rule on the rival claims. However, even as the state attempted to render the territory knowable through mapping in order to project power over it, the magistrate remained dependent on local descriptions to draw its map. The clerk had no independent knowledge of local geography or land-holding patterns, and thus remained dependent on local knowledge.

The magistrate's efforts failed to settle the matter. According to Zhou, Wu had not respected the court settlement and continued to violate the property lines. In the midst of this litigation, Zhou's eight-*sui* son, Zhou Dongyang, died. At the time of his son's death, Zhou was being held in chains by the court. Zhou seized the opportunity presented by his son's death to accuse Wu's sons, Wu Gui and Wu San, of poisoning his son. In his plaint, Zhou stated:

> My wife, Yuan Shi, and my eight-*sui* son, Zhou Dongshang, were at home as usual. Suddenly, this month on the night of the eighteenth, Dongyang cried out that he was having stomach pains. My wife feared his food had something bad in it. She asked him to come tell her what he had been doing. Dongyang said he hadn't eaten. He had only had dried beef with Youheng's sons, Wu Gui and Wu San, while they were playing. And Wu Gui had given him a ball of sticky rice to eat.[42]

This accusation was a clear escalation of the conflict, ratcheting it up from a simple land dispute to a homicide case. Wu quickly submitted a counter-plaint denouncing Zhou's claims as pure fabrication. In that document and elsewhere, Wu argued that his sons had not been playing with

Dongyang because they lived far apart, that his sons would not have played with Dongyang because they were much older, and, finally, that no one had seen them playing together. The accusation seems to have been Zhou's final card to play in a case in which he seemed to be slowly losing ground.

The case file still holds the map of landholdings that was entered as evidence in this intractable conflict (Map 1.1). A first question is: who should draw maps used in court? Official procedures for the creation and use of maps at court are not clear. For example, Huang Liuhong's magistrate's handbook, *Fuhui Quanshu*, offers no guidance for the production or use of maps.[43] The Qing Code offers no help either. However, in this case at least, it is clear that the magistrate ordered the map drawn, and then used it to make a judgment. A report from community leaders included in the case reads in part: "Your honor personally interrogated [the parties], issued a vermillion rescript, inspected the map, and established the boundaries."[44]

The map submitted as part of this conflict demonstrates the use of vernacular maps in court. This map has no single orientation and makes no reference to the four cardinal directions. Instead, it is oriented around the center of the map, as if the viewer were standing in the landscape. This is the world as the individual might confront it. The map is an accurate description of meaningful relations between known objects and markers.

A map is "an interpretive abstraction of the material space."[45] Within this space, our map focuses on dry fields [*tu*] and rice paddies [*tian*]. In addition, it depicts streams, bridges, paths, woods, graves [*fen*], defensive earthen mounds [*tubao*], and an empty weir. The undulating contours of the fields and path suggest a description of the topography. The trees in particular are rendered with an artistic flourish reminiscent of Chinese landscape painting. The map is at once crude (compared to contemporary scientific maps) and cultured (drawing on a rich artistic tradition).

The map is principally concerned with delineating landholdings and is instrumental: the map is a tool used to describe holdings in order to support claims made at court. Curiously, although the land is divided into discrete parcels, the map does not indicate ownership of those lands. By itself, the map is open to a host of interpretations. The map could not stand alone as a description of local landholding patterns, but instead required an interpreter with local knowledge to move the magistrate through the terrain. While the lands are fully bounded, the interpretations one could derive from them are not.

Presumably, the litigants' land contracts were also examined as evidence. Contracts often "walked" the reader through the space of the holding, with specific language about the boundaries of fields: "to the east it extends to Zhang San's field, to the west it extends to the main road." Locally informed interpreters (the middlemen or witnesses listed on the contract) were necessary to make sense of the explicit local terms of the contract. This map appears as an extension of, or appendix to, the contracts that provided the main evidence about who owned what, although they were not included in

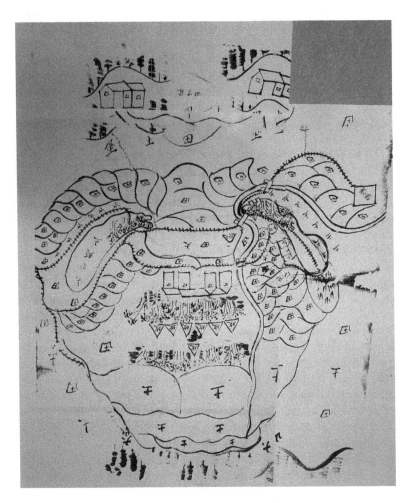

Map 1.1 Vernacular map from local dispute (BXDA 7782).

the court documents. These documents would have to be read all together and explained by local people.

One could consider the map a failure because it does not make clear its principal concern: ownership of land.[46] On the other hand, perhaps the map does succeed in its intent. This map cannot be fully divorced from the local context in which it was created precisely because it is incomplete as it stands. This design prevented the usurpation of meaning by the court, and forced a dialogue between the state and the local society. It discouraged imperial monologues and gave voice to alternative forms of authority. Local knowledge was essential to interpreting this evidence, and locals were often deeply interested in the outcome of the dispute and in the manufacturing of local justice in general. The magistrate, in his frustration, sent a clerk out to map the site, but the locals stayed in the conversation when the process yielded still-encoded maps.

Another case provides a clear example in which the maps themselves might become the subject of contention as locals compete to have their representations of the local order ratified at court, a contest to create local reality. In 1896, a long-standing dispute found its way to the court, with one party again dating the conflict to a land sale in the reign of the Jiaqing Emperor (r. 1796–1820). The case concerned property boundaries in the coal-rich mountains of the county.[47] Ding Jitian, 54 *sui*, reported that he had inherited a coal mine from his ancestors and that the land deed clearly marked the boundaries of his property. Ding's neighbor had rented his land to Li Yushan, and the dispute arose after the Dings apparently dug a new channel for the stream, diverting it around a spring located on Li's rented land. Since the middle of the stream was the agreed boundary between their holdings, this was effectively an attempt to move the boundary and encroach on Li's land. In the end, the magistrate used a map to establish the borders, restoring the original boundaries and ordering both parties to stay on their respective sides of the stream.

This case presents a series of competing maps and offers a clearer picture of how maps were generated and used at court. Moreover, the maps themselves became the object of contention, with competing maps supporting competing claims. The rival maps are direct extensions of the rival plaints, each having been drafted to tell a particular story. The first map in this case was produced by the state. Court clerk Li Chengxi reported to the court that he had gone to the village, a distance of roughly eight miles, on orders from the magistrate and produced a map in consultation with community leaders. On this report, the magistrate wrote: "Your report is noted. The map is filed."[48] Offering only the vaguest sketch of the land and claims, the map in question offers little to clarify the dispute (Map 1.2). Much like the previous case, land ownership of individual properties is not indicated on this map either.[49] In fact, one of the only labels that appears on the map, the four cardinal directions, is incorrect. There are two directions labeled south, with the one on the right-hand side appearing to have been changed from north. Beyond this problem of orientation, the lack of labels again requires a translator to describe the contents of the map to the magistrate. Clerk Li was unlikely to have a sufficiently accurate understanding of local geography and landholdings to render a map. Instead, he had to go to the village, consult with community leaders, and rely on their information to produce a map. Locals had already shaped the reality presented as objective to the magistrate.

The map depicts the stream, the central concern of the case, running down the center of the view, while a dotted line representing a path meanders back and forth. Mine entrances are on both sides of the water, as are two structures. The hillside is dotted with tufts of grass, and the vaguest

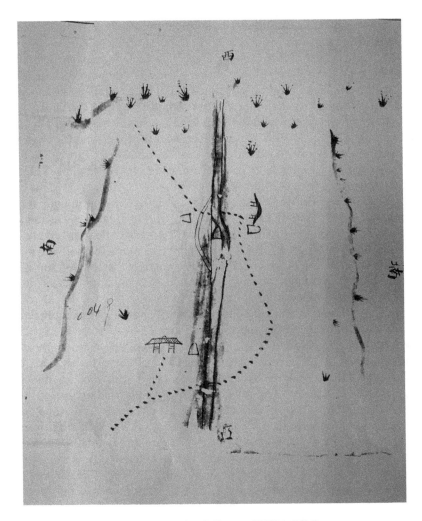

Map 1.2 Vernacular map one from land dispute (BXDA 7704).

outline of the hillside is suggested. This is all the description offered by the map. My frustration with the haziness of Clerk Li's map was seconded by Ding and his supporters.

In a plaint filed three days after Clerk Li submitted his map, Ding offered a meticulous description of the site and appended his own, detailed map (Map 1.3). This map was apparently drawn, or at least commissioned, by Ding himself. Following the main text of the plaint is a small notation stating: "A single map drawn by the plaintiff himself is attached."[50]

This map, mirroring the geography conjured by the written plaint, clearly describes the landscape and Ding's concerns within that space. It is a richly

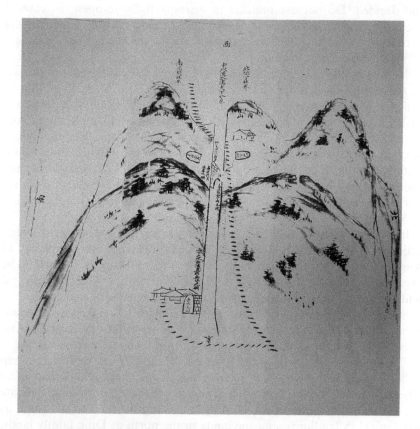

Map 1.3 Vernacular map two from land dispute (BXDA 7704).

drawn scene. In addition to the four cardinal directions (with north supplanting the erroneous second south of Clerk Li's map), the map further describes the setting by referencing the "inner mountains" [*neishan*] and "outer mountains" [*waishan*]. These are not absolute directional markers like east, west, north, and south. Rather, these terms express a relational understanding of the landscape, expressing a specifically local conception of the mountains' orientation. In addition to more-fully orienting the reader, the map also clearly marks the objects of contention. This map could stand on its own within the context of the case, masking its partiality with its seemingly neutral and comprehensive presentation of the land.

However, like everything in this case, the cartographic evidence did not go unchallenged. In a subsequent plaint, Li Yushan criticized both Clerk Li's and Ding's maps. This plaint came nearly a month after Ding's and followed a written agreement signed by all parties stating that the matter was settled. The intractability of the litigants drove the magistrate to frustration. He wrote on Li Yushan's plaint: "The case was already interrogated clearly and decided. Do not use pretexts to disrespectfully re-open the case."[51] From the magistrate's response, it seems clear that Ba County's landholders were willing to engage in complicated litigation, even in the face of the magistrate's explicit consternation.[52]

So, despite the magistrate's clear displeasure, the case went on. In fact, on the plaint that had drawn the magistrate's ire, Li Yushan noted that he had also attached a map (Map 1.4). In terms of composition, this document strikes a middle ground between Clerk Li's first map and Ding's submission. In fact, it looks a lot like Clerk Li's map with clear labels. The plaint does not make clear who drew the map, as opposed to the note in Ding's plaint stating that the plaintiff had produced the map. Since Li Yushan's map had been submitted as an attachment to the plaint (as had Ding's), and not reported internally by the court (as Clerk Li's map had been), it appears that Li Yushan had this map produced.

It is clear, however, that this final map was part of a rebuttal to Ding's claims and a denunciation of Clerk Li's incompetence. In the plaint, Li Yushan argued that the map drawn by Clerk Li was "vague."[53] Further, he argued that Ding had produced a "fraudulent map."[54] The miniaturized and abstracted representations of space had themselves become objects of contention. While the case was still concerned with actual landholding conflicts, it had also become an argument over representations of space. And these abstract representations helped determine who really owned what.

The arguments made by both Ding's map (Map 1.3) and Li Yushan's map (Map 1.4) are clearer when they are put in dialogue. First, Ding's map offers a broad sense of the two properties. The notes at the top of the map indicate the general orientation of the holdings, marking the land to the south as the Liu's (Li's landlord), and the lands to the north as Ding family lands. Between these two notations, the map declares that the stream forms the boundary between the two properties. Farther down on the map, the mining operations of both families are marked. The picture the map draws is of two clearly defined and distinct holdings separated by an unambiguous and agreed-upon natural marker: the stream. To further emphasize this understanding, the note on the lower left of the stream remarks that its waters flow freely and do not block the Li's mine. Everything is clear and there seems little ground for contention.

Li Yushan's map, however, suggests a different situation. His map also makes clear the general lay of the land. On the left, the entrances to Li Yushan's mines are noted, the old mine at the top and the new mine at the bottom. The map marks the left-hand side of the stream as Li's land and the right-hand side as Ding's land. The writing in the stream states that the middle of the stream was the agreed-upon border. Ding's coal mine is labeled on their side of the stream. The map indicates that the hillsides on both sides are planted with dry fields.

So far, Li Yushan's map does not seem to differ from Ding's map. However, the source of the conflict can be found in the small, secondary stream that curves off into the Li's side and around a structure marked as Li Yushan's

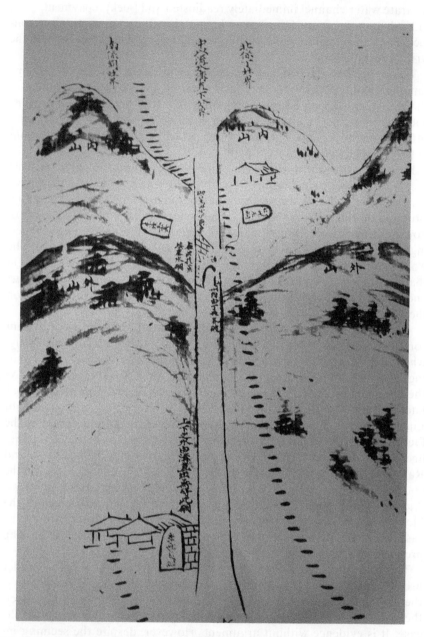

Map 1.4 Detail of vernacular map two from land dispute (BXDA 7704).

mine's dam. According to Li Yushan, this small tributary, which does not appear on the other map, was Ding's attempt to unilaterally alter the borders and usurp land that rightfully belonged to Li Yushan. Next to this channel he wrote: "The Ding family has jumped over the border. [We want] this new separate water channel immediately readjusted and [seek] repayment."[55] In Li Yushan's map, it was Ding's new channel that threw the parties into conflict. Thus, the map mirrored and supported the arguments presented in the written record.

Taken together, the two maps present very different pictures of the same supposed reality. Ding's map emphasizes stability, while Li Yushan's stresses change. What they do have in common is that they both make arguments and each presents its argument as an accurate reflection of the objective situation on the ground. The magistrate was left with visual representations of two competing depictions of reality.

In this dispute within the dispute, the ability to convincingly construct the world on a page and arguing using that map – in order to have the magistrate recognize that representation – had become as important as the actual situation on the ground. Of course, these maps did not carry some sort of power entirely divorced from reality, but, in court, these abstracted renderings of the world could carry as much meaning as the "real" landscape. The world had been fully translated into a simplified picture for the court. On that basis, the court issued its ruling – a decision that would leave the court and return to local communities where it would have a tangible impact on the real landscape.

A final case is slightly more puzzling and comes from an entirely different sort of conflict. This case concerned the alleged murder of Luo Hongsheng, whose death resulted from a fight at a local market.[56] Luo was demanding repayment of a debt from Carpenter Ran when Xie Jiu intervened. As the argument escalated, they came to blows. Xie immediately fled but was later captured. He then testified that he had intervened because he thought Luo was being "unfair" to Ran. Xie's role in the fight is complicated by the fact that he seems to have been acting at the behest of the market's security agent, who apparently asked Xie to break up the fight between Luo and Ran. Whether or not Xie felt he was acting in a semi-official capacity, the court adjudicated the case as a simple homicide resulting from an affray. As part of this investigation, the court attempted to determine precisely the blows struck and received by each party. As part of its prosecution of the case, the court investigated the scene of the fight and, it seems, had a map produced as part of this investigation (Map 1.5).

This case hints at a wider role for maps at court and suggests a broader use of maps in a range of conflicts beyond land disputes. Unfortunately, the case offers little explanation of the map or its use at court. In fact, the numerous structures that populate the map were not mentioned in the case. It is evidence without argument. However, despite the seeming incongruity between the map and the contents of the case, it is clear that the homicide case produced the map. In response to a report from court clerk Deng Yutang, the magistrate wrote: "Your report is noted. You should gather the parties together, draw a detailed map, and submit it for me to look at."[57]

Map 1.5 Vernacular map four from land dispute (BXDA 7704).

What purpose did the map serve? In this case, as in the others, the map was part of an attempt to fix subjects and their holdings in space. Qing courts exhibited a strong interest in spatially defining their subjects. This desire is evident in the detailed information litigants were required to enter in their plaints. Following name and age, the first piece of information the court collected was where the subject lived permanently and where s/he was residing during the court case. This information, part of a generic questionnaire at the beginning of each plaint form, referenced the individual's security and tax units, the closest market town to the village, and its distance from the county seat. These are notions of space intimately connected to power. The state had the power to mediate disputes and alter the landscape – physical and social – on the litigant's behalf. While power clearly resided at court, it

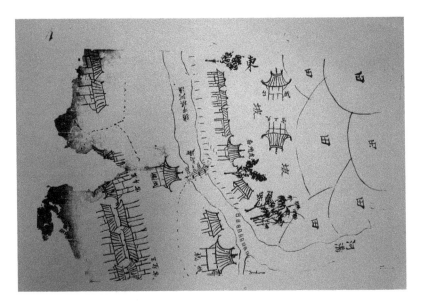

Map 1.6 Vernacular map from homicide case (BXDA 711).

was only brought to bear once locals had sought it out and only on the basis of local information and knowledge. Maps were used *in addition* to oral testimony and contracts as evidence in order to make local *spatial* knowledge comprehensible to the magistrate. Cordell Yee has written that maps "worked in tandem with language to communicate something about space and place."[58] Here, he refers to the heavy use of text within traditional Chinese maps, but this dynamic was also at work in court, where maps served as another kind of proof and worked in tandem with testimony. Here, then, is the magistrate's gaze, as he uses maps to "see" and judge spatial relations within his county without ever leaving his *yamen*. Locals brought their self-serving maps to him, but he also sent out his own clerks to produce presumably more objective maps. His challenge was how to get beyond the walls of his *yamen* in order to make informed judgments. Yet, these maps – like all the intelligence the magistrate could gather – were first shaped by locals, who were often deeply interested in the outcome of legal cases. Justice was shaped by local truths.

The court formed only one element in the creation of local justice in Ba County. The use of maps in court cases reveals the driving role locals played in this legal culture. Here, at the very end of the Qing dynasty, people still turned to the state as arbiter and sought to manipulate its authority. In this process, locals transmitted and translated local realities for disputative use at court. Indeed, "the state had no unmediated access to local 'truth,' and...could resolve nothing without that truth."[59] The magistrate was routinely ignorant of local circumstances. Maps were another tool litigants could deploy when engaging with the court.[60] All of these factors suggest a great willingness to use the court, and a fairly sophisticated understanding of its procedures and possibilities. In these conflicts, local actors took a variety of steps to control the information that flowed to the court, and to make local truths key to the production of legal truth.

Local influence over state authority

My examination of both vernacular maps and false accusations stresses the shaping role locals played county-level legal culture. While the lion's share of power undoubtedly rested with the magistrate and the county court, information empowered locals in their attempts to leverage state power to further specific aims in ongoing local disputes. Indeed, false accusation cases reveal not only the centrality of locals in the creation of local justice during the late-Qing period, but also expose the county court's expanded sphere of engagement. Instead of turning away cases based on hollow accusations, magistrates went out of their way to rule on the often-petty disputes that lay at their core. Indeed, this is what local governance looked like in the late-Qing period. In Ba County, at least, magistrates exhibited a surprising willingness to adjudicate and turn a blind eye toward the false accusations that landed a case in court. The examination of false accusation cases exhumes an expanded role for the state at the local level, one that saw locals pull the state into their disputes. Moreover, the county magistrate's engagement with the communities he oversaw enhanced the Qing's vitality and legitimacy at the local level even near the dynasty's collapse. In meaningful ways, the Qing state still worked at the end of the nineteenth century.

Further, given the number of non-elite and rural actors actively (and illegally) pursuing their interests at court, scholars must imagine an enlarged and rowdy legal culture at work in the county. I understand *legal culture* as transcending individual experience to encompass understandings of the law and its use that existed in the community more generally, even removed from direct experiences of the legal system. This broader scope allows for ideas about the law derived from second-hand experience: from rumor, from gossip, from scandal, from stories.[61] This wider web of legal action connected local communities (local leaders as well as common peasants) to the state, in as much as the county court was the face of the state at the local level.

The negotiation of state authority is also visible in the use of vernacular maps, which illuminate a process in which depictions of local realities were brought to the magistrate, who attempted to use them to solve a specific dispute. The magistrate possessed great power, but the magistrate was isolated by both the vastness of his territory and by his frequent ignorance of local circumstances. As a result, locals were able to shape the narrative presented to the court by shaping the intelligence the magistrate received regarding local conditions. Of course, these representations of local realities were not limited to maps (in fact, they were more often in the form of contracts[62]), but this conjuring of local realities and using them to argue in court is particularly clear in cases with maps.

These maps make clear the process of translation – from distant local circumstances into clear, disputative representations of reality in court – that occurred as locals sought out state power and invited it into their disputes. In doing so, they attempted to control how the magistrate "saw" the communities under his authority. In these encounters between the local state and various communities within the county, the legal system also acted as a conduit through which the state reached out into local society. Local people were *pushing* their way into the court by deploying a variety of shrewd strategies to guide the outcome of their interactions with state authority. The court, for its part, seemed to welcome these engagements by ignoring the sometimes-illegal tactics employed to bring matters before the state's authority.

Focusing on these twin techniques for the negotiation of state authority makes clear the full sweep of these conflicts, and puts locals (and their communities) front and center. These disputes were mobile. They began in local communities, where various individuals, or groups of individuals, came into conflict. After this initial phase, which was usually followed by repeated local attempts at mediation, disputes entered the state's gaze as the yamen took up the case. This shifting of the geography of the dispute – from local authorities to the state's courtroom – was a choice made by one of the contestants. Following this change in venue (and authority, tactics, and stakes), both sides in the conflict attempted to manipulate their encounter with state authority in order to achieve their aims. False accusation and vernacular maps were local tools in this drive to shape the contours of the state's interactions.

Sensitivity to this shift into the courtroom underlines the prehistory of legal cases, which took place in local communities, away from the state's view and power. The county court, even as the court of first instance, entered conflicts late in the process.[63] The local interests already in conflict then turned to the court, marshaling competing and disputative accounts of local realities. In the case of vernacular maps, disputants mapped competing local realities and argued with them, bringing visions of local circumstances into the courtroom. In instances of false accusation, these claims served as a hook to grab the magistrate's attention and force the dispute into court.

Both false accusation and vernacular maps were tools deployed by contestants to increase the likelihood of a favorable outcome at court. Local information was a powerful resource on which locals had a monopoly. Kentaro Matsubara has described how the Qing government was dependent on local reporting of landholding for tax collection.[64] He finds that registered land was entirely unrelated to actual local landholding patterns, leaving the state with no record of actual landholding patterns. Similarly, the county magistrate also relied on local information to form legal judgments, and thereby govern. He was divorced from the social realities of those communities, and consequently relied on local intelligence to rule. Both false accusation and vernacular maps presented local truths about that local order. These depictions were presented as accurate, but both were attempts to exert control of the framing over the dispute as it entered a new arena, and became subject to a new authority. The two techniques could also be considered "false maps" and "vernacular accusations." They presented argumentative visions of local realities in order to manipulate state power and shape the production of justice in court. Locals continued to make justice, even in court. While individuals sought to shape state authority in the courtroom, most justice in Ba County was made outside the court, or at least through the interaction between state and non-state authority, which is the subject of the next chapter.

Notes

1 This is true not only for the Ba County archive but across central-level records and other local archives as well.

2 While *wugao* was a legal term in the Qing, the cases considered in this chapter were not archived according to the term. I have named these cases as instances of false accusation based on their content in order to consider the *wugao* as a routine legal strategy.

3 When referring to someone making a "false accusation" or even "lying," I use these terms not in relation to some objective truth but rather describe claims they made at court. These claims illuminate the ways in which individuals, including the rural poor, attempted to use the legal system to their benefit.

4 DLCY, 336.00. There are 27 sub-statutes elaborating statute 336.00. False accusation is also mentioned in several other places in the Code in relation to the commission of other crimes.

5 The increasing burden that fell on county magistrates was largely a product of the Qing's failure to increase the size of the bureaucracy in the face of a surging population. Consequently, the relative size of the bureaucracy fell, and the magistrate's legal and administrative responsibilities grew. See William G. Skinner (ed.), "Introduction: Urban Development in Imperial China," in *The City in Late Imperial China* (Stanford: Stanford University Press, 1997), 19–23.

6 DLCY, 336.00.

7 Legal culture was not neatly bracketed from other aspects of local culture. Yasuhiko Karasawa has demonstrated the degree to which oral and written traditions mingled to create storytelling tropes and stereotypes for use in court, and Ting Zhang highlights commercial publishers' role in the widening circulation of legal texts across the Qing. See Yasuhiko Karasawa, "Between Oral and Written Cultures: Buddhist Monks in Qing Legal Plaints," in *Writing and Law in Late Imperial China*, ed. Robert E. Hegel and Katherine N. Carlitz (Seattle: University of Washington Press, 2007), 78; and Ting Zhang, "Marketing Legal Information: Commercial Publications of the Great Qing Code, 1644–1911," in *Chinese Law: Knowledge, Practice, and Transformation, 1530s to 1950s*, eds. Li Chen and Madeline Zelin (Leiden: Brill, 2015), 250.

8 Melissa Macauley describes this as the "opportunistic use of cadavers." See Macauley, *Social Power and Legal Culture*, 197–214.

9 BXDA 7918.

10 Ibid.
11 Ibid.
12 Ibid.
13 Ibid.
14 Six witnesses signed the pledge.
15 BXDA 7918.
16 Robert H. Mnookin and Lewis Kornhauser, "Bargaining in the Shadow of the Law: The Case of Divorce," *The Yale Law Journal* 88, no. 5 (April 1, 1979): 950–997. Mnookin and Kornhauser explored how the anticipated outcome of a future court case led to pre-courtroom settlements. In this way, the legal system exerted influence even before a dispute reached the court.
17 BXDA 7863.
18 Ibid.
19 Ibid.
20 See Chapter 4 for a detailed discussion of this issue.
21 I would not push this point too hard. This was not some widespread saturnalia turning orthodoxy on its head. Instead, it was a small moment in which hegemony was disrupted.
22 Theiss, *Disgraceful Matters*, 9.
23 For his full elaboration of the "third realm," see Huang, *Civil Justice in China*, 110–137.
24 Ibid., 110.
25 Ibid., 135.
26 That is after "the first actions of the formal system" and before "the final action of the formal system." Ibid., 111.
27 BXDA 7660.
28 I discuss kidnapping in greater detail in Chapter 2.
29 Sun was a "doctor" as well as a landlord, suggesting that his family had at least some means at their disposal, particularly compared to a tenant farmer such as Chen.
30 Macauley, *Social Power and Legal Culture*, 166.
31 I borrow this term from James Scott. See James Scott, *Weapons of the Weak: Everyday Forms of Peasant Resistance* (New Haven: Yale University Press, 1985), xv–vii.
32 Macauley, *Social Power and Legal Culture*, 142. She also argues that false accusations had to be skillfully written in order to prove effective, thereby stressing the role of the litigation master. But in cases drawn from Ba Country, many of the false accusations have a more *ad hoc* or even casual feel, suggesting less the careful and skillful hand of the litigation master at work, more the clumsy deployment of a sturdy and proven tool. This difference may in part be a consequence of Macauley's use of central-level records, rather than those from the bottom of the legal system [Her work is based on materials circulating at the highest levels of the Qing bureaucracy: *zhupi zouzhe* (palace memorials), *lufu zouzhe* (copies of palace memorials including depositions and other evidence), and *xingke tiben* (routine memorials to the Board of Punishments)].
33 Attempts to stress the emancipatory power of false accusation must be tempered by the routinely conservative cast of legal power in the Qing. Magistrates often relied heavily on those in positions of local power to make their decisions. So, while the court could be a site of resistance, legal truths often reinforced normative power structures. In this way, the court often acted as a conservative force, rewarding normative social organization and behavior, and confirming the power of local elites. In Ba County, this could be done by labeling claims

made at court as "false accusations," thereby dismissing one rendering of reality and enshrining another as "true." See Chapter 3 for further discussion of this issue.

34 Linxia Liang, Delivering Justice in Qing China Civil Trials in the Magistrate's Court (Oxford: Oxford University Press, 2007), 221–230.

35 DLCY 336.09.

36 DLCY 386.00.

37 Tristan Brown considers mapping, particularly in regard to property rights, and geomancy's critical role in interpreting the land. See Tristan Brown, "The Veins of the Earth: Property, Environment, and Cosmology in Nanbu County, 1865–1942" (PhD dissertation, Columbia University, 2017).

38 John Brian Harley and David Woodward, *The History of Cartography, Volume 2, Book 2: Cartography in the Traditional East and Southeast Asian Societies* (Chicago: University of Chicago Press, 1995). Other scholarship focusing on Qing cartographic practice also overlooks this form of mapping. For example, see Emma Teng, *Taiwan's Imagined Geography: Chinese Colonial Travel Writing and Pictures* (Cambridge: Harvard University Asia Center, 2004) and Laura Hostetler, *Qing Colonial Enterprise: Ethnography and Cartography in Early Modern China* (Chicago: University of Chicago Press, 2001).

39 Ibid., 228.

40 In addition to the maps found in the Ba County archive, maps can be found in a number of archives, including those for Danshui-Xinzhu, Nanbu, and Baodi counties, as well as in archives in Xinjiang and Gansu.

41 BXDA 7782.

42 BXDA 7782.

43 Liuhong Huang, *Fukkei zensho* (Tōkyō : Kyūko Shoin, 1973).

44 BXDA 7782.

45 Thongchai Winichakul, *Siam Mapped: A History of the Geo-Body of a Nation* (Honolulu: University of Hawaii Press, 1997), 53.

46 Thongchai has defined mapmaking as follows: "The cartographer observer surveys the geographical terrain (A) with specific objectives for each kind of map. Then, by cartographic methods, he or she conceptualizes it (B), transforms the data into mapping form (C), and the map is produced." In his terms, our map can perhaps be seen as a failure because it fails in step A by not making its "specific objectives," land ownership, clear. Thongchai, *Siam Mapped*, 53.

47 BXDA 7704.

48 Ibid.

49 Unlike Map 1.1, however, this map depicts the landscape from an abstracted and inhuman bird's-eye perspective. The viewer is no longer situated in the terrain.

50 BXDA 7704.

51 Ibid.

52 Philip Huang has speculated that the legal system in Ba County transitioned from a simple, relatively well-functioning arrangement primarily serving small landholders (typified for Huang by Baodi County in North China) to an unwieldy and highly differentiated one that was overwhelmed by clever and cynical litigants, frequently large landowners (as seen in Huang's depiction of Danshui-Xinzhu in Taiwan). In this latter system, conflicts in court grew more protracted and complicated. Huang, *Civil Justice in China*, 138.

53 Ibid.

54 Ibid.

55 Ibid.

56 BXDA 7711. This case also appears in BXDA 7698.

57 Ibid.

58 Harley and Woodward, *The History of Cartography*, 228.

59 Valerie Kivelson, *Cartographies of Tsardom: The Land and Its Meanings in Seventeenth-Century Russia* (Ithaca: Cornell University Press, 2006), 49.

60 Kivelson also argues that maps sometimes "armed local litigants with new and creative ways to lie, falsify, and misrepresent the lay of the land and to turn the state's own regulation to their own purpose." Ibid.

61 Paul Katz argues that Chinese legal culture consists of three components: "structural (legal institutions), substantive (laws), and cultural (values, ideas and practices, including religion and rituals)." The legal culture described in this chapter is largely focused on how the last of these sites interacted with the first two. Paul Katz, *Divine Justice: Religion and the Development of Chinese Legal Culture* (New York: Routledge, 2009), 7.

62 For a fuller description of land contracts, see Christopher Isett, *State, Peasant, and Merchant in Qing Manchuria, 1644–1862* (Stanford: Stanford University Press, 2006), 78–95.

63 By taking court documents as the start of the clash, historians too tend to enter these conflicts in their later stages, thereby obscuring local aspects of the production of justice.

64 Kentaro Matsubara, "Land Registration and Local Society in Qing China: Taxation and Property Rights in Mid-nineteenth Century Guangdong," *International Journal of Asian Studies* 8, no. 2 (2011): 163–187.

2   Local violence
Kidnapping, sexual impropriety, and community discipline

Most justice in the Qing was made in local communities, forged without state intervention through a frequently violent expression of everyday politics. In this way, violence or the threat of it played a regular and constructive role in the county's communities, where bloodletting formed a regular practice of rough justice rather than an anarchic force. This sort of violence had a specific and local social meaning, and instances of private justice expose the extended ties that held communities together (individuals coming together to commit these acts) as well as the disciplinary force of the community (groups acting against the alleged transgressor(s)). While these acts of rough justice may not precisely mirror practices of "rough music" (or *charivari*) in early modern Europe, they were similar acts of community policing. E. P Thompson writes: "Rough music belongs to a mode of life in which some part of the law belongs still to the community and is theirs to enforce."[1] In this mode, community justice was enacted on the spot, and the individual was constrained by the community. In Ba County, informal, extra-legal clashes served didactically to enforce community standards. These clashes were often a contest in which the meaning of abstract norms was being inscribed on actual events.

These community-based means of non-state dispute settlement formed part of a parallel, and dominant, alternative to the state's courtroom, and magistrates were aware of these routine practices. The seventeenth-century magistrate Huang Liuhong warned against young men who came together to practice this sort of violence: "Whenever someone complains about injustice, these young men volunteer their services to avenge him. Street fights and brawls are their obsession, attacking and plundering are their chosen profession."[2] Huang's comments were directed at rowdy young men who exploited disputes as opportunities for recreational violence and profit.[3]

In addition to these opportunists, he also warned about fights that broke out after verdicts were announced, continuations of the very disputes that the magistrate had hoped to settle. Clearly, he did not always have the last word in these conflicts, and brawls could form a bloody coda to the state's intervention. This post-trial fighting stresses an extended lifespan for disputes. Moreover, just as the magistrate's verdict did not always end the conflict, entry into the court was not the beginning of these clashes. They had local origins. Taken together, these prehistories and postscripts expose an enlarged process of disputation. The state – in the guise of the local magistrate – was a late entrant into the clash. Local disputes raged on both before and sometimes after the state's intervention, marking the state's periodic interventions in local life.

The Qing state had a rather limited presence in local communities, and, consequently, the dynasty relied heavily on forces of local order to carry out some of the routine work of the state. Many depictions of this hybrid rule suggest that local control emerged rather neatly from the "natural" village leadership, and focus on the tension between the state and its local deputies.[4] Local legal records, however, detail the tensions within these communities as well as rough-and-tumble forms of local authority and control. In these instances, the lines of division were not between the state and the local communities, but within the communities themselves. In these societies, justice often came in the form of violence wielded by normative forms of local authority to protect their interests.

In Ba County, rough justice ran the gamut from petty street fighting to well-organized kidnapping. The court's handling of these matters suggests that a degree of private violence was tolerable and indeed expected. The magistrate routinely failed to punish offenders for these transgressions. This official acceptance of local justice and private violence should not be surprising. In fact, in at least some circumstances, this official tolerance was written into the Qing Code. If a husband caught his wife having sex with another man, he was legally permitted to kill both his wife and her lover as long as he did so immediately.[5] This statute led to an involved discussion and definition of the acceptable parameters of this space for personal justice, resulting in a Legalist parallel to question of "how many angels can dance on the head of a pin." What if the husband catches his wife's lover exactly in the doorway of the house? What if the lover makes it one step outside the house? Can the husband still legally kill him? What about two?[6]

At its root, though, this section of the Code grants formal legal protection to an act of private vengeance. In fact, with the statute, the Code transforms this killing from personal vengeance to state-sponsored justice. The state recognized and legitimized some private justice (while denying others). From this precedent, local magistrates' unwillingness to aggressively punish many forms of rough justice becomes easier to understand. But if some forms of local violence were acceptable, where should magistrates draw the line? While the commoner head of household was given a wide prerogative to defend his patriarchy, a similar ambit was extended to creditors as they worked to recover debts. The exact scope of the power was less clear, and it is difficult to precisely delineate the ends of this authority, but the debtor's death, by suicide or other violent means, was not tolerated. Yet, the punishment for even these actions often failed to elicit the Code's most severe punishment. These deaths were often presented as no-fault suicides, requiring monetary compensation, rather than the capital crime of driving someone to commit suicide. Clearly the state did not approve of this outcome, yet the imposition of this reduced penalty suggests a knowing tolerance of practice, even when it was abused.

Further, given the sojourning magistrate's numerous responsibilities and, at least partial, alienation from and dependence on local society, the magistrate must have picked his battles. However, despite these concerns, the magistrate often went out of his way to rule on rather petty disputes. This expanded sphere of state engagement often saw a reactive state dragged into local disputes. Despite the strictures of the Code, the magistrate was brought into these quarrels, bringing state authority to bear in local disputes. In this pursuit, some forms of private justice were sanctioned, others merely tolerated.

Two forms of rough justice in particular expose local patterns of justice making: kidnapping (or private detainment) and violence surrounding sexual impropriety. Both of these practices also stress the importance of *simultaneity* for our understanding of conflict and community in the late-Qing period. Disputes emerged from local communities, where they had active social lives before they entered court. Once in front of the magistrate, many of these clashes continued to play out at the local level. Disputes could exist simultaneously in both local communities and at the county court, and often the magistrate's yamen was not the most important venue among these competing sites of contestation. The court was one venue among many to find resolution, and individuals might work all of these sites at once – with each holding its own potential for satisfaction.

In many disputes, one party, along with a group of relatives or friends, descended on the home of their adversary and destroyed property, perhaps assaulting the victim as well. On occasions, these clashes generated lists of objects damaged or stolen during the affray, and this property would be listed in an appendix attached to a plaint from the victim seeking redress. Catalogues of destroyed or missing objects constitute the material culture of disputation in the late-Qing period, and expose routine practices of local violence. This ritualized smashing and looting appears in many legal cases.[7] With this petty violence, individuals were not acting randomly, but were drawing from a shared social script, which shaped the performance of conflict in the county.[8] Acts of violence, sometimes lethal, were given form and meaning by local understandings of justice, inscribing local values on others (fellow community members as well as strangers). Smashing, looting, and violence in Ba County proceeded along known and regular routes. These conflicts were values made visible, and one of the most visible acts of private justice was kidnapping.[9]

Kidnapping

The goal of many "private detainments" was to force payment of a debt. This practice was not sanctioned in law, and, in fact, the Code explicitly forbade forms of aggressive dunning.[10] Kidnapping an individual in order to recover a debt was punishable by a set number of strokes of the heavy bamboo, determined by the amount of the money in question or, depending on the magistrate's interpretation, 80 strokes of the heavy bamboo. However, despite official prohibition, the practice endured. Official tolerance of kidnapping was perhaps a simple acknowledgment of its prevalence as social practice, and the magistrate's routine failure to prosecute kidnapping itself as a criminal act suggests an official disinterest in these acts. Indeed, kidnapping of this sort appears to have enjoyed at least implicit support from the state. Even when this practice went wrong and the dispute ended up in court, the magistrate often intervened to settle the underlying economic dispute, rather than the issue of detention. Like so much of local life, this strategy only appears in the legal archive when it failed. Still, kidnapping appears as a regular strategy for recovering debts. The deceased's family often presented the event as kidnapping, while those instigating the abduction framed their actions as acts of semi-official detainment. Petitioners' characterizations of kidnappings were, in part, an element of the fairly routine repertoire of exaggeration employed to gain the magistrate's ear and secure a hearing at court. However, regardless of how the abduction was framed, these cases reveal a violent and informal practice of debt collection.

This custom is clear in the following case. On the fifth day of the fourth month of 1891, Liu Mou Shi, aged 72 *sui*, submitted a plaint regarding the suicide of her 17-*sui* grandson, Liu Jialiu:

> This month, in the afternoon of the third day, I encountered Guo Heshang, who snarled at me saying my grandson, Liu Jialiu, owed him 350 *wen,* and he was pressing for repayment of the debt. [Guo] forced [Liu] behind Yuantong temple and ordered my grandson beaten repeatedly. Ran Liushi, Peng Zhengwen and Wang Sanmao [then] held him at Li Laochi's teahouse and drank tea. At that point, my grandson became desperate and ran to the Number Three dock and threw himself in the water and drowned.[11]

Her explanation of the situation is clear. Debt led to the "kidnapping" and beating, which directly resulted in her grandson's suicide. The causality seems obvious, as is the seeming guilt of the "kidnappers." This version of events was supported by her son (the deceased's uncle), Liu Kaiwen. Subsequent testimony from the "kidnappers," however, suggests an alternate reading of the conflict.

The accused kidnappers, Ran Liushi, a boatman, Peng Zhengwen and Wang Sanmao, who both sold sugarcane, testified that they had met Liu

Jialiu at the teahouse and were casually drinking tea together. They claimed that they were preparing to leave when Liu went outside to "relieve himself," and that they were unable to prevent his death because they had no idea he was going to kill himself. Liu's death, in this rendering, was an awkward and unexpected end to a pleasant afternoon at the teahouse.[12] Further support for this story was provided by the owner of the teahouse, Li Laochi, who made no mention of Liu being held against his will or having been beaten. In his testimony, Li laid out the same story as Ran, Peng, and Wang: Guo joined the others at the teahouse and then, within an hour, Liu threw himself in the river.

Community leaders challenged this account and reiterated the story that the deceased's uncle had told them. Despite the astonishing and vital difference in the two narratives, these local leaders had tried to broker a settlement, ignoring the precise terms of Liu's death. Local security head [*boajia*] Liu Jinyi testified that he, along with other community leaders and neighbors, brokered a signed agreement in which Liu Mou Shi was paid 15,000 *wen*. The court recognized this settlement, and the claims submitted by Liu Mou Shi were ignored. The case moved quickly from the cause of the death to the terms of the settlement, obscuring the kidnapping by focusing on the settlement following a suicide.

This alteration in the character of the case elides the enormous gulf between the events described by the various contestants. One version of this case described a vicious attack ordered by a creditor against a debtor. After the beating, the victim was held against his will by at least three men. Driven beyond desperation, the young man escaped his captors and threw himself into the river. The second description of this episode centers on an afternoon at the teahouse, where four men drank tea together. After an hour, one member of this party excused himself, saying he had to micturate, and then, for reasons entirely unknown to his fellows, he plunged to his death. Local leaders – and indeed the magistrate as well – left aside the shattering gulf between these two accounts and moved to settle the affair by paying the mother 15,000 *wen*. The questions of violence and of kidnapping were both ignored.

So, the local leaders first, and then the magistrate, disregarded the aggressive dunning and proceeded directly to the issue of compensation. The complete abandonment of the issue of the beating and kidnapping suggests that these were not concerns for local mediation or legal intervention. The settlement suggests that it was not the tactics of debt collection that were the problem – the issue was Li's suicide. His death required the attention of the community and court, not the acts that drove him to self-annihilation. Yet, even if the magistrate was simply adjudicating based on the most severe crime, which was a common legal practice, the unexamined context of the suicide is odd, particularly as he was not punished according to the Code's prescription for driving someone to suicide. The formal legal consequence of Liu being driven to commit suicide was dropped in order to pursue no-fault compensation. Indeed, the court's actions rephrased the issue from one of criminal justice to state-backed financial restitution. This is particularly striking given that, following the Code, the guilty parties would have been sentenced to, at least, 100 strokes of heavy bamboo.[13] Explicitly no-fault suicides often still required compensation to be paid to the family of the deceased.[14] In this case, however, compensation was mandated even though the issue of fault has been entirely left aside. Guo Heshang's actions, and those of his myrmidons, were left unexamined. Practices of rough justice did not warrant explanation or justification. As a routine part of the social landscape, they escaped mention, as local and state authorities moved to only consider the issue of suicide. Moreover, even if the compensation that Mou Shi received was, in part, also a rebuke of the aggressive debt collection and not just compensation for the suicide, then the punishment was still at odds with the Code and shows the magistrate going off-script to involve himself in the community. Instead of being punished with a beating, the perpetrator paid compensation.

This death also lays bare the social power of suicide. Through his death, Liu Jialiu converted his family's debt into a payoff, moving his family from the red into the black (from 350 *wen* down to 1,500 up). Liu paid with his life, a potent sacrifice, and, perhaps, a powerful "weapon of the weak."[15] This suggests another choice, a drastic and final one, available to the poor. Moreover, it also sketches the fine line that existed between pressing for compensation and going too far. Those with power, creditors for example, could (and did) harass the less fortunate within an inch of their lives, but moving beyond these bounds resulted not in repayment but in financial penalty. The community (and the state) respected local power, but punished its excesses. Moreover, since these practices tend to enter the legal record only once they had failed in some way (thereby producing a dead body), the usual, uneventful versions of these strategies are nearly invisible to the historian.

Debt was also at the center of the kidnapping case that followed Zeng Yuanchun's suicide, although the exact nature of the act is unclear.[16] Zeng's wife, Zeng Zhang Shi, at first claimed her husband had been abducted by his creditors over a debt of 50 *wen*. In her initial plaint, she stated: "[My husband] was detained at [his creditor Zhou's] store. They demanded the money and tried to force him to pay, and they would not release him."[17] Her husband has been abducted by his creditors over a debt of 50 *wen*, she pointed out. She later testified: "[Zeng] was privately detained at [Zhou's] home, and they would not release him."[18]

Zhang Shi's claims were, not surprisingly, supported by her son, but Zhou, community leaders, and others involved in the case made no mention of the alleged kidnapping. In this telling, Zeng went to Zhou's house willingly. In fact, Zhang Shi also went to Zhou's house in order to see Zeng there after he "fell sick."[19] By the case's end, there was no accusation of kidnapping. In fact, the settlement signed by Zhang Shi and her son does not mention kidnapping at all. This, of course, does not necessarily mean that it never occurred. There are two likely scenarios. The first is that Zeng Yuanchun was kidnapped because of the money he owed. It is possible that Zhang Shi told the truth, but that Zhou and his accomplices were able to marshal community leaders to simply deny that it had ever occurred. This would be a productive deployment of social power in order to avoid further charges at court. The second scenario is that the kidnapping never occurred and Zhang Shi made it up.

Why might she do that? Lies told at court are useful to historians because they must be plausible both in the eyes of the court and in terms of local circumstances to have their desired influence on the proceedings.[20] If the kidnapping never occurred, Zhang Shi could have used the accusation to further defame her antagonists. She would have to draw on her knowledge of local practices and been aware that in a situation like this – the non-payment of debt – kidnapping was a tactic employed to compel payment. Rough justice was part of the social landscape that she could exploit to construct an advantageous account of her husband's death. These alleged kidnappings adhered to patterns and scripts that were known within the community.

In this way, local practice was ritualistic in the sense that there were known ways to proceed and that the actions had shared meaning. Local rituals are also seen when widows were "seized in adultery" [*zhuo jian*] in order to separate them from property that they were entitled to control only by virtue of their chastity. Matthew Sommer has described this practice as having a "ritual quality" in that "there seems to have been a well-known, established way of doing things."[21] If a widow's in-laws suspected her of adultery, they would stalk her and try to catch her with her lover (in the act if possible). The in-laws would then beat the couple, tie them up, and immediately drag them off to the magistrate. This was another regular and ritualized form of violence that expressed the local norm (patriarchal control of property), while also exploiting a state-sponsored value (widow chastity).

Indeed, in the following case, kidnapping takes on an almost official cast. In the wake of Li Zhengyou's death, the three men hired to detain him described the circumstances surrounding Li's abduction and subsequent suicide.[22] Yuan Tai, Zhang Sheng, and Liu Kunshan testified:

> I, Yuan Tai, am a night watchman in the village. We, Zhang Sheng and Liu Kunshan, are security guards [*xiaojia*] in Xiema market. We do not serve as runners at the court. This month on the sixth day, Zeng Dexuan hired us to detain into custody Li Kunshun's son, Li Zhengyou. He said that during the previous winter sacrifice,[23] Li, along with Zeng Yizheng, carried off [Zeng Dexuan's] food and grains. On the eighth day [of the month], community leaders mediated a settlement according to which Li paid two *dan* of foods and grains, 8200 cash, and eight hundred cash in port money [*kouan qian*]. This money was to be delivered to Chen Bingnan who would leave it at the village office. We certainly did not

demand the money. On the ninth, Li Zhengyou returned home, and on the eleventh, we heard that Li Zhengyou had the night before, in the middle of the night, hanged himself at home.[24]

In their description of the "detainment," it sounds rather official. The three men hired were apparently some sort of security officers, and much of the language they employed mirrors that used by court runners. The slippage between official and unofficial roles was such that they felt compelled to clarify the point that they were not in fact court runners. It, apparently, would have been possible to mistake the three men for official agents of the state. The amount owed was coolly calculated, and the "payment" was to be handled properly and deposited with a formal office. The general impression is that this detainment was an acceptable practice carried out with the approval of the village authorities.

Li Zhengyou's father, Li Kunshun, framed the dispute in different terms. He argued that his son had not stolen anything, and that, in fact, it was Zeng Yizheng who had stolen from his uncle, Zeng Dexuan. Li insisted that Zeng Dexuan had demanded 13,000 *wen* to pay his son's debt, and stated that he had paid Zeng 9,000 of it. Li's son was then released, but became "desperate" [*qingji*] and killed himself.[25] In this telling, the problem was not really the kidnapping. Instead, the problem was the false information that served as the basis for the abduction. The process was fine – it just had the wrong man.

Li expressed no shock or surprise that someone would be kidnapped for owing money. In fact, despite his conviction that his son had been falsely accused, he had worked through the local system: he brought his son clothing and arranged to pay what he could. Li gave the payment to Chen, who then deposited it at the village office – again, suggesting that this was locally acceptable behavior, if misdirected in this instance. Community leaders were aware of kidnappings, but only moved to settle the dispute, not to challenge the legitimacy of the practice. Even the magistrate did not punish this kidnapping, instead instructing that payment be made to Li as restitution. Again, kidnapping went unchallenged and unpunished. Only the resulting death was the issue.

Up to this point, I have mainly considered kidnapping as it was deployed to recover debt, but this was not the only motivation for this act. In a case from 1900, a Buddhist nun meted out a similar sort of private justice to her defiant subordinate. This case began with the brutal murder of a Buddhist nun named Zhilu.[26] Her father's report describes how he had sent her to live at Yueming Temple at the age of five.[27] Fifteen years later, things went very badly for her. According to her family's testimony, another nun, Deming, was having a sexual affair, and as rumors of her misdeeds spread, Deming murdered Zhilu to cover her tracks. Zhilu's father had gone to the temple looking for his daughter only to be told by another young nun that Zhilu had been tied up, poisoned, beaten, had the lower parts of her body branded by a pair of fire tongs by Deming and others, and that her body had then been secretly buried. On hearing this, he brought a suit to the county court.

Parts of this shocking account were challenged by the autopsy that was conducted. The coroner found extensive injuries from beatings (likely from a wooden object) and ligature marks, but no burns or evidence of poison. The examiner concluded that Zhilu had died of the injuries she had sustained. Even though this new evidence proposed a slightly less savage scenario, the young nun clearly had been brutally beaten to death. This salacious tale of sex and murder in the temple was not refuted by a series of nuns brought to court to testify.

In fact, although they rejected many aspects of Zhilu's family's account, the nuns painted a no less sensational picture of sex, scandal, and violence in Yueming Temple.[28] In her testimony, Deming presented this version:

> I am from Ba County originally. I am 34 *sui*. My common surname is Ding. Both my parents are dead. I was seven *sui* when I entered Yueming Temple to become a nun; my father was already dead. This nun Dequan is my senior fellow apprentice. Nun Yuejiang is my apprentice. The deceased, Zhilu, is [also] my apprentice.... Because Zhilu did not follow the monastic rules, last year [she] and this nun Qingtao were having an affair [and] they were found out by a nun, Qingtao was expelled. After this, Zhilu [became] very lazy; [she] wouldn't keep within bounds. She frequently stole things and privately sold it [while working] with that Mou Yushun's brothers.[29]

Deming claimed to have expelled Zhilu from the temple because of this theft. At this point, the head nun's story seems rather clear, if still rather surprising.[30] A sexual relationship was discovered between two nuns, who were required by their vows to remain chaste regardless of the gender of their partners.[31] One of the offenders was expelled, which led to the souring of the other's attitude and behavior. However, this was not the end of Zhilu's interactions with the temple or with the power dynamics that entangled these relationships. Another nun, Dequan, mirroring accounts given by Deming and another nun, testified:

> This year on the 27th day of the first month, Zhilu secretly returned to the temple and snuck in under my bed. I realized and shouted: "There's a thief!" Then, along with a tenant farmer, Mou Yushun, [we] captured her and tied her hands to a temple column. Word reached Deming and she returned to the temple. Relying on He Bingyuan and others, [we] brought the temple together and [they] advised us to send Zhilu under guard to an empty building. For two or three days we regularly sent food. I had no idea she wouldn't repent. She completely smashed the building's window – she wanted to escape. When Deming saw this, she used a short hoe made from oak to hit her several times.[32]

Zhilu's ordeal continued. On the second day of the second month, while still detained, Zhilu quarreled with Mou over some stolen goods, and he too beat her, this time using a bamboo cudgel. At some point during her ordeal, she was brought back into the temple. There she was offered food, but she refused it and, apparently, vigorously cursed the nuns. At this, Deming saw red and again beat Zhilu with the hoe.[33] Zhilu was then held captive for over a week. During this time, she was beaten repeatedly and had refused to eat. On the fifth, she died, and on the sixth a coffin was purchased. Deming, with help from a tenant farmer, secretly buried the body on the night of the seventh. While Zhilu's demise may not have been as scandalous as first reported by her father, it was by any account a vicious and brutal end.

There was more than simple theft at work in this murder. This case exposes the working of power, authority, and reputation in very specific community within the county. In this conflict, Deming's authority was challenged in a variety of ways: her own reputation was sullied, and her subordinates were seen to be running amok. Moreover, according to the testimony from Zhilu's family, Deming herself was having an affair, which Zhilu threatened to expose. All of this imperiled her authority.

Deming occupied an accepted and legitimate position of authority within the larger community. Her status was highlighted by her control over various men affiliated with the temple: men such as the tenant Mou Yushun and his brothers, as well as He Bingyuan. These men, either as tenant farmers on temple grounds or as temple employees, were clearly subordinate to Deming, and perhaps to other senior nuns as well. This exception to gender norms underscores Deming's elevated status. However, her position as a recognized authority figure was predicated on her performance of her role as temple head, and this role was challenged by the public exposure of her own sexual indiscretions, Zhilu's relationship, and Zhilu's open challenge to Deming's standing. She held a fragile authority that, in many ways, paralleled chaste widows' autonomy. In both of these limited spheres for female empowerment, women's authority was precarious and dependent on the ongoing performance of certain norms. These empowered women had to appear chaste or pious to continue to hold their relative autonomy.

In light of these dynamics, Deming's violence is easier to understand. Rather than simple disobedience, Zhilu's actions represented a direct challenge that imperiled Deming's privileged standing within the temple and in the larger community as well. Moreover, given nuns', and particularly older nuns', alienation from the normative roles available to women in the late-Qing dynasty, the stakes were quite high. Defrocked, where would she go? Who could she be? Having exited the family [*chu jia*] to become a nun, there was no way to return.[34]

Despite the particular environment in which this case unfolded, its dynamics of authority and violence are largely congruent, if perhaps in an exaggerated form, with broader norms. Local power holders operated with a great deal of autonomy (an autonomy often recognized, and indeed encouraged, by the state). Violence, such as kidnapping, was available to them as a tool for both protecting their interests and displaying their power.

Sex and violence

The private spaces for rough justice and violence in local communities are also clear in other instances of sexual impropriety.[35] The intersection of sex and violence highlights a geography of private justice in the very same space (the normative family) in which the Qing state was strongly interested in enacting formal justice, suggesting the possible tensions between the two (as well as the doubled power formed by the overlapping of these two systems of authority). The Qing state had strong interest in defending and strengthening sexual orthodoxy.[36] Although there were nodes of resistance to this project for moral transformation [*jiaohua*], in the main, the state's views accorded with popular visions of normative sexual roles. In these cases, then, state authority was all too ready to police sexual transgressions. Locals, however, often ignored the state's desires in favor of private justice. Sexual violence or other transgressions often required immediate reprisals, and this need for immediacy often favored private justice over state intervention. In general, however, both the state and local communities agreed and flagged sexual impropriety as a special circumstance, one that often legitimated violence. The added space for acceptable interpersonal violence carved out by sexual impropriety is clear in a dispute over vegetables that flared into violence that left a pregnant woman dead.

In a plaint from 1896, Zheng Yiting described the murder of his wife.[37] The 35-*sui* Zheng Yiting reported:

> I am an apprentice in Tianxiang Building on Chaoyang Street. I have only my widowed mother and my wife, Yu Shi, in my house. This year in the middle of the day on the 29th of the fourth month, my wife, Yu Shi, was at the front gate [of our house] when the vegetable vendor Zhang Ba came out of the Chen family's house. He saw my wife and used obscene language to try to seduce her, but my wife was not won over and rightfully put him in his place. This enraged him and he beat my wife on her chest and belly, and he pushed her to the ground with the palm of his hand and kicked her. My wife's stomach was already sticking out because she was four months pregnant. At dusk, she was lying on the ground when a neighbor…helped her.[38]

Yu Shi died later that night. In subsequent testimony, Zheng slightly altered his story, now saying that he had witnessed the attack himself and had run to the scene along with another man, Li Songbai. Moreover, he described a much more heated argument between his wife and Zhang. Li also testified that the two men had run to intervene in the shouting match. He added, however, that Yu Shi had told him that the conflict started because she had not wanted to buy vegetables, not as a result of Zhang's lascivious advances. In fact, there was no mention of Zhang sexually propositioning Yu Shi in Li's testimony.

In his own testimony, Zhang did not deny that he beat Yu Shi, but he argued that he had been acting in self-defense. His account offered the same explanation for how the fight started:

> I am from Bishan County [west of Chongqing]. I am 30 *sui*. My father and mother are both dead, and I have no brothers. My wife, Lu Shi, is alive, and we have one daughter.... I sell vegetables for a living....[On the day of the attack], I was carrying vegetables on a pole and selling them on the streets. I came along the street to Zhang Yiting's front door. His wife, Yu Shi, called out saying she wanted to buy vegetables. We had already settled on a price when Yu Shi became suspicious about the vegetables she had selected. [She thought] something was wrong with her selection. I considered upbraiding Zheng Yu Shi that it was not so. Zheng Yu Shi cursed me and I cursed her back. Zheng Yu Shi wouldn't listen and pounced on me. She grabbed my clothes and head and made a lot of noise. I couldn't get away. In a moment, I became angry and desperate. I used my foot and kicked her to scare her off. I had no idea she was pregnant. She loosened her grip and fell to the ground. Zheng Yiting returned; he had run into Li Songbai. Together they came to help, but not in time.[39]

In their report to the court, the local authorities supported this version of events, testifying that the clash began with a dispute over vegetables rather than from Zhang's come-ons, although they learned of events second-hand and did not have direct knowledge of the encounter. Confronted with these competing claims, I can imagine two possible origins for Zheng's tale of sexual impropriety. The first scenario is that Yu Shi told her husband after the attack that Zhang had propositioned her. This was possibly an accurate account of the conflict's roots, yet it is also possible that Yu Shi misled Zheng, possibly because she was embarrassed by the pettiness of the dispute that led to her injuries (and the potential harm done to the baby she was carrying).[40] Or perhaps, she wanted to ensure a more severe set of consequences, legal or extra-legal, for Zhang. The terms of the conflict would have been fundamentally redrawn with Zhang sexually propositioning a pregnant married woman. His violation would have been much more severe (in her husband's eyes, the community's eyes, and in the eyes of the state). A second possible origin for this account is that Zheng himself conjured the tale of inappropriate advances to ensure that Zhang would be severely punished for murdering his wife and his unborn child.

In this conflict, multiple contestants competed to shape the contours of the dispute. In doing so, all participants tried to control the meaning of the violence. Zhang argued that he acted in self-defense in a petty fight on the street. He saw the violence as unintentional and caused by Yu Shi's actions. Yu Shi's unforeseen (and unforeseeable) death, however, required explanation. Common violence, uncommon consequence. Zheng and Yu Shi, on the other hand, steered the dispute toward an acceptable, and even mandatory, form of violence on their part, and a grievous transgression by Zhang. The accusation of sexual impropriety was instrumental in this case. His salacious affront required Yu Shi to defend herself such that this recasting of the dispute rendered Zhang doubly guilty: of sexual impropriety as well as murder. Zheng's framing essentially paints Yu Shi as martyring herself in the cause of the Qing's normative gender order: she defended her honor against his sexual aggression, and died for it. Her violence was normative and positive, while his was transgressive and negative.

Policing sexual reputation often required violence – an immediate form of rough justice. Moreover, acts of vengeance following sexual violations, particularly rape, further make clear the role of private justice in these communities. In these instances, the individuals involved could certainly have gone to the magistrate, who was deeply interested in defending the male householders' sexual monopoly, but they chose not to. Following the rape of Zhang Li Shi, Zhang San Wu'er, aged 50 *sui*, brutally stabbed to death her attacker, Zhang Yingyuan.[41] All the individuals involved in the case were related.[42] In the wake of this violation, two motivations were perhaps present. The first, and most easily recognized, would be sheer horror at the act. The records report that Zhang San Wa'er felt a "surge of anger" after witnessing the attack on Zhang Li Shi. After this, Zhang San Wa'er recruited Li Si'er to help him murder Zhang Yingyuan. The severity of the violation was sufficient motivation to violence.

A second, if more slippery, possibility relates to reputation. The assault on Zhang Li Shi was not only an attack on her; it was also an affront to her family's reputation. Her family was responsible for safeguarding her husband's sexual monopoly. Zhang Li Shi belonged exclusively to her husband, Zhang Laoyao. By violating this understanding, Zhang Yingyuan threatened the family's reputation as a place of order and uprightness, particularly since the attack occurred amongst members of the same (extended) family.

Another aspect of this case is suggested by the "*laoyao*" in Zhang's name, which refers to the youngest member of a family or group. San Wa'er acted to defend the youngest/weakest member of the extended family group, defending both Li Shi's honor as well as her husband's. The young and the female both required safeguarding by violent adult males. The family's reputation was held collectively, such that all family members would feel slights against the common honor. This reputation could also be policed collectively, as we see with San Wa'er's murder of the rapist, which upheld his family's reputation as a place of moral order. The policing of reputation, particularly in matters relating to sexual propriety, is present in many criminal cases.

For example, in 1897, Xu Xinyuan, 45 *sui*, was stabbed to death by his landlord in the house they shared.[43] At first, none of the several people who lived in the house offered any explanation for the brutal murder. Each of these individuals rigorously confined themselves to describing the general contours of the situation, pleading ignorance as to the specific motivations for the crime. The dead man's cousin explained how the two of them had traveled from a county northwest of Chongqing (Xichong County) on business, reporting that "[I] along with him [Xu] trade precious jewels in Chongqing's parade grounds to make a living."[44] The cousin also described how Xu had rented parts of the upper floors of Gao Yutang's building for them to live in, along with Xu's two apprentices.

As for the murder, Xu's cousin testified: "On the morning of the ninth day of the sixth month, [one of the apprentices] came to me and said that his master had been murdered that morning while in bed."[45] The cousin then alerted the authorities. The same apprentice offered a few more details: "I...was upstairs and heard my master crying: 'Save me!' I hurried downstairs and saw my master lying on the bed not speaking."[46] His landlord's wife, Gao Zou Shi, was also at Xu's side and attempted to save him. In her account, Zou Shi repeated nearly the same tale, adding only that her husband had gotten up and left the home at some early, unknown hour.

As details emerged over the course of several rounds of testimony, blame gradually coalesced around the still-absent Gao Yutang. He was now presented as the known killer, although there was still no comment as to his possible motivation for murdering a tenant of nearly ten years with whom he was not known to have any conflicts. The artifice of this collective ignorance was finally shattered in Xu's cousin's fourth round of testimony. The sudden clarity that descended on all involved seems to have been provoked by Gao's return.

At this point, a full ten days after their initial testimony, the cousin reported that Xu had been having an affair with his landlord's wife, Zuo Shi. With fresh lucidity, Xu's cousin testified that, on the morning of the murder, one of the apprentices had told him: "Xu Xingyuan was having an affair with Gao Yutang's wife. He got caught and killed."[47] The two apprentices then confirmed this revelation in new testimony. Zou Shi herself, finally, came clean:

> I am originally from Ba County. I am 42 *sui*. When I was a child I was married, through a matchmaker, to Gao Yutang as his legal wife. I've given birth to two daughters. We get along well, there's no ill will. In 1897, to my surprise, my husband, Gao Yutang, rented to Xu Xinyuan the adjoining rooms [in our house] to live. My husband [later] left on business and was not at home. As a result, Xu Xinyuan tried to seduce me. I didn't give in to him. My husband's luck did not follow him

into business; he lost money in business. Xu Xinyuan's [apprentices] add big amounts – every month [they pay] 1,800 *wen*. Later on, Xu Xinyuan and I committed adultery, and not just once. My husband didn't know.[48]

She then explained how her husband learned of the affair. In her account, Gao discovered the pair in the middle of the night but only returned at daybreak to attack and murder Xu.[49] In his own account, Gao said he knew of the adultery before the attack, which occurred on the ninth day:

On...the afternoon of the eighth day of the sixth month, I returned home from being away. I ran into Xu Xinyuan coming out of my wife's room. [He] appeared very flustered and I knew that they were having an affair. Then I interrogated my wife. She was not able to hide it and she said that in the fourth month she started having an affair with Xu Xinyuan. I was angry and cursed my wife. I said I was going to capture Xu Xinyuan and deliver them together for an investigation. On the morning of the ninth, I went and grabbed a sharp knife and went to Xu Xinyuan's room. I saw Xu Xinyuan was already up. I cursed him and said that he should not have had an affair with my wife. I grabbed him – then he wanted to escape. I used the knife to cut him once on his left rib and on his right side.[50]

Gao then described each wound and his victim's vain attempt to defend himself, adding that he had not meant to kill Xu, only to injure him. Gao was apparently attempting a solo performance of "seizing an adulterer."

Despite these admissions, the exact relationship between Zou Shi and Xu remains unclear. There was an economic angle to their sexual encounters. In her own testimony, Zou Shi stressed the economic troubles her family was having as well as the crucial importance of the rent that Xu and his fellows contributed. Her explanation flows directly from money to sex. She may not have been explicitly obligated to sleep with Xu, but the financial circumstances entangling the pair put her in a position where she perhaps could not have refused his advances. It is also possible that Gao knew about, or even encouraged, the affair. Husbands did sell their wives into prostitution when faced with dire circumstances.[51]

Matthew Sommer has argued that sex work, and specifically polyandry, served among non-elites to preserve the family as a basic social unit. In these situations, "the distinction between marriage and sex work collapses, as a wife exchanges her sexual and other domestic labor with one or more outside males, with her husband's approval, in order to help maintain her family."[52] In Zou Shi's predicament, this may have been the case, but it is clear that at some point, Gao had withdrawn his consent. These relationships were a complex mix of sex and money.

On the other hand, perhaps their relationship was consensual. Zou Shi and Gao had been married as children. As a result, they would have grown up together something like brother and sister. The often-awkward transition to a sexual relationship after marriage could have an adverse impact on the couple's later sexual life.[53] Moreover, Zou Shi and Gao both said that he was frequently away on business, which provided opportunity, as well as perhaps for the emotional space, to seek other relationships. Perhaps there was something to their relationship after all.

For Gao, his humiliation was both personal and public. The adultery forced him to personally confront his failed family. He testified that he was forced to "see through" the sham of his family and bear the disgrace of a cuckold. During the case, Gao confessed that the entire incident had forced him to "become disillusioned" with his family. This sense of personal failure was coupled with the public knowledge of his humiliation, as Zou Shi's affair was commonly known. While there was perhaps little Gao could do to erase his own sense of disgrace and failure, he could work to reverse, or at least moderate, the public verdict on his manhood by attacking Xu.[54] Violence can be a form of communication, and, in this way, Gao's acts were a performance of his honor, a public declaration of his continuing status as a man, despite his "wearing a green hat."[55] A local sense of justice required that he act violently. This performative aspect of justice is visible in many of the conflicts considered in this chapter. Acts of private justice communicated local norms and announced power structures. In instances of sexual transgression, locals could have taken their complaints to court, but they often chose not to. Instead, they drew on locally acceptable forms of violence to defend reputations and right wrongs. Here, we see the face of a local – and immediate – system of justice that used violence to enforce local norms and discipline its members, even if this system's acts were subsequently challenged by state prosecution.

These local acts of violence offered an emotional outlet to individuals confronting the loss or violation of a loved one, or a violation of their own honor, as in the preceding case. While practices of rough justice in Ba County served to punish wrongdoers (from the community's perspective), they also provided an emotional release for the injured party. This was a rough and rowdy informal justice: one that held the possibility for abuse, for the strong to take from the weak, and for the desperate to extort the secure. I do not take an overly romantic view of these practices, as they could easily be deployed against innocents who simply inhabited marginal spaces in the community or to beat down non-conformists of a variety of stripes.[56] Indeed, these acts often policed sexual norms. These performances could have baser motivations as well: opportunities for economic gain and brute acts of vengeance. Marking the boundaries of acceptability, these assaults were public statements of accepted community standards.

Simultaneity

Disputes in court were often static snapshots of social conflict that formed one expression of an often-ongoing clash. While the court case unfolding in the county seat was distant and periodic, the quarrel often continued to have an active – and often violent – social life in the local community. As a forum for dispute resolution, the county court was exploited in concert – *simultaneously* – with a range of other strategies, including local mediation, private justice, and outright violence. Disputes originated in local communities and in many ways never left, despite the county court's taking up the case. This multiplicity of dispute-resolution practices was a fundamental feature of disputation in the Qing. Conflicts did not simply progress from local community to the county court. Instead, state authority remained in contest with other forms of power. Everyday politics drew in and could subsume state power, and through this process, the local community could push for its own justice. This complex matrix of justice-making complicated, and could dilute, the state's authority.

The Qing state was powerful, but individuals lived in local communities where other forms of authority worked in more immediate ways, and often entirely without the state's notice (and occasionally in direct opposition to the state's interests). The limited role of state authority and the power of local forces is highlighted in the following case. In 1893, Cheng Xingfa protested against his mistreatment at the hands of Wang Gui, the sub-district head runner.[57] Wang had opened an opium bar next door to Cheng's home and soon started an affair with Cheng's wife. Local authorities had already intervened and punished Wang (including forbidding him from associating with Cheng's wife), but he persisted in bullying Cheng. Cheng's complaint that day was that Wang had stolen things from his home. He pleaded that in the past he had "feared [Wang's] wickedness but didn't have the courage to accuse him at court."[58] Since Wang had already been implicated in a separate legal case, however, Cheng had found the mettle to bring forward his own accusation.

The primary dispute considered in this case was the suicide of a young man, and the conflict between Cheng and Wang appears in the file as a minor complaint involving some of the same individuals. This conflict's convoluted path to the magistrate's court exposes the crucial interplay between ongoing local conflicts and state authority. While the dispute was not directly related to the suicide, Cheng seized on the state's intervention in the suicide as an opportunity to accuse Wang. Despite Wang's ongoing torment, Cheng was only able to escape his local contexts by piggybacking his complaint onto a more serious one. It was a rather accidental encounter with state authority that worked to break Wang's control over Cheng. But even in this chance meeting with the state, Wang continued to press Cheng, even as the court case continued. As the local fight continued to evolve, court proceedings fell further behind the clash's development.

While local power and state power formed overlapping sphere of contestation, developments in the community outpaced the state's awareness and ability to act.

In his complaint, Cheng included a list of 19 items allegedly stolen by Wang: a pair of gold rings; a silver ear pick; a black lined coat; an oilcloth woman's shirt; man's sateen mandarin jacket; a chest; a pot; a silver hair clasp; a silver *ruyi* (an S-shaped ornamental object that was a symbol of good luck); a woman's blue shirt; a man's lined black coat; a cotton-waded bedspread; a crib; a pair of silver earrings; silver flowers; two pairs of blue underpants; two blue men's shirts; a mosquito net; and a cabinet.[59] This raw display of power mirrored Wang's earlier usurpation of Cheng's wife – first Wang stole his marital bed and then he stole his bedspread. Wang's actions were didactic. Through this brazen theft, Wang asserted – and publicly performed – his dominance over Cheng. No wonder Cheng was afraid of him. After all, local authorities had already proven ineffective in controlling Wang. This, of course, was Wang's point. The routine structures of authority were unable to countermand the immediate neighborhood clout brought to bear by Wang.

He embodied the layering of authority extant in the Qing. The state could intervene, and had the potential to be enormously powerful should it become interested.[60] But most of the time it was not. In these vast expanses, local forms of authority dominated. Moreover, even when one was able to occasionally bring the state, local authorities continued to exert daily pressures to shape to contours of local life. Ironically, this street power was enabled in part by Wang's position as court runner.[61] He was empowered by the state, but Wang co-opted state authority to enhance his own local power, and in his performance of power asserted the primacy of day-to-day social reality on the ground over distant efforts by the state to order local life. The interplay between the local expressions of power and state efforts at control is apparent in many disputes.

In 1890, Zhu Qingsan found himself embroiled in conflict with his concubine's family following her suicide.[62] The family blamed Zhu for Gan Shi's death. At one point, Zhu reported that the deceased's relatives "swarmed" his house, beat him, and smashed and made off with his property. Moreover, they demanded payment of 1,000 ounces of silver before they would drop their agitation. Zhu appended a list of items lost in this assault. His catalogue had 58 entries, including eight "red" contracts for land sales (that is, officially endorsed contracts that served as deeds to land); a jade ring; a gold hair clasp; two silver bracelets; a range of men's and women's clothing; two chiming clocks; a silver bracelet; a gold *ruyi*; two pairs of gold earrings; a gold bracelet; and a gold ear pick.[63]

In another plaint, filed roughly two weeks after the first, Zhu complained that Gan Shi's family had stolen things from him on a second occasion, this time while he and his wife were not at home. He attached another list of items stolen from him. This list had 16 entries: a gold bracelet; a gold ring; a gold ear pick; an ivory opium case; silk underwear; a bloodstone chop; a water pipe; a copper stove; a gold hairpin; a gold *ruyi*; a jade bracelet; a gold-leaf folding fan; a large copper ink stone from Suzhou; a silver opium case; a gold staff; and ten silver flowers. He further admitted to having already paid his antagonists 50 *taels* of silver. Here, rough justice produced immediate material benefits, and resembles the aggressive dunning practices discussed earlier in the chapter. These were forms of disputing that settled accounts as well as scores.

In addition to the possible material benefits of these attacks, they also perhaps satisfied a desire for revenge. If Gan Shi's family believed that Zhu had caused her death, then these were acts of retribution. As such, they conformed to customary understandings regarding the proper performance of vengeance, even vengeance often followed in social scripts.[64] Ritualized collective acts of looting, smashing, and extortion enforced norms and imposed consequences for proscribed behaviors. This violence marked the boundaries of acceptability and helped to construct the community as a social whole. In these processes, the comingling of various forms of conflict and resolution is clear. This complexity is particularly well defined in a case from 1894, when three men reported the death of their nephew, Deng Guomo. This case was complicated by the suicide of Deng's wife, Wu Shi, who killed herself soon after her husband's death. Indeed, this second death would also become a subject of contention. In their initial plaint, Deng's uncles claimed that his tenant, Jin Yimei, had caused their nephew's death.[65] They also noted that Jin had been sleeping with Wu Shi. This plaint was followed by one from a neighbor, who described the circumstances of Deng's death. The neighbor explained that Deng had rented some of his property to Jin, who had opened an opium bar, and that the two men, along with Wu Shi, all lived together (Figure 2.1).[66]

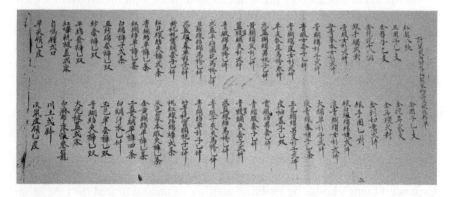

Figure 2.1 List of items appended to Zhu Qingsan's Plaint [BXDA 7666].

The neighbor further explained that earlier that month, he had seen Deng, who appeared "terminally ill," lying by the edge of his property, and that later that afternoon, the neighbor's tenant had gone to the market and reported then that Deng was dead. The neighbor returned home and called local leaders to investigate.[67] Wu Shi had quickly ordered him buried, which struck the neighbor as odd.

About a week later, Jin Yimei's mother filed a plaint defending her son and accusing the dead man's uncles of attempting to profit from their nephew's death. She reported:

> My second son Yimei had married Long Shi and had four sons. In the past he had rented Deng Guomo's house to live in. He paid a deposit of 27 taels of silver. He sells fruit for a living and he lived there over ten years without any trouble. How can I sing the praises of Guomo when he smoked opium? Last month on the 22nd, Guomo fell ill and he died at the edge of Cen Mingde's property. It doesn't have anything to do with my son. This Deng Taishun and others planned a swindle to get silver. They planned to take advantage of his death to demand payment of a debt. So they trumped up this case and falsely accused my son and Guomo's wife, Wu Shi, of having an affair and other lies. Obviously, Yimei has a wife and has sons of his own. His relations with Guomo's wife were just business. If they were having an affair we'd all know. But they've ridiculously [and] falsely accused him of having an affair.[68]

In this plaint, Jin's mother drew a clear contrast between her son and Deng. She lambasted Deng for smoking opium, and stressed her son's respectability, presenting him as an upright family man. She also refuted the notion that her son ran an opium bar, noting his pedestrian life as a fruit vendor. Her simple narrative constructed clear types: family man with sons versus drug addict.

On the same day, Deng's three uncles submitted a plaint expanding their previous accusations. In this account, they accused Jin of covering his tracks. They reported that "[Jin] feared punishment for his crimes" and had taken action.[69] They alleged that he had instructed his younger brother, Jin Si, to pass opium to Wu Shi. She, in turn, used it to commit suicide, adding the second corpse to this single case. Deng's uncles claimed that Jin "sent his brother [to give her the opium] so he wouldn't have to face Wu Shi in court."[70]

In testimony following this expanded accusation, a clearer picture of the power relations between Deng and Jin emerged. This portrait was first sketched by the uncles' testimony. They described their nephew as "simple" before explaining how Jin had moved in and opened an opium bar. He then expanded Deng's house by building another room and forced the renegotiation of the rent. Seeing that Deng was "simple and cowardly," Jin next took up with Wu Shi. The description charted Jin's expanding power over Deng, a domination that led to Wu Shi's death as well as Deng's. In his own testimony, even Jin depicted Deng as a weak opium addict.[71]

Deng's aunt, who also lived with them, then testified that on the night before she died, Wu Shi had called out in the middle of the night. Wu Shi allegedly confided to her that Jin, through his brother, had passed her opium, which she had used to commit suicide. This account was the basis for Deng's uncles' claim that Jin had seduced Wu Shi into suicide. The convoluted and multi-sited development of this conflict was further stressed in a notice from the local community reporting Jin's return to the village.

Following the two deaths, Jin had been ordered by the court to move out of Deng's home, but village leaders now accused him of stealing the contents of the house when he left. They also complained about Jin's intransigence in the face of village mediation and his hampering of a proper burial for Wu Shi. Deng's uncles also accused Jin of making off with the contents of Deng's house and added that Jin's wife, Long Shi, was also causing trouble by behaving like a "rude and unreasonable scorpion" and by shouting that she would have the uncles and others "put to death" for their crimes.[72] The uncles reported that they and community leaders were "making an all-out effort to ensure law and discipline," but it sounded as if they were having a hard time of it.[73]

These interactions illustrate Jin's continuing local power. Despite the explicit intervention of the state and the efforts of local leaders, he continued to plague Deng, and much of the community. The layering of power in these communities privileged the petty local tyrant over state agents in everyday interactions. Moreover, even as Deng's relatives (and community leaders) attempted to pull the state's power into this conflict, clashes with Jin continued to build at home. The court case was not the totality of the conflict, but simply one node in a complex matrix of dispute resolution. The state existed in local society, but it competed with other – sometimes rather petty and arbitrary – forms of authority.

In addition to the complaint, Deng's uncles appended a list of 14 household items that Jin had allegedly absconded with: a blue wadded-cotton quilt; two blue women's shirts; a set of blue undergarments; a silver ear pick; two wooden cabinets; "all" of the pots, dishes, and bowls; a light blue hemp mosquito net; a cotton woman's vest; a silver hairpin; a pair of silver bracelets; two flat beds; and a copper water pipe.[74] The looting of these objects was an extension of the conflict. Theft formed another mode of disputing, along with outright interpersonal violence and attempts at mediation both at court and informally. The ritualized smashing and stealing of things was a vital part of the performance of local clashes. Assaults on property were often linked to legal wrangling already underway at the county court. In his study of informal social control, legal scholar Robert Ellickson writes: "One reason people are frequently willing to ignore law is that they often possess a more expeditious means for achieving order."[75] In Ba County, however, there was no stark choice between informal resolution and formal adjudication.

Individuals exploited all available venues to pursue their interests, and pursued these sites simultaneously. Conflicts did not ascend neatly from one level to the next; rather, they advanced on all fronts, with the court proceedings often lagging behind the dynamic reality on the ground. The lists of objects contained in case files lay bare the complicated chronology of ongoing conflicts that drove disputes, revealing the dynamism and fluidity of disputation in the late-Qing period. These assaults took place within a multi-sited landscape of dispute resolution. Violent acts occurred *at the same time* as both state-led attempts at resolution and local informal mediation, and this simultaneity is key to understanding disputing in Ba County. Because, as we see, individuals worked concurrently on multiple fronts to solve conflicts, employing the layered authorities of personal connections and family, the community at large, and the state. Often there was no binary choice between formal and informal, or even the simple influencing of the former by the latter. The process was messier and more complex than that.

Indeed, my conception of justice making stresses the simultaneous pursuit of resolution across multiple sites, and places greater emphasis on the local "prehistories and postscripts" of conflicts mentioned at the beginning of this chapter. Disputes began in local communities, could re-erupt there after court intervention, and were often adjudicated simultaneously in both formal and informal venues. This expanded sense of justice making in the county makes clear the state's often limited presence in this key process and reduces official power to an ephemeral contestant in a crowded field of authority. Justice making was routinely dominated by locals, and not just by gentry and other elites. All members of the community could participate, however, unequally in this process.

Violence as a tool for community building

Violence often had a prescribed and routine presence in the community. Acts that might seem as anti-social were in fact deeply social and could drive social organization. In this way, they were constructive and constitutive. Indeed, one practical reason for son preference in the late-Imperial period was that the raw manpower they provided was necessary to defend family interests. Elderly men without sons might more easily be victimized by the predatory behavior of others.[76] Sons (and male relatives in general) enlarged the body of men available for violence. Elizabeth Perry has described the essential work performed by the ubiquitous surplus males in the endemic violence of North China. She notes that the same people, often dismissed as "marginal men," played crucial and recognized social roles – often violent ones – that benefited the local community. Violent predation on rival communities "need not be seen as the domain of solitary individuals, forced into asocial behavior by their lack of communal bonds."[77] Perry has also described how this practice involved family organization as well as that of neighbors or even hired guards.[78] She further notes, "collective action implies organization, but this may be variously based upon kinship, settlement, class, friendship, occupation, or a number of other ties."[79] These men and their violent acts were integral parts of local society, especially when locals could not rely on state interventions alone to secure one's property or defend homes.

These constructive acts of bloodletting reveal the importance of properly locating violence within local communities. Violence, most often wielded by neighbors and kin rather than by "rootless rascals" or other outsiders, was not outside the community but was instead a constituent part. The violence that sometimes animated private justice can also be seen in other aspects of informal security strategies. Collective organization of crop watching ensured order and relied on extended ties and networks for success. Philip Kuhn noted that crop-watching organization existed as a "purely non-official effort, based on local initiative and management."[80] Both Joseph Esherick and Kenneth Pomeranz have stressed crop watching as a tool for both promoting security and defusing class tensions within the village.[81] Crop watching, which carried with it the potential for violent interactions, was foundational in the organization of village security, and facilitated the militarization of the local community to defend its interests or attack other communities. These small-scale communal ties have been explored mainly in connection to their revolutionary potential. My investigation, however, takes a broader view, returning to the quotidian use of community bonds in informal dispute resolution to consider the resting temperature of violence in the county.

In many of the cases presented here, individuals rallied neighbors and kin to descend on the home of their adversary. Once there, they stole or broke household items, often beating the owner as well and making demands for greater cash payments. Each of these assaults in the chapter also led to a court hearing, which formed yet another stage on which to enact the conflict. Such theatrical clashes had both economic and emotional components. They were simultaneously constructive (of close kinship bonds, identities, and values) and destructive (of broader community bonds and property). At the same time, they were public performances of outrage that served to shame and punish the attacker's target. They were attempts to fix the social meaning of the conflicts, the local truths of them. The assaults in these *ming'an* cases are not carbon copies of each other, yet they do display important similarities and possess a ritual-like quality.

In these acts of rough justice, the community policed itself against transgressors, but, moreover, these acts also continually constructed these same communities by practicing its norms and inscribing them on actual events and individuals. Violence was made available to individuals based on their membership in the community. This was a fundamental benefit – and obligation – that accrued from association. The power of a particular form of association, the family, is the subject of the next chapter.

Notes

1 E. P. Thompson, "Rough Music," in *Customs in Common: Studies in Popular Culture* (London: Merlin Press, 2009) 530.
2 Huang Liuhong, *A Complete Book Concerning Happiness and Benevolence: A Manual for Local Magistrates in Seventeenth-Century China* (Tucson: University of Arizona Press, 1984), 265.
3 In a very different setting, Carolyn Conley argues that "recreational violence was also a response to the monotony of rural life. Fighting was often one of the very few leisure activities available in the countryside." Moreover, she stresses that violence was one of the only roads to individual social status open to young, unmarried men. Carolyn Conley, "The Agreeable Recreation of Fighting," *Journal of Social History* 22, no. 1 (1999): 59.
4 For examples, Kung-Chuan Hsiao referred to the "uneasy tranquility" that existed at the local level, and T'ung-Tzu Ch'ü stressed the seemingly natural emergence of local power holders. Hsiao, *Rural China*, 503. Qu, *Local Government*, 168–193.
5 The Code defines this as catching the lovers in the location where the act occurred [*jiansuo*] rather than stating specifically that the couple must be caught in the act, but the implication is the same. *DLCY* 285.00.
6 The parsing of these questions required a full 36 sub-statutes. *DLCY* 285.01–285.36.
7 I employ a rather loose definition of ritual that emphasizes Durkheim's conceptualization of its constructive aspects: "it is by uttering the same cry, pronouncing the same word, or performing the same gesture in regard to some object that [rituals] become the necessary way for achieving group cohesion." David Kertzer, elaborating on this Durheimian approach, writes: "What is important about rituals, then, is not that they deal with supernatural beings, but rather that they provide a powerful way in which people's social dependence can be expressed." In this view, the lived *experience* of ritual is its key element. The groups strengthened by this cohesion were nested inside still larger groups, with ritual serving to divide as well as unify. In short, ritual was a social tool. This definition, and the acts it seeks to describe, moves beyond the more formal ritual and ritual practice described by other scholars. For example, in *Spectacle and Sacrifice,* David Johnson focuses on local festivals and opera, but my enlarged concept of ritual allows me to consider a range of acts that fall outside more strict consideration of ritual. Emile Durkheim, *The Elementary Forms of Religious Life* (New York: Free Press, 1995), 272. David I. Kertzer, *Ritual, Politics, and Power* (New Haven: Yale University Press, 1989), 9. Johnson, *Spectacle and Sacrifice.*
8 The anthropologist Robert Redfield has noted that "retaliative force is stylized by custom into a sort of ritualistic revenge, and something like the legal process." Redfield's discussion concerned "primitive" societies that had not developed codified systems of law but had built informal systems that exhibit a "legalistic point of view." While the Qing certainly had a robust tradition of codified law, there remains something law-like in these local processes of dispute resolution. Robert Redfield, "Primitive Law," in *Law and Warfare: Studies in the Anthropology of Conflict*, ed. Paul Bohannan (New York: The Natural History Press, 1967), 12.

9　The word most often employed to describe these acts was "private detainment" [*siya*].

10　See *DLCY* 273.00 and 312.00.

11　BXDA 7694.

12　Teahouses were well-known sites for dispute resolution, where individuals would gather to negotiate their grievances, so perhaps they were meeting to settle their conflict. For a full discussion of the social role of teahouses, see Di Wang, *The Teahouse: Small Business, Everyday Culture, and Public Politics in Chengdu, 1900–1950* (Stanford: Stanford University Press, 2008), 175–199, 203–223.

13　*DLCY* 299.00.

14　I consider this issue more fully in Chapter 4.

15　I do not intend to posit the strong class connotations of James Scott's own interpretation, particularly given the apparently low standing of all the parties involved in this case. Instead, I use the term to highlight the potential for forms of positive action "hidden" within diverse social practices. See, Scott, *Weapons of the Weak* and James Scott, *Domination and the Arts of Resistance: Hidden Transcripts* (New Haven: Yale University Press, 1990).

16　BXDA 7806.

17　Ibid.

18　Ibid.

19　Zhang Shi claimed that this illness was the result of a first, unsuccessful suicide attempt made by eating opium. He was later found dead at Zhou's home after he had succeeded in killing himself (this time by cutting his own throat).

20　My views on this are shaped by Natalie Davis' insights and Walter Johnson's further discussion. See Natalie Zemon Davis, *Fiction in the Archives* (Stanford: Stanford University Press, 1987) and Walter Johnson, *Soul by Soul* (Cambridge: Harvard University Press, 1999), 183.

21　Sommer, *Sex, Law and Society*, 197.

22　BXDA 7738.

23　The winter sacrifice [*la*] was held three days after the winter solstice in the twelfth lunar month.

24　BXDA 7738.

25　Ibid.

26　BXDA 7985 (This case is continued in BXDA 7986).

27　In the Qing (as in other periods), children were often given to religious orders for reasons of poverty as well as piety.

28　In late-Imperial China, temples often enjoyed a rowdy reputation as sites of sex, violence, and assorted heterodoxy. Temples were spaces that fell outside sexual and familial norms, and were consequently suspect. For an example of a less decorous vision of a temple, one has only to think of the tattooed monk Lu Zhishen's outrageous behavior in the classic novel *Water Margin*.

29　BXDA 7685.

30　Descriptions of female same-sex relationships are extremely rare in Qing legal documents, although they do appear in literature. In fact, this is the only legal case featuring female same-sex desire that I am aware of. Perhaps these relationships were less visible, and the Qing state was clearly less concerned with these relationships than with male same-sex encounters. While male sodomy was expressly prohibited by the Code, sexual affairs between women go unmentioned. For a fuller discussion of these issues, see Tze-lan Sang, *The Emerging Lesbian: Female Same-Sex Desire in Modern China* (Chicago: University of Chicago Press, 2003), 37–65.

31　Again, the question of female/female sexual relationship in Buddhism is a tricky one. According to Bernard Faure, "what we would call lesbianism, but for which

the Buddhists have no name, was at best perceived as a poor imitation of het-
erosexual relations – or a preparation for them – and as such condemned." For
Buddhist clergy, all forms of promiscuity were theoretically condemned, those
between women included. Faure notes that that it was

> prohibited for a nun to undress in the presence of another woman…, to be
> massaged by her, for two women to examine each other while joking, to dis-
> cuss sexual matters, to sit on the bed of a young woman or girl, or to examine
> her wardrobe.

More generally, there was no clear discourse surrounding these practices,
unlike male/male sex acts, and, perhaps more importantly, as sex was largely
understood in terms of penetrator and penetrated, female same-sex acts fell
outside this imagery. Bernard Faure, *The Red Thread: Buddhist Approaches
to Sexuality, Revised and Expanded Edition* (Princeton: Princeton University
Press, 1998), 81, 82.

32 Ibid.

33 Deming's repeated use of the hoe, its apparent constant availability (she employs
it in both the empty building and in the temple), suggests a degree of premedi-
tation to the beatings – she was sure to have to hoe at the ready, presuming that
she would have to use it again. Deming may have been provoked by Zhilu's ob-
scenities, but she was prepared to administer the beating.

34 For a general discussion of the place of nuns within the Qing sexual pantheon,
see Matthew Sommer, "The Gendered Body in the Qing Courtroom," *Journal
for the History of Sexuality* 22, no. 2 (May 2013): 293–295.

35 Most acts of sexual violence are not found in the *ming'an* category of the archive,
and it is unclear how precisely these cases ended up in this file. In this section,
I consider some of the cases that found their way into the *ming'an*, and use sex-
related violence as a view on private justice.

36 Over the Yongzheng and Qianlong reigns, there was a massive expansion of new
sub-statutes governing the sex lives of Qing subjects. In this period, Janet Theiss counts 25 new sub-statutes parsing various illegalities in the contracting of
marriages; over 40 new sub-statutes covering homicide resulting from sexual
assaults, adultery, and prostitution; and 25 more fresh sub-statutes related to
causing a woman to commit suicide through improper behavior. Theiss, 47.

37 BXDA 7815/7818 (The relevant records span two separate case files. The first file
also contains scraps from other cases).

38 Ibid.

39 Ibid.

40 Zhang Yitang testified that he was 35 *sui* and still had no children. This would
have put enormous pressure on him to ensure the viability of Yu Shi's pregnancy.

41 BXDA 7927.

42 The men, including the rape victim's husband, are all described as "*xiaogong
tangdi*." *Xiaogong* refers to the length of mourning required (five months) and
was both a ritual and legal description of the closeness of relations. *Tangdi*
means "younger paternal cousin." The combination of the two is slightly con-
fusing because paternal cousins usually fell within a "closer" mourning relation,
that of *dagong* (seven months of mourning). However, the impact in the case is
the same, they were related, a fact which increased the severity of both the crime
and the punishment. For further elaboration of family structure and its legal
ramifications, see Qu, *Law and Society in Traditional China*, 15–20.

43 BXDA 7896.

44 Ibid.

45 Ibid.

46 Ibid.
47 Ibid.
48 Ibid.
49 The Code did not allow for this sort of killing. The jilted husband had to act immediately since only the passion of the moment excused his act. *DLCY 285.00*.
50 Ibid.
51 For a complete discussion of the dynamics of wife selling, see Matthew H. Sommer, *Polyandry and Wife-selling in Qing Dynasty China: Survival Strategies and Judicial Interventions* (Berkeley: University of California Press, 2015), 117–276.
52 Matthew H. Sommer, "Making Sex Work: Polyandry as a Survival Strategy in Qing Dynasty China," in *Gender in Motion: Division of Labor and Cultural Change in Late Imperial and Modern China*, eds. Bryna Goodman and Wendy Larson (Lanham: Roman and Littlefield, 2005), 50.
53 For more on this topic, see Arthur P. Wolf, *Sexual Attraction and Childhood Association: A Chinese Brief for Edward Westermarck* (Stanford: Stanford University Press, 1995), 439–475.
54 Anton Blok writes that "violence often has the character of theater and performance in which things are 'said' as much as they are 'done.'" Anton Blok, *Honour and Violence* (Cambridge: Polity, 2001), 111.
55 This expression [*dai lü mao*] for a cuckold comes from sumptuary laws introduced in the Yuan Dynasty (1271–1368) that required the heads of prostitute households and their male relatives to wrap their heads in green scarves.
56 Barend ter Haar considers oral traditions of popular fear in *Telling Stories: Witchcraft and Scapegoating in Chinese History* (Leiden: Brill, 2006), particularly 9–26.
57 BXDA 7881.
58 Ibid.
59 Ibid.
60 For focused expressions of this power, see Philip Kuhn, *Soulstealers: The Chinese Sorcery Scare of 1768* (Cambridge: Harvard University Press, 1990) and Jonathan Spence, *Treason by the Book* (New York: Viking, 2001).
61 Wang's actions also conform to the classic trope of a corrupt and abusive runner. For a fuller discussion of runners, and court staff in general, see Reed's *Talons and Teeth*, where he challenges this stereotype.
62 BXDA 7666.
63 Ibid.
64 The sociologist Jonathan Rieder has noted that revenge "obeys basic social laws, conforms to ethical mandates, considers its usage with cunning, consults the calculus of power, flows through well-worn channels, pays homage to cultural etiquette." Jonathan Rieder, "The Social Organization of Vengeance," in *Toward a General Theory of Social Control* (New York: Academic Press, 1984), 159.
65 BXDA 7796.
66 What went unspoken here was the distinct possibility that Deng was renting his wife's sexual services to Jin.
67 Since the neighbor had not stopped to help Deng when he appeared to be dying, perhaps he was prone to passing out in strange places, which accords with subsequent accusations of his opium addiction.
68 Ibid.
69 Ibid.
70 Ibid.
71 Of course, one of the subtexts of this case is that Jin was Deng's drug dealer, placing him in a further weakened position.
72 Ibid.

73 Ibid.
74 Ibid.
75 Robert Ellickson, *Order Without Law: How Neighbors Settle Disputes* (Cambridge: Harvard University Press, 1994), 28.
76 Arthur Wolf suggested this idea in private conversation.
77 Perry, *Rebels and Revolutionaries*, 63.
78 Ibid., 81.
79 Ibid., 49.
80 Ibid., 154.
81 Esherick, *Origins of the Boxer Uprising*, 65–66; Kenneth Pomeranz, *The Making of a Hinterland: State, Society, and Economy in Inland North China, 1853–1937* (Berkeley: University of California Press, 1993), 88–105.

Part II
Webs of power

3 Family conflict

Contesting and constructing local authority

This chapter turns to a key source of local authority, the family, and considers the forms of everyday politics kin deployed to work with the state to extract resources and maintain power or, less commonly, to challenge state authority. As twin sites of authority, the family and the state often reinforced each other's power to achieve shared ends. The state was committed to defending the normative commoner family as both a source of revenue extraction (for the state and local elites) and as an ideological project that saw the hierarchical relationships embedded in the patriarchal household as a miniaturized version of the state's own connections to its subjects. The local community too was largely committed to defending the family, as it represented the means to controlling land and ensuring survival. Indeed, the family was recognized by both locals and the state as the basis for social order and social reproduction, as the foundation of political order.

This chapter also returns to the issue of local knowledge introduced in Chapter 1. Specifically, I consider the family's role in making what I have called local truth, the accepted version of a conflict, often connected to a specific demand for justice, that community leaders presented at court. Local truth was not necessarily a disinterested expression of some objective reality, yet, when presented in court, it was key in the state's production of its legal truth, which was the state's official rendering of the conflict and its meaning. The state's "truth" then moved out of the courtroom and back to the community, where it altered local politics with its verdicts.

Families were central to the tales these authorities constructed and were consequently essential to the production of local justice. Sometimes kin looked to the court to challenge local truths, in an attempt to use state authority to cut against local power. Skeptical of local norms and local verdicts on relatives' deaths, kin appealed to the court to reinterpret what had happened. These insurgent interpretations could also rally local connections for acts of violence, bringing their challenges home.

Family and the production of local order

A messy range of everyday politics animates a case from 1891 and reveals the importance of the family in local order. In particular, the interplay between the family, as both a site of social and economic reproduction, and economic unit, and various forms of authority, including village leaders and the state, makes clear the inherent tensions in the local order, as well as the shifting authorities that sought to regulate and perpetuate this system. In this conflict, adoption, as a strategy to continue the patriline and ensure the economic vitality of the family, played a central role, revealing the reproductive burdens placed on rural women and the pressures of eking out a living. The family, in its manifold assemblages, drove conflict and settlement as enduring familial connections, and competing kinship ties worked to serve their members. This case began when 47-*sui* Jin Wu Shi filed a plaint accusing Peng Zifa of beating her 17-*sui* son to death.[1] Five days later, an initial examination of the body was submitted to the court:

> [The corpse] is facing upward, the facial expression is serene; both eyes are slightly open; the mouth is [also] slightly open; the ribs have a line of three wounds on the left side; the first wound runs obliquely for two *cun* two *fen* in length; the second wound is one *cun* and seven or eight *fen*; each wound is uniformly three *fen* wide; they are purplish red in color; they are all wounds from a bamboo rod. The belly is flat; the two legs are extended together; the left and right arms each have one wound; each [wound] runs obliquely for one *cun* and eight or nine *fen* in length; they are all purplish red in color; they were made by a bamboo rod. On the back of his left leg there is an oblique wound two *cun* eight *fen* in length and one *cun* five *fen* wide; it is discolored black and blue; it was made by a wooden cudgel.[2]

The coroner's report concluded that the deceased had died from these wounds. Wu Shi followed this examination with a request to bury her son, which was granted. She explained:

> The deceased, Jin San, also known as Peng Chengshou, is my son. Because my husband died, my family is very poor. Getting food every day was extremely difficult until, after discussing it with my relatives, I gave Jin San up in adoption to Peng, who took him as his heir.[3]

Her testimony went on to explain that following the adoption, she left to work as a casual laborer in Jiangbei, immediately across the Jialing River from Chongqing. Earlier that month, her brother-in-law, Jin Wenming, had come to Jiangbei and told her that Peng had beaten her son to death after the ox he was driving had trampled the neighbor's graves, and that Peng was planning on concealing the circumstances of her son's death from her. She returned home to examine the body, but Peng would not let her in his home, locking himself inside with the corpse until she called village leaders for help. This account was supported by Wu Shi's brother-in-law's testimony, and lineage leaders also supported her story, although without the same degree of detail. They testified that they had overseen the adoption, which had gone smoothly, and that Wu Shi later reported to them that Peng had beaten her son to death. These lineage represent-atives had gone with village leaders to see the corpse and reported that it showed severe wounds.[4] They then came to court with Wu Shi to report the matter.

The deceased's wife, Peng Xu Shi, testified next. After establishing her relationship to those involved, Xu Shi noted that Peng was not in court, the first explicit reference to his absence.[5] She did not explain this but instead simply narrated her version of the events leading to Jin San's death: on the fourth of the same month, Jin San was working with the ox in the fields when the animal trampled on the Du family's grave markers, destroying them. The Du family was Peng's landlord. That night, the family told Peng what had happened and he flew into a rage, beating Jin San with a bamboo cudgel. When Xu Shi and Peng's wife, Peng Yu Shi, tried to protect Jin San, Peng beat them as well. Terrified, Xu Shi fled outside to hide and, less than an hour later, her husband was dead. Jin San was buried the next day, and Xu Shi claimed that her husband had been buried quickly to prevent her from discovering the cause of death.

Eleven days after this testimony, Peng's wife, Yu Shi, filed her own plaint. In this document, she described a very different clash:

> Jin Wu Shi, along with [her husband] Pockmarked Jin the Fourth, had given her young son, Jin San, in adoption to my husband, Peng Zifa, as his son. We changed his name to Peng Changshou. The adoption con-tract was clear and witnessed. This year [he turned] 17 *sui* and we have already taken Xu Shi as a daughter-in-law without any problems. Out of nowhere on the third, Changshou was cutting the grass and somehow encountered disaster, whereupon he came back home and hanged him-self. Then his birthmother, along with Pockmarked Jin the Fourth, with the backing of their neighbors, demanded six strings cash. Then on the 12th, Pockmarked Jin the Fourth and six others... repeatedly came to the house smashing things to bully and intimidate us. My husband fled and hid.[6]

Not only did this testimony offer an explanation for Peng's absence, it also fundamentally altered the terms of the conflict, depicting Peng as the victim and denying the homicide charge, as well as altering the timeline of Peng's adoption. Moreover, this description shifted the crux of the conflict away from Jin San's death and onto his birth family's behavior following his de-mise, altering the case from an accusation of homicide to one of bullying and intimidation. The case appears to be a conflict between competing wings of the family. Evidently, separation by both distance and adoption could not fully sever their blood ties and the enduring connection between the two drove the birth mother to intervene.

Yu Shi's recasting of the conflict was followed by dramatic news of Peng's arrest. A brief report from village leaders in a nearby market town announced that they had detained Peng and turned him over to court runners. Following his capture, Peng filed his own plaint, reiterating his wife's claims regarding the Jin family's attempt to extort money for the burial. Moreover, Peng alleged that a village leader, Wu Yuanyi, had conspired with the Jin family to intimidate and bully him. To add further specificity to his accusations, Peng appended a list of 14 items stolen by his adversaries: over eight *dan* of food grains; four *dan* eight *dou* of sorghum; over one *dou* of green peas; blue wadded cotton quilts for three beds; a man's gown, underpants, and undershirt; a tin vessel for tea or wine; over 120 *jin* of cured meat; over four *dou* of glutinous rice; over two *dou* of rice beans; over two *dou* of soy beans; two burlap mosquito nets; four hoes and rakes; silver ornaments worth three *liang* eight in cash; and a range of household items such as pots bowls and a table. The list also notes that various other odds and ends were damaged but not included on the list.[7]

The magistrate's rescript on Peng's plaint ordered the careful investigation of the cause of Jin San's death, particularly whether he died of his injuries or from hanging, and, following this, the magistrate brought the parties back to court to testify yet again. While Wu Shi and her family reiterated their account, Peng now dramatically altered his story:

> I am a Ba County native, and I am 48 *sui*. I am married to Yu Shi, but we had no sons or daughters. I adopted Jin Wu Shi's third son, Jin San, as my heir. We changed his name to Peng Changshou and arranged for him to marry Xu Shi. Because he was born outside our family I had to repeatedly warn him about his errors, but he would not change. Last year on the third day of the twelfth month, I was returning from the market when Yang Lao told me that while tending the ox my [adopted] son had trampled and destroyed the Du family's graves and that he wanted to tell the Dus. Because I was drunk I lost control and picked up a wooden cudgel and beat my son on the back of his left thigh. [Then] I was afraid and fled.[8]

Yu Shi then abandoned her claim that her adopted son had hanged himself and echoed her husband's account, with both of them dropping any mention of intimidation by the Jin family. As a sad coda to having drunkenly beaten his adopted son to death, Peng languished in jail for a month after his confession before finally dying in custody.[9]

What does Peng's sad fate say about local justice in the late-Qing dynasty? What role do mosquito nets and soybeans play in this story? Peng's mundane inventory of stolen property and damaged goods reveals the complicated roles of family in local society. Families were communities of potential violence, meddlers, and guardians. In this case, the Jin family worked as a group to punish Peng, whom they blamed for the death of their relative, and extract compensation. Moreover, Peng's testimony stating that village head Jin Yuanyi assisted or oversaw this violence suggests a normative role to these acts, casting them as village practice. Wu Shi's connections to her son were not severed by adoption, and she still demanded satisfaction following his death. The persistence of familial bonds is clear in legal cases in which natal families sought justice for their kin, including daughters, after their deaths. There were complicated webs of responsibility and oversight that patterned local power.

In this case, stealing and smashing things, as well as physical intimidation, exacted a financial penalty on Peng and publicly shamed him into paying "burial expenses." This confrontation also served as an emotional release for angry family members who continued to live in the same community as Peng. Social obligations were not easily broken. The public performance of outrage, of grief, of accusation can be seen in this account of Jins' assault on Peng's home. The soybeans and the mosquito nets were props for this performance. The destruction was a public notification of conflict and discord. By attacking Peng Zifa's home, the Jin family asserted the legitimacy of their claim, and their notion of local order. They demanded justice and reified the conflict into stark categories of right and wrong.

Equally clear among this destruction are the ways in which families were constructed and worked to protect their members. The most obvious issue in this particular conflict was adoption. Practices varied widely across the Qing, but, in this case, adoption was an essential strategy that produced (in theory) an heir for Peng, as well as means for Wu Shi to escape the burden of another child.[10] Adoption formed families, and also worked to reproduce local order. The family was an economic unit, as well as a ritual and reproductive one, that controlled land and labor for its own survival, while also serving the extractive needs of the state and local elites, such as Peng's landlords – the Du family. Adoption, consequently, was a form of everyday politics that provided a workaround that served the needs of the patriline, local elites, and the state.

Indeed, producing a male heir was the central task confronting families in late-Imperial China. Male heirs carried on the patriline, delivered support to parents in their old age, and provided important labor. As Mencius famously wrote: "There are three ways of being a bad son. The most serious is to have no heir."[11] Peng was facing just this tragedy. As stated in his testimony, Peng and his wife were unable to have children, and turned to the Jin family, who had three sons, to find an heir. The process was carried out formally, with a contract signed by witnesses. In this particular instance, this local solution failed. Peng seems unable to have seen Peng Chengshou fully as his son: "he was born outside our family," "he would not change."[12] Peng echoed a widespread fear that sons adopted from outside the lineage would never truly be loyal to their new families, particularly when adopted at such a late age.[13] This fear testifies to the enduring connection between adopted sons and their natal families.

This anxiety came to life with the continuing involvement of Peng Cheng-shou's natal family, who first brought the case to court, and continued to pursue justice well beyond the scope of official sanction. As Peng dreaded, Peng Chengshou was not cut off from this family by the process of adoption, and his natal family's obligations to him had not ended. Peng Changshou's complicated family demonstrates how kinship ties aggregated, enmeshing individuals in dense webs of relations and responsibilities, without alienating former bonds. Despite the formality of the contract, family relationships were not fully alienable, particularly when members of the families remained in relatively close proximity. Peng Zifa knew it, and Jin Wu Shi knew it too.

This conflict reveals two key aspects of local order. The first comes as the case's backstory, and centers on Wu Shi's poverty and Peng's use of his economic means to acquire an heir (as well as a daughter-in-law). Adoption relieved Wu Shi of the burden of another mouth to feed, provided Peng with a means to continue the patriline, and allowed the landlord and state to extract surplus from Peng's labor. The construction (and destruction) of a family served the needs of local order. The second essential element of local politics visible in the cases emerges from Peng's murder of his adopted son, and features new authorities and various modes of contestation. Following Peng Chengshou's death, Wu Shi and her relatives intervened, smashing and looting, demanding justice for her son's death. Village leaders also moved to interpret the conflict, and formulated a local truth that demanded justice for Peng's homicide. The county court also intervened and investigated the meaning of the violence, building on the community's local truth and reinforcing its verdict. In both of these key aspects, the family was central – it provided local solutions to enduring problems, disciplined community members who violated norms, and sought justice for its members. This case suggests the diffused but powerful ties that surveilled social relations and could be marshaled to demand justice.

Suicide

The family's essential role in the making of local justice is perhaps most clear in legal cases following suicides, particularly those of women.[14] They expose practices of contestation and the construction of both local and legal truths.[15] In particular, the legal record makes clear the meanings survivors attributed to acts of self-annihilation as well as the instrumental use of suicide to reach desired ends. These acts only enter the historical record as a potential crime. Officially, Qing courts were committed to getting to the bottom of suicide cases. Huang Liuhong urged magistrates to actively investigate them, boasting: "During my tenures of magistracy I strictly ordered all village headman and local elders to report suicide cases with accurate descriptions and to designate them as such."[16] Huang devotes several pages in his magistrate's handbook to the subject of suicide.

Song Ci's *Xiyuan ji lu*, completed in 1247, served as a guide to court medical examiners [*wuzuo*] down to the Qing, and explained how to determine if suicide was the cause of death.[17] In this foundational text, Song writes: "begin by asking the original informant what sort of person the victim was. Was the suicide committed early or late in the day.... It is always necessary to examine the marks with great care."[18] Driving someone to commit suicide was a crime punishable by 100 strokes of the heavy bamboo in the Qing.[19] Consequently, the accusation of this crime carried with it power and a potential for economic reward through various settlement practices. Some of the legal cases that followed suicides can be interpreted as acts of extortion by the family of the deceased. Families might demand remuneration for their loss and, when refused, bring the suit to court. Beyond these simple acts of extortion, the suits filed by relatives often sought postmortem justice for a relative. Having failed to provide appropriate care and oversight in life, kin often worked to ensure that justice was done, or that their relatives at least received proper burials.

While existing scholarship on female suicide in the Qing dynasty has focused on suicide as a site of agency, and as a means for finding female voices in male-dominated historical records, the county-level legal cases from Ba County do not allow for strong affirmation of personal dignity or intent.[20] Moreover, much of this scholarship has focused on elite women, which leaves the vast majority of female suicides unexamined. As illuminating as elite suicides can be, they are the expressions of an elite minority whose choices were shaped by the cultural access granted by literacy and wealth, and who represented perhaps 0.1 percent of the population, with 70 percent of these women being from the Lower Yangzi region.[21]

Janet Theiss has attempted to move the discussion away from social elites by examining legal sources to consider female suicide's rich cultural and social life.[22] Her analysis focuses on the individual and her death, and interprets the meaning of these suicides for the individual involved. While examining a very different set of sources, Theiss too finds agency in suicide, and argues that affronts to public reputation, inappropriate interactions, sexual violence, all required violent and public vindication, and so women resorted to suicide as an assertion of their essential human dignity.[23] Suicide was "an aggressive act" that shouted these women's humanity.[24]

In my reading of court cases, the woman is largely absent, but what remains are other people's interpretations, their deeply partial understandings. The individual, and her specific motivations, were replaced by a *void* at the center of the conflict. There is simply not enough in records collected after the fatal act to parse intent or agency. As an instigating and central act in the court case, suicide removes the only individual who might offer the most insightful interpretation. Without her, there is a darkness at the heart of all these cases.

In court, the void that the women left at the center of the case was given name. Time and again, in the moments before they killed themselves, individuals are described as becoming "greatly distressed" [*qingji*].[25] *Qingji* was shorthand for the intense personal drama that remained largely beyond survivors' ability to comprehend fully. The consistent repetition of this term in the case records suggests that this phrase had become a stand-in or place-holder for a range of human sentiment. As they distilled and compiled tes-timony, court scribes used "great distress" to signify whatever emotional process led the person to kill her/himself. Since that moment is lost to histo-rians, I too must rely on *qingji* and talk around these deaths. Not knowing the intention behind these acts, it is very difficult to portray them as heroic, as futile, or as powerful acts of agency.

> What was left was a body, and this could be endowed with multiple meanings.[26]

A suicide case from 1890 includes the inventory of a young women's coffin, which contained 28 entries, including a solid gold hairpin, a solid gold *ruyi*, a handkerchief, and a variety of garments.[27] This inventory was followed by a parallel list from a medical examination detailing the appearance of Liu Shi's corpse. The coroner determined that Liu Shi had died of illness, and described the body as follows:

> 23 years old, the body measures four *chi* two *cun* in length; it is facing upward; the face has already changed in color; the two eyes are slightly open; the two eyeballs are completely dull; [the corpse] is blue/green from top to bottom; the lips are completely dull and also blue/green; the mouth is slightly open; the gums are completely dull and the throat is blue/green in color; the fingers on both sides are stiff and there are red cholera blisters; the hands are slightly open with the left grasping the right across the breast; the hands are stiff and have red cholera blisters; the abdomen is not distended; the relatives have requested that we not examine the lower body [i.e. sexual organs]...; the cause of death was certainly cholera.[28]

These mirrored lists demonstrate the multiple meanings her body assumed. It was a ritual object in a burial, the subject of forensic investigation, a legal question requiring state intervention, and a social body that rearranged the possibilities for social action and interaction. Her corpse contained all of these multiple meanings. So, while suicides tend not to illuminate the in-dividual, they do make clear the social relations activated by this dramatic act, which can be seen in the justice claims individuals made to interpret the death, to affix a local truth to it so as to define its meaning.

In the wake of suicides, competing meanings were proposed in court. The parties in court, frequently relying on cultural tropes and types, prof-fered their respective versions of the death, and the court, employing its own investigatory techniques, and with a seemingly genuine interest in and commitment to finding out what happened, attached its authority to one version. A verdict may not have been accepted by all parties and could provoke further contestation in the form of violence or continued court action, but the rendering of a decision at court fixed the official meaning of each death to create a legal truth, and these meanings could bring punishment or compensation.

Moreover, opium's dominance as the means of suicide in Ba County ensured that suicide was frequently a *process* rather than a single *act*, and suggests an important new social role of opium in the late-Qing period.[29] Opium overdose resulted in a lingering and unpleasant death, with symptoms including slow breathing, nausea, constricted pupils, moist, cold bluish skin, and uncontrollable drowsiness. Drowsiness could lead to respiratory failure, and to death.[30] The threat of death by opium kickstarted the social machine: families intervened (or not), doctors were called (or not), community leaders may have arrived, and various meanings for the act began to coalesce. The act sent the community into action, and individuals began to construct their local understandings of the events. As these coalesced, questions of blame and justice emerged to expose the roles and expectations that undergirded local life. These crises had to be fit into existing power structures or marshaled against them. In these moments, the individual is less clear than the community's competing assertions of the meaning of her death. Suicide was a social act that activated local justice making, as her death was interpreted again and again.

Natal bonds and postmortem justice

Susan Mann has written that "marriage was the ladder of success for women in late imperial China."[31] There were substantial hazards involved in climbing this ladder, and no rung was more perilous than the first. Young women and girls entering marriage faced a structural imbalance of power that left them vulnerable.[32] Frequently, women remained caught between the competing claims of their natal and married families and, despite talk of women "marrying out," natal families could still lay claim to their daughters, and, through their daughters, even make demands on their new families. This complicates notions of a family headed by a male commoner as a discrete, foundational unit of society.[33] The family unit remained linked to the other families they interacted with.

The ebbing and flowing of these ties, as well as their occasional exploitation and competition, was an important part of local life, and key in the creation of local justice. Cases following suicides further caution against seeing "marrying out" as an end to rights and responsibilities, and instead stress the deep ties that endured across marriage.[34] Indeed, legal cases, however, often make clear the strategies natal families deployed in order to remain visible in the lives of their daughters, or to provide a corrective to the authority of the marital family. This network of care and supervision is visible in the suicide case of Zhou Runxiu from 1891.[35] Her brother, Zhou Liancheng, aged 28 *sui*, described the circumstances of his sister's marriage and characterized the life she married into:

> Last year my sister, Runxiu, had illicit sex. Matchmaker Li Huishan's brothers made an agreement to marry her to Wu Huosan, the son of her older sister's husband, Wu Qiaogui. After they were married, we began to realize that Qiaogui's wife, Li Shi, simply had a shrewish temper. She disliked and scolded my sister until she couldn't stand it, and still she [Li Shi] repeatedly reprimanded her.... This was because my sister was pregnant."[36]

Sadly, in his subsequent testimony, Zhou made no further mention of either his sister's sexual history or her pregnancy. Instead, he detailed an assault on his sister by her mother-in-law, saying Li Shi had beaten Zhou Runxiu with a bamboo stick. Zhou Liancheng further claimed that it was Wu Huosan who had told him about Zhou Runxiu's beating as he explained her death.

Wu, aged 22 *sui*, subsequently filed a counter-plaint in which he stated that he and Zhou Runxiu, whom he refers to as Zhou Shi, were engaged as children and that they were happy even though they had not had any children of their own.[37] He reported that Zhou Runxiu consumed opium on the seventh of the previous month, and that she had lingered until finally dying on the seventh day of the following month. Wu stated that he had hired a doctor to try and save his wife, and that Zhou Runxiu's mother had come and seen the treatment she was receiving. Finally, Wu alleged that Zhou Liancheng and others assaulted his father and damaged their property.

As a result, Wu and his father had agreed to "help" by contributing 20 *liang* of silver for Zhou Runxiu's funeral rituals, and also arranged for another 20 *liang* in compensation. This payment followed an explicit agreement by all parties that her death was of her own doing, and could not be blamed on anyone, seemingly shielding him from formal legal wrongdoing. The court found that the deceased was not driven to take her own life – a criminal offense – but still ordered a payment from her husband's family to the deceased's natal family, a *formal* backing of *informal* compensation. In this moment of state intervention, the magistrate moved beyond the strict confines of the Code in order to mediate the strife caused by her death. Although the law did not require prosecution, social norms still demanded reparation for Zhou Runxiu's death, and her family used the court to enforce its local claim for justice. In this instance, the formal power of the state worked to impose the expectations of informal forms of authority rooted in local norms of fairness. The state lent its authority to justice claims that saw marital families as bearing a clear responsibility for their daughters-in-law's well-being. This was a recognized social expectation that had to be asserted, rather than a self-evident norm. In this way, justice was an act of assertion rather than a hand-out from the court.

The conflict that could surround a wife's entry into a new family was, in many ways, the archetypal family strife and appears frequently in the legal record. The tension between the natal and marital families suggests that although girls may "marry out," natal families continued to track their children, and were often present to demand restitution and justice in the event of suicide. In this way, the local community placed an additional expectation on marital families, and this cost is particularly clear in cases that were explicitly no-fault suicides. These understandings of familial responsibility animated a dispute from 1890. In this case, a woman demanded justice and accused her granddaughter's mother-in-law, Li Zhu Shi, of causing the girl's death, and complained that her granddaughter had been mistreated almost immediately upon her arrival in her new home.[38] The plaintiff, Old Zhou Zhang Shi, reported that her granddaughter's father-in-law had died just after the girl was married. Following his death, Zhu Shi began to harass and mistreat her granddaughter. Zhang Shi claimed that this abuse caused the girl's death (from illness), although she did not explain how the two were connected. Zhang Shi further complained that Zhu Shi had failed to inform her promptly about her granddaughter's death, and that the girl had been given a cheap and unworthy burial. Finally, Zhang Shi alleged that Zhu Shi had had her and her daughter-in-law bound and beaten.

Zhu Shi's family, responding to this pile of accusations, claimed that the girl had been chronically ill since her marriage nearly three years earlier. They further stated that they had agreed when the girl's relatives wanted to take her to see a doctor, and even paid the costs for the medicine. Zhu family members further testified that Zhang Shi had been included in every stage of her granddaughter's illness and burial. Finally, they alleged that once they were at the temple for the funeral, Zhang Shi went berserk and "ran around like crazy," smashing windows and tools.[39] Her actions were a public performance of her displeasure that served to shame and humiliate her adversary. This emotive act was a precursor to Zhang Shi's engagement of the legal system. Indeed, the performance of displeasure continued at court. Litigants used the courts to gain emotional, as well as economic, satisfaction in their search for justice. Indeed, one scholar has written that

> part of the reason why certain people chose to invest in litigation lies in its publicity. Hatreds and social sanctions of all types are useless unless they are advertised to a general public, and the courts of law were geared toward publicity.[40]

Zhang Shi's performance shifted from the funeral to the courtroom, but its meaning remained the same. Going to court was an extension of Zhang Shi's efforts to publicize her demands for justice.

Following Zhang Shi's performance, Zhu Shi's sought redress through community mediation. This should have augured well for Zhang Shi since the man leading this local effort was her relative, but this attempt at settlement was largely ineffective in this case. Although they began immediately after the girl's funeral, these efforts failed to prevent Zhang Shi from bringing the case to court. Zhang Shi, unable to find satisfaction at the local level, sought out intervention from the court. In order to do so, she needed the power of a false, if vague, homicide accusation.[41] The court, however, offered her no escape either, finding that the girl had died of "blood stasis."[42]

Despite the court's unwillingness to accept Zhang Shi's narrative, this case suggests the ways in which family members used litigation to press for the proper treatment of dead relatives. At its root, this case stemmed from a dispute over the proper burial of a dead girl. Zhang Shi pressed her demand for better treatment while the girl was alive. Then, following her granddaughter's death, she intensified her demands by making a violent public scene at the funeral. Finally, finding no redress, she took her complaint to court. While Zhang Shi was unsuccessful in this instance, her case illuminates the court's broader role as part of the repertoire available for the enforcement of familial responsibility, particularly when individuals challenged the authority of marital families.

A similar dynamic can be seen in a case from 1890, which began when Liu Luo Shi filed a plaint following the death of her daughter:

> My husband is dead and I look after the family. Last winter, my second daughter married Li Fangqiao's son, Jingxiu, supposedly as his second wife, but after they were married he made her his concubine instead. The ill will between them grew and grew. Out of nowhere, this month on the 20th, Jingxiu sent his servant to get in touch with me and told me that my daughter, Liu Shi, had suddenly fallen ill. That night I went to his house. All I saw was them putting my daughter's corpse into a coffin. I was overwhelmed and had to be helped to stand and was taken into the house. Jinxiu took advantage of my incapacitation and buried her [quickly].[43]

Luo Shi began by impugning Li Jingxiu's character, accusing him of marriage fraud: she had believed that her daughter was joining his house as a second wife, but she was actually a concubine (she claimed that at the time she "overcame her suspicions" to avoid trouble). She concluded her plaint by saying that Li Jingxiu's servant, Xiong the Youngest, had also told her (after she had "interrogated" [*pangjie*] him) that Li Jingxiu had beaten her daughter to death. Luo Shi said she became determined to examine her daughter's corpse for injuries.

Li Jingxiu's father, Li Fanggu, challenged this account in his own plaint. He stated that Liu Shi had been his son's concubine, as has always been intended, and reported that there had been no ill will after she joined his family. Li Fanggu then described a chronic ailment that plagued Liu Shi, claiming that she often fell ill with scarlet fever. He noted:

In the third month, her illness flared up and a doctor treated her. Then last month, on the 17th, Liu Shi's younger brother, Liu Zaizhi, came to my home for a large banquet. Then on the 19th, Liu Shi's scarlet fever suddenly came back…. The doctor's medicine had no effect. Liu Zaizhi had his hands on her shoulders when she died.[44]

Li noted that Liu Zhaizhi and other relatives came and verified that Liu Shi had indeed died of illness. She was then buried, with proper ceremony and relatives as witnesses, according to Li. Despite his proper conduct, "Luo Shi came to town and began listening to scurrilous talk," which led her to court.[45] The magistrate ordered the examination of Liu Shi's body to determine the cause of death. The coroner's report determined that Liu Shi had died from disease, not from violence.

Moreover, Luo Shi's accusation continued to fall apart when Xiong the Youngest testified that he had not told her that Li Jingxiu had beaten her daughter to death. In her subsequent testimony, Luo Shi altered her account, now saying that her daughter had been married as a concubine, and made no mention of violence of any sort. She continued to claim that Li Jingxiu's servant had come to tell her of her daughter's illness, but no longer alleged that he had whispered to her about a beating. Despite these changes, Luo Shi claimed she was innocent of any "plotting."

Despite Luo Shi's seeming acquiesce, in a final round of testimony, Li Jingxiu claimed that a gang of people was harassing him. He reported that on the day after Liu Shi's death, "[Liu] Zaizhi [Liu Shi's younger brother] led a bunch of his relatives by sedan chair from Chongqing to my house to recklessly stir up trouble."[46] After appealing for local mediation, he had paid over 20,000 cash for "sedan fees." This seems to have satisfied Liu Zaizhi's mob and they dispersed. Li Jingxiu said he had no idea that Luo Shi would be incited by empty gossip. But rumor led Luo Shi to seek justice, in court and in the street. She imposed responsibility for her daughter's death on Li and, through violence as the court failed her, extracted justice from him.

Mothers were not the only individuals who attempted to police their kin's marital families. Brothers (as well as other relatives) also played this part. For example, in 1900, Yang Jinyuan, 31 *sui*, filed a plaint claiming that his younger sister had been beaten to death by her husband, Wang San.[47] According to Yang, the friction between the couple was driven by Wang's laziness and his sister's frequent criticism of his sloth. Wang's mother, by contrast, argued that Yang was trying to profit from his sister's death, and that everybody knew the girl had died from illness. She further claimed that Yang was not present for his sister's death because of his own mother's funeral, and explicitly blamed his absence from the local community for leading to the conflict. Disconnected from local visions of justice, he attempted to use the power of the court against the local knowledge of the community in the service of their shared uterine family.

In late-Qing Ba County, this form of physical separation was not unusual. Family members often became separated from another, frequently due to economic necessity, and thus were unable to exercise regular oversight and protection of relatives. Moreover, given the dominance of virilocal marriage practices, natal families were routinely physically separated from the sisters and daughters. Consequently, at times, family members intervened through the court, rather than using informal local processes, to fulfill familial obligations. While family members were perhaps unable to intervene in life, they could still work to secure a semblance of a good death for their loved ones. Indeed, many of these cases seem to be fundamentally concerned with securing a proper burial for a relative.[48] These legal interventions were expressions of familial responsibility and postmortem attempts to perform the protective role that was an essential element of kinship bonds. In these cases, the enduring power of normative family obligations, and corresponding demands for justice, are clear. Moreover, these conflicts also expose the incongruence between these expectations and lives people often led – lives characterized by mobility and change.

Returning to the case at hand, Yang was attempting to fulfill these normative obligations. His attempt to use the court to achieve this goal was weakened, however, when the autopsy report undercut his claim, concluding that the girl had died of disease. Despite this contrary evidence, Yang persisted in his accusation of murder. This perseverance prompted testimony from Wang, who described the circumstances of his wife's death:

> We were married three years. During that time, she frequently fell ill, of this there is no doubt. This year, last month, my wife suddenly fell ill. The doctor treated her without success. On the sixth day of the month, she died as a result of the illness. At that time, we notified her mother, Yang Mou Shi, who came to our house and saw [everything].[49]

In addition to the participation of his wife's mother, Wang further claimed that the burial had been cleared with community leaders, suggesting that he had indeed provided a good death for her. But, despite the seeming absence of conflict surrounding the girl's death, Yang arrived the next day at Wang's house and smashed things. Wang reported that he had responded to this violence by calling on community leaders, who were unable to mediate a settlement. At court, these leaders buttressed Wang's account by filing a plaint detailing both the conflict and their interventions.

Faced with this comprehensive rebuttal, Yang backed off his claim slightly, acknowledging that there were no injuries visible on his sister's corpse. Finally, after much court wrangling, Yang admitted that his sister had not been killed: "In fact, she died from illness and there was nothing else to it."[50] In this same court session, the deceased's other natal relatives testified that the girl was often sick and had died of illness. That same day, Yang signed documents ending the court case.

Despite his failure, the state recognized his actions as a particular and protected form of legal advocacy. The *Xing'an Huilan* [*Conspectus of Penal Cases*] presents several similar cases in which lies spoken as attempts to ensure justice for family members were treated by courts as less pernicious than "normal" false accusation cases, suggesting that the state was sensitive to this other type of lying, and that it should be treated differently.[51] Given that the aim of the *Conspectus* was to provide guidance for magistrates in adjudicating tricky cases, the attention given to compassionate false accusation suggests that these were singled out as deserving special sensitivity.[52] After all, the individuals in these cases were attempting to fulfill their familial responsibilities by seeking justice for family members, a pursuit generally supported by official Qing ideology. In this way, families pursued multiple courses of action and remediation – both in court and outside it – to find satisfaction.

Kin played pivotal roles in agitating for justice. Natal families served as a check on patriarchal authority, playing a key part in conflicts over women's behavior, as well as serving as strong allies in their daughters' conflicts with their new, marital kin.[53] At the same time, natal and marital families' authority could overlap to form a powerful corrective to improper behavior, particularly in the case of adultery.[54] The suppleness of these connections allowed for their selective and strategic deployment as a means for effecting change in women's lives.[55] Natal families played important roles in non-elite (as well as elite) women's attempts to activate webs of connections to promote their own interests.

Many of the cases in my study suggest an additional aspect of these relationships. Not only could women reach out to pull their natal family into their lives, natal kin could also pull on these ties, often to demand postmortem justice. Natal connections worked in both directions, and continued to be exploited even *after* the woman's death. Beverly Bossler has criticized a gendered analysis of family ties that describes male use of kinship as "strategic" and female exploitation of these same ties as "emotional." Instead, she argues that both strategic and emotional elements can be found in the behavior of both women and men.[56] The same complex coupling of motivations is present in cases from Ba County. Natal families acted on the basis of both emotional bonds and calculated assessments of benefit. In these acts, natal families often used the court as a vehicle to collapse the distance between them and their daughters' marital kin, and to intervene in the circumstances of their deaths. Relatives separated from kin exploited state power to play the protective role inherent in kinship ties, even if these efforts were initiated postmortem.

A web of relationships endured between natal and marital homes, and these ties are clear the moment they were monetized following a suicide. Natal families often demanded restitution, primarily financial, for the loss of their daughters. They often agitated for a proper burial. These kin continued to take an interest in their well-being (perhaps as much as they could), and punished in-laws who failed to take appropriate care of the new members of the family. Indeed, rather than the alienation of daughters from their birth families, natal families continued to make claims and assert rights to deceased daughters and granddaughters. Moreover, these claims make clear the additional burden placed on marital families to ensure the well-being of their daughters-in-law. If they failed to do so, they could be forced to compensate natal kin. This was true even in cases in which the court explicitly found that the marital family was criminally responsible for the woman's death. With these acts, the magistrate moved beyond the exclusively penal confines of the Code to enforce a local settlement. The court backed elements of the local community to construct justice.

The state and the tales families tell

In many legal cases, the events themselves were obscured or contested. In these instances, the court played its role as arbiter: first establishing an official narrative, and then affixing value to people's actions by judging them good/legal or bad/illegal. The court was a center for the production of truth: not of objective truth, but of legal truth. Bestowing the mantle on one version of a conflict was not arbitrary; magistrates based their decisions on the available evidence, which often included flawed, incomplete, and disputative accounts. Once fixed, the official narrative could have powerful, even fatal, consequences. As anthropologist Sally Engle Merry has written: "Law works in the world not just by the imposition of rules and punishments but also by its capacity to construct authoritative images of social relationships and actions..."[57] The power of the law's images did not vanish outside the courtroom. Instead, meanings affixed in the courtroom traveled beyond its confines and returned to local communities, where they acted on social relations and realities. These were not simply abstract constructions. They were intended as transformative forces of social change.

Local informants were central to the creation of official narratives, and often most important among these were heads of families. These individuals constituted a recognized body of normative authority, and they were instrumental in the court's interventions in local justice. So, while the court could be a site of resistance, legal truths often reinforced normative power structures. In this way, the court acted as a conservative force by rewarding normative social organization and behavior, and confirming the power of local elites, heads of households, and even mothers-in-law. A case from 1890 demonstrates the fragility of social norms as well as the lengths the state would go to prop them up.

When Zuo Shi hanged herself, her son, Zuo Guilin, was forced to offer an explanation.[58] He reported that his wife, Zuo Chen Shi, and her ex-husband, Yang Chengzhang, had gone to his mother and demanded money to pay for the debts they had run up smoking opium. This convoluted tale only became clear when Chen Shi's father, Chen Zhankui, explained in court the backstory to this affair. Chen Shi had been married to another man, Zhu Xingfa, at a young age, but Zhu's poverty forced him to marry Chen Shi off to Yang Chengzhang. There was then some non-specific altercation and "further misfortune," the details of which are not given in the case records. This state intervention ordered Chen Shi to return to Zhu. But this was not the end of Chen Shi's complicated marriage history. Her father alleged that Zhu would disappear for days, leaving Chen Shi without anything to eat. Once again, this dire poverty led to Chen Shi being married off, this time (and finally) to Zuo Guilin, a widower (Figure 3.1).

Poverty drove these marriages – Chen Shi was married and remarried to fit economic necessity. In this case, the family, as a sturdy social unit, looks somewhat disposable. For Chen Shi, economic privation trumped any semblance of a normative household. The Confucian family was not possible here, and perhaps not even desired.[59] Zuo Shi's suicide was no longer the subject of contention in this case. Instead, the magistrate intervened to support Zuo's fragile household. Yang Chengzhang was ordered beaten with the light bamboo for "stirring up trouble," a seemingly informal and ad hoc punishment that did not explicitly hold him liable for the suicide. The magistrate intervened outside the explicit confines of the Code. In this case, there was not even a veneer of the normative family unit, but the state did act to support the family unit that had been tenuously created in these dire circumstances. To do so, the state stepped outside its formal procedure, mirroring locals' own poverty-driven departure from normative family structure. Zuo's household may have been far from ideal, but the state went to lengths to defend it.

The court's interest in backing local power structure is also seen in a case from 1890. Wu De'an, 41 *sui*, filed a plaint claiming that his nephew had been beaten to death. Wu stated:

When my sister was young she was married to Cheng Huitang and gave birth to a son, Pinsan. When he was only two, my sister died from illness. Huitang took a second wife, Lin Shi, and had two more boys: Cheng Er (who became a Buddhist monk) [and] Cheng San. Huitang followed [my sister] in death. Lin Shi then plotted to dominate the family mill. In a hundred ways she was ill willed and petty to my sister's son [and] particularly cheated the weaklings in her family. To me and others and [even] to her kin she was distant, particularly in her treatment of my nephew. Her heart was wicked and she plotted murder. Last year on the thirtieth day of the twelfth month, she had the audacity to order Pinsan bound and beaten and he fell to the floor. In protest, he went on a hunger strike and died, and she ordered him secretly/privately buried. The family didn't find out that any of this had happened until later.[60]

This case is another attempt by a family member to exact postmortem justice for a relative. But this version of the conflict was contested the very next

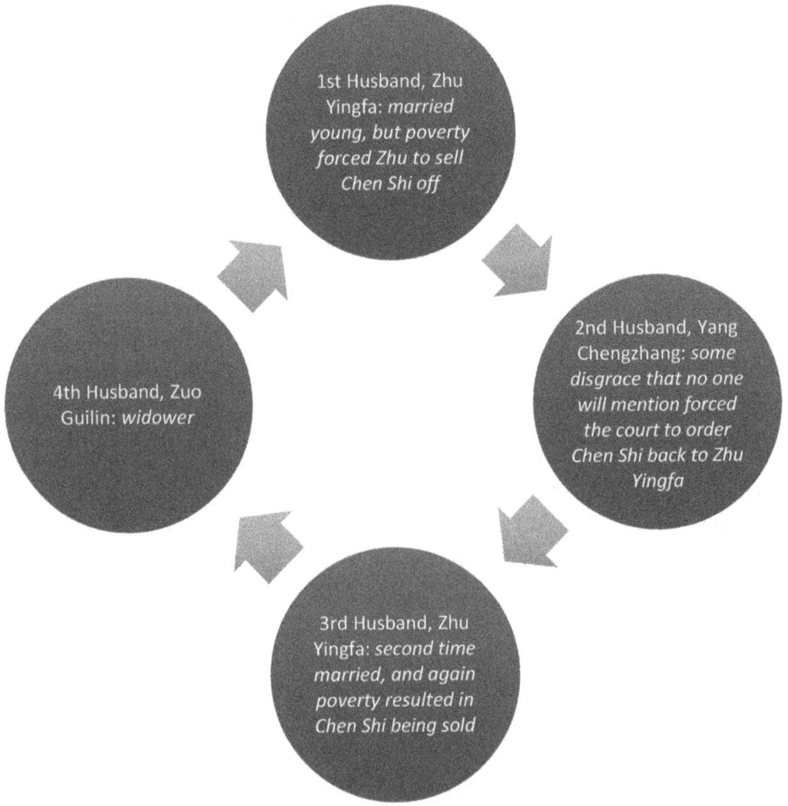

Figure 3.1 The many marriages of Zuo Chen Shi.

day in a plaint submitted by the deceased's paternal grandmother (that is, Cheng Huitang's mother), 74-*sui* Cheng Xie Shi. She accused Wu of black-mail and presented the conflict in starkly different terms. In her version, her grandson had been given his inheritance of over 120 ounces of silver, but he had squandered it. After his own wife died, Cheng's grandson had become reckless and wild. In her subsequent testimony, she elaborated on his irre-sponsibility, saying he smoked opium until his debts "overflowed" and that he would "stop at nothing."[61]

Community leaders repeatedly weighed in on Xie Shi's side, stating that they had seen the body and that her grandson had been properly buried. In the end, the court accepted their version of events. But perhaps this was not what had happened at all. Perhaps Wu De'an had it right the first time. After all, Xie Shi's grandson was superfluous and a drain on family resources. Per-haps he was murdered to cut the family free from him. However, the court, in its ruling, bestowed the mantle of truth on Cheng's version of events. Given that the magistrate was not in a position to know the local realities of the situation, he was forced to rely on the deeply interested intercession of family heads and community leaders to (re)construct a vision of this social reality and then, based on this profoundly partial local intelligence, render his judgment, which then returned to the local community, where it altered local realities to make them conform to the magistrate's vision.

Historians must be wary of unknowingly replicating the biases and power imbalances that existed in a given conflict, and legal records are ripe with this danger.[62] The law works to label individuals and their actions in order to punish them. This is precisely the point of branding an individual "criminal." In many conflicts, the power of the court to name and create truth, as well as the power of local actors to shape the truth presented to the court, is clear. Cheng was able to have her version of the truth accepted and sanctioned by the court largely as a result of her ability to marshal family authority and local community leaders. Her use of these tactics highlights the means by which legal truth was created, and the degree to which this process was framed by existing power relations. This tendency must caution us against overstating the social leveling potential of court intervention.

In a similar cautionary tale, a tailor claimed that his cousin-in-law had been murdered.[63] Zhong Maolin, 26 *sui*, filed a plaint in which he reported:

> I am a tailor. This year in the first month, I went to Jiangjin[64] to practice my craft. My wife's uncle, Guo Liang, died of illness in the fourth year of the reign of the Guangxu emperor. He left behind [his son] Liuyuan. The next year [Liuyuan's] mother, Huang Shi, remarried to Zou Guirong as his legal wife. Liuyuan followed his mother to live in Zou's home and was raised there for ten years. Suddenly last month on the 23rd, Liuyuan died. I was not informed. Guirong's servant secretly buried him. This month on the 11th, I returned and went to Guirong's to call on him. Guirong blurted out that Liuyuan had been beaten to death by someone. I was shocked. I asked all around. It seems that Guirong's sons, Zou San and Zou Qi, had argued [with Liuyuan] on the street, and they beat him to death. I reported this story to the [community leaders] for investigation.[65]

In this document and others, Zhong presented himself as an interested family member and advocate. He argued that shifting family dynamics left his cousin-in-law vulnerable to his stepbrothers' predation. However, Huang Shi and community leaders submitted their own plaint, offering a radically different depiction.

In this account, the young man, who was 15 *sui*, had gotten into an argument while playing. When he returned home he was "admonished" by his mother. He then "timidly" swallowed a large amount of opium and died the following day. The local community contributed 15 strings of cash to the funeral expenses, and produced a public burial notice. This notice, included in the court file, carefully details the cause of death, the monies given, and an explicit statement that all family members –both those present and absent – should accept the death and get on with their own lives without causing trouble. This document was signed by several family members and included the names of 22 witnesses. This public fixing of the terms of the young man's death was an effort to anticipate Zhong's complaints and render them null.[66]

Describing his own motivations, Zhong said he had misgivings about the death, which would not go away. These reservations challenged the local community's agreed-upon understanding of this death. In the end, however, the court upheld this local truth, and Zhong was ordered flogged with the light bamboo. Curiously, while Zhong was punished for false accusation, a rarity in the hundreds of cases I have read, that punishment seems rather ad hoc since it deviates from the prescriptions of the Code.[67] Consequently, the beating seems less like an official verdict than an informal expression of the magistrate's displeasure with Zhong for causing trouble.

Zhong's beating was in part a result of the united stand of the local community, including both family and community leaders. These local power structures influenced the court's understanding of the situation. The court then added its weight to this asymmetry, reinforcing normative social relations – and local power holders' privileged place within them. In demarcating local roles and obligations, the court often backed local authorities, basing its ruling on the "realities" drawn by the local power holders, and particularly family members. Whether state authority upheld local authority or cut against it seems – in part – based on local power holders presenting a unified judgment on the social meaning of the actions under consideration. Gross violations of local norms or deeply divided local authorities tended to open the door to more unpredictable state interventions.

Contesting local verdicts

The family was an influential force in local society and an essential part of the local justice system. Kinship networks were a form of oversight that surveilled social relations and could make demands, both locally and in court, for justice. They were essential in creating local and legal justice. This power is visible when natal families reached across and make demands on their married daughters and their new families, demanding justice and restitution for the mistreatment of their daughters. Sojourning or otherwise distant family members could use the power of the local state to intervene in the deaths of their relatives. Skeptical of local norms and local verdicts on these deaths, relatives appealed to the court to reinterpret what had happened. These insurgent interpretations could rally local connections for acts of violence, bringing their challenges home. The magistrate sometimes recognized the legitimacy of these claims and ordered some form of restitution, even if it fell outside the confines of the Code, demonstrating the role of state authority in supporting familial and local power. The court could not "see" what had happened, and often fell back on supporting local power structures rather than overturning them. Magistrates were routinely constrained by local truths.

In suicide cases, the state often supported a no-fault settlement. While explicitly rejecting any criminal wrongdoing, the court routinely intervened to support local claims for compensation following suicides. The court pushed its authority into local life in matters that explicitly fell outside criminal matters. These extra-legal interventions did not cite Code. Instead, they were predicated on an enlarged sense of the court's informal role in enforcing local patterns of behavior. The barrier between the formal and the informal was porous.

Marriages, in Ba County, were long-term socials bonds, yet when these ties were severed, local justice could impose – both informally (in the form of mediated settlements) and formally (working through the county court) – compensation for loss. Restitution was often economic, although it could also be expressed (simultaneously) violently. When these conflicts appeared in the county court, the magistrate often – but not always – reinforced local understandings of the conflict, reinforcing local justice. In this way, the local state was both quite active in upholding local justice, with the county court engaged in petty disputes, and rather conservative, by supporting local authority. Moreover, family conflicts make clear the immediate and essential role of forms of local justice, a power that is also evident in economic conflicts, which are considered in the next chapter.

Notes

1 BXDA 7728.
2 Ibid.
3 Ibid.
4 The two individuals representing the clan Wu Shi had married into, Jin Hongfa and Jin Dexuan, refer to themselves as *zuzheng*, or lineage representatives, and the village leaders are, in this case, the *baozheng*, the security head, and the *jianzheng*, the warden. Another village leader, the *xiangyue*, a village head, testified along similar lines.
5 The list of individuals involved in the case [*shendan*] also notes that Peng was not present.
6 Ibid.
7 Ibid. This list is an inventory of the contents of a fairly prosperous farmer's house, and Peng Zifa's status as fairly prosperous – at least compared to Wu Shi – is further marked by his ability to adopt a son, a transaction that required him to pay the boy's family.
8 Ibid.
9 BXDA 7736. This file is the continuation of the same case and contains both the jailor's requests for a doctor to treat Peng, which were approved, as well as a report announcing Peng's death.
10 For more on adoption in China, see Arthur Wolf and Chieh-shan Huang, *Marriage and Adoption in China, 1845–1945* (Stanford: Stanford University Press, 1980); and Ann Walter, *Getting an Heir: Adoption and the Construction of Kinship in Late Imperial China* (Honolulu: University of Hawaii Press, 1990).
11 *Mencius*, Book Four, Part A, 26 (translated by D.C. Lau, 1970).

12 BXDA 7728.
13 Wolf, *Marriage and Adoption*, 208–213.
14 I consider male suicide in Chapter 4.
15 Differing cultural attitudes toward suicide, human life, and the individual all have been posited as holding the key to understanding differences between suicides in the "West" and in "China." Suffice it to say, at least from a generalized "cultural" standpoint, one could find a number of bulwarks against suicide as well as celebrations of it in Qing China. For Confucians, suicide was unfilial inasmuch as it destroyed the body and life given from parent to child. This same understanding informs the Qing Code's hierarchy of capital punishments – decapitation was a more severe punishment than strangulation expressly because it violated the body's somatic integrity and insulted the ancestors. For Buddhists, a host of injunctions to preserve life could also militate against suicide. Drawing on both Confucianism and Buddhism, the Qing jurist Huang Liuhong writes: "The human body is not only a bequest of one's parents but also a result of countless cycles of reincarnation. That anyone can be degraded enough to destroy it with his own hands...is something I detest most vigorously." Broad-brush cultural arguments offer little heuristic insight, and I instead focus on individual acts. Huang, *A Complete Book Concerning Happiness and Benevolence*, 357.
16 Ibid., 358.
17 Ci Song, *Xi Yuan Ji Lu: 5 Juan* (Beijing: Falü chubanshe, 1958). The bulk of the discussion of suicide comes at the end of the third *juan*, and at the beginning of the fourth *juan* in discussions of drowning and wounds from edged weapons. The copies used by Qing-era *wuzuo* contained additional information and commentary in addition to Song's text.
18 Ci Song, *The Washing Away of Wrongs: Forensic Medicine in Thirteenth-century China*, trans. Brian McKnight (Ann Arbor: Center for Chinese Studies, University of Michigan, 1981), 127. Also see, Asen, *Death in Beijing*, 60–63; and Pierre-Etienne Will, "Developing Forensic Knowledge through Cases in the Qing Dynasty," in *Thinking with Cases: Specialist Knowledge in Chinese Cultural History*, eds. Charlotte Furth, Judith T. Zeitlin, and Ping-chen Hsiung (Honolulu: University of Hawaii Press, 2007), 62–100.
19 DLCY, 199.00. The punishment was increased to strangulation if it was a younger relative who pushed an elder relative to commit suicide. If the pressure was motivated by either theft or sex, then the punishment was increased to beheading.
20 For example, Lu Weijing has considered female suicide in her examination of the late imperial female chastity cult. Her work primarily focuses on the cultural, political, and intellectual history of this phenomenon, basing her study on literati perspectives found in sources such as poetry. Lu Weijing, *True to Her Word: The Faithful Maiden Cult in Late Imperial China* (Stanford, CA: Stanford University Press, 2008), 129, 159. For an overview of the development of suicide studies in China, see Paul Ropp's Introduction to *Passionate Women: Female Suicide in Late Imperial China*, eds. Paul Ropp, Paula Zamperini, and Harriet Zurndorfer (Leiden: Brill, 2001), 3–22.
21 Susan Mann, *Precious Records: Women in China's Long Eighteenth Century* (Stanford: Stanford University Press, 1997), 4.
22 Theiss, *Disgraceful Matters*, 13, 206–207.
23 This work is primarily based on central-level documents, such as *zhupi zouzhe*, *lufu zouzhe*, and *xingke tiben*.
24 Ibid., 207.
25 The other term frequently found in the records is *yuxie*, "to encounter disaster." *Xie* has medical and spiritual connotations, as both an environmental influence

that causes disease and as a ghost or spirit that brings disaster. Interestingly, *xie* also means heretical, irregular, and abnormal, evoking an idea that people who killed themselves had fallen out of the normal and acceptable and become polluted. Thomas Buoye has studied similar linguistic placeholders for eighteen-century homicide cases. See Thomas Buoye, "Murderous Intent Arose: Bureaucratization and Benevolence in Eighteenth-Century Qing Homicide Reports," *Late Imperial China* 16, no. 2 (December 1995): 72–74.

26 Writing about the body's manifold significances, the Dutch philosopher and anthropologist Annemarie Mol writes of the two "creatures" present during medical procedures. While witnessing a dissection, she noticed this twinning as the pathologist covered the corpse's face with a simple white cloth: "One [of the creatures] is having its insides taken out and its organs are being cut into slices. The other is being accorded human dignity and treated with respect." The multiple meanings of the body, one a corpse and one a social being, existed simultaneously and in tension. Annemarie Mol, *The Body Multiple: Ontology in Medical Practice* (Durham: Duke University Press Books, 2003), 126.

27 BXDA 7662, although the case also appears in BXDA 7664. This case is discussed further later in the chapter.

28 Ibid.

29 Of the 64 cases of suicide found in my sample, opium was the method of choice in 39 cases, followed by 12 hangings, four cut-throats, two drownings, one leap off a cliff, and one case of arsenic poisoning.

30 For more on overdose symptoms, see the Substance Abuse and Mental Health Services Administrations Opioid Overdose Toolkit (https://store.samhsa.gov/ shin/content//SMA18-4742/SMA18-4742.pdf).

31 Susan Mann. "Grooming a Daughter for Marriage: Brides and Wives in the Mid-Qing Period," in *Chinese Femininities, Chinese Masculinities*, eds. Susan Brownwell and Jeffrey Wasserstrom (Berkeley: University of California Press, 2002), 93.

32 The roles women were supposed to play were not static over her lifetime: daughter, daughter-in-law, mother, chaste widow, and so forth. To stress women's changing roles over a lifetime, Margery Wolf described the Chinese family as "cyclical." Margery Wolf, *Women and the Family in Rural Taiwan* (Stanford: Stanford University Press, 1972), 170.

33 Margery Wolf has convincingly challenged this conception with her assertion of the importance of the "uterine family," which included a woman's mother and her mother's children. Wolf contrasts these persistent ties with women's changing connections to her father's household and her marital home. I draw on Wolf's work to broaden the definition of family to expose the enduring connections that persisted once a daughter left her natal home. Wolf's work examines twentieth-century Taiwan, but her insights are a productive point of departure. See, Wolf, *Women and the Family*, 32–41.

34 The ideal of women "marrying out" derives from the virilocal expectations of the normative family.

35 BXDA 7696. Interestingly, Zhou has a proper given name, rather than simply being referred to as Zhou, daughter of so-and-so.

36 Ibid.

37 As mentioned before, while adopting a daughter-in-law was a fairly common practice, it was recognized as potentially causing trouble as the relationship between the two young people switched from something broadly akin to brother/ sister to husband/wife. Years of youthful cohabitation could complicate a now sexual relationship. See Wolf and Huang, *Marriage and Adoption*, 230–241.

38 BXDA 7651.

39 Zhang Shi's behavior resembles a solo form of "rough music" (or *charivari*), discussed in Chapter 2, used to shame the deceased's in-laws. E. P. Thompson described rough music as "a rude cacophony, with or without more elaborate ritual, which usually directed mockery or hostility against individuals who offended against certain community norms." Rough music was often a conservative tool to enforce normative local values. Zhang Shi's actions do not perfectly mirror the European practice, particularly as she acted as an individual rather than as part of a collective, but there is a parallel to rough music's public performance of community standards and disputes. E. P. Thompson, "Rough Music" in *Customs in Common*, 467. Also see, Natalie Zemon Davis, *Society and Culture in Early Modern France: Eight Essays* (Stanford: Stanford University Press, 1975), 97–103, and Edward Muir, *Ritual in Early Modern Europe* (Cambridge: Cambridge University Press, 2005), 98–104, 135–136.

40 Daniel Lord Smail, *The Consumption of Justice: Emotions, Publicity, and Legal Culture in Marseille, 1264–1423* (Ithaca: Cornell University Press, 2003), 132.

41 I considered false accusation in Chapter 1 and earlier in Quinn Javers, "The Logic of Lies: False Accusation and Legal Culture in Late Imperial Sichuan," *Late Imperial China* 35, no. 2 (December 2014).

42 "Blood stasis" [*gan xue lao*] refers to tuberculosis or a host of blood disorders. For more on the subject, see Gunter R. Neeb, *Blood Stasis: China's Classical Concept in Modern Medicine* (London: Churchill Livingstone, 2006).

43 BXDA 7664.

44 BXDA 7662.

45 Ibid.

46 Ibid.

47 BXDA 7974.

48 For more of Chinese death ritual, see James Watson and Evelyn Rawski, *Death Ritual in Late Imperial and Modern China*, particularly Watson's "The Structure of Chinese Funerary Rites," 3–19; and Susan Naquin's "Funerals in North China," in *Death Ritual in Late Imperial and Modern China*, eds. James L. Watson and Evelyn Sakakida Rawski (Berkeley: University of California Press, 1988), 37–70.

49 BXDA 7974.

50 Ibid.

51 *Xing'an Hui Lan San Bian* [Conspectus of Penal Cases, with Sequels] (Beijing: Beijing gu ji chu ban she, 2004), 1712.

52 These compassionate cases also account for the majority of the false accusation cases presented by Bodde and Morris. See Bodde and Morris, *Law in Imperial China*, 402–404.

53 Theiss, 83.

54 Ibid., 95.

55 Beverly Bossler, "'A Daughter is a Daughter All Her Life:' Affinal Relations and Women's Networks in Song and Late Imperial China," *Late Imperial China* 21, no. 1 (June 2000): 79.

56 Ibid., 98.

57 Sally Engle Merry, *Getting Justice and Getting Even: Legal Consciousness among Working-Class Americans* (Chicago: University of Chicago Press, 1990), 8.

58 BXDA 7653.

59 I cannot assume that the individuals in this case, or any other, were interested in forming normative households (even if their finances had allowed for it) or that they ascribed to moral norms. Non-normative households perhaps might not represent failures to form normative households so much as realizations of different goals. Matthew Sommer's work on wife-selling and polyandry makes

clear sweeping range of marriage practices and desires, as well as the state's sometimes winking involvement in these processes. See Sommer, *Polyandry and Wife-Selling*, 55–85, 341–375.

60 BXDA 7650.
61 Ibid.
62 B. J. ter Haar's study of the White Lotus makes clear the dangers posed by an historian's uncritical acceptance of labels used by figures or institutions of authority to denounce those less powerful. He writes: "Labels form a kind of closed system, always accurate for those who apply them, and providing justification for actions against the labeled phenomena." Barend J. ter Harr, *White Lotus Teachings in Chinese Religious History* (Leiden: Brill, 1992), 14.
63 BXDA 7652.
64 Jiangjin, also on the Yangzi River, is southwest of Chongqing.
65 BXDA 7652.
66 This practice parallels the role of wife-selling contracts, which documented a formally illegal transaction, played as a bulwark against future litigation or contestation. See Sommer, *Polyandry and Wife-Selling*, 244–246.
67 I considered false accusation, and the Code's views on it, more fully in Chapter 1.

4 Economic disputes

Social meanings and market-based exchange

Like the family, the local economy was a site of conflict, and, in this chapter, I examine dispute stemming from debt, land transfers, and employee suicide. These three forms of economic conflict illuminate key aspects of justice making in Ba County. First, debt, particularly resulting from small-scale loans, was a common source of violence, and these clashes illuminate a clear and violent form of justice at work in the county. This rich vein of bloodletting stresses the routine place of violence within the community as a tool to police norms. Second, conflicts surrounding land transfers reveal individuals drawing off of shared social scripts to assert competing justice claims. In these conflicts, the multiple meanings of land are visible: land was a measure of one's standing, a tie to the patriline, a ritual space filled with geomantic significance, and the rich array of landholding practices further attest to the centrality of this form of ownership.[1] Here, social norms did not automatically provide a clear resolution. Instead, conflict and attempts at resolution were both expressed through contesting appeals to shared expectations. Finally, legal cases following employee suicides reveal enduring non-economic meanings embedded within putatively economic relationships, and the ways in which both the community and court used these other meanings to impose extra-economic burdens of support and care on employers, as well as to extract compensation from them when they failed to meet social expectation.

All of these conflicts underline the extent to which economic exchange was a social act, one that often relied on preexisting relationships and could be superseded by competing social norms. Debt cases make clear the social relationships that patterned small-time loans, as individuals leveraged preexisting bonds of trust and obligation for financial assistance. In this way, non-economic ties shape "the costs and techniques available for economic activity."[2] When employees killed themselves, employers were required to compensate surviving family members. This extra-legal economic burden, often in the form of no-fault compensation, demonstrates the endurance of the familization of the employer–employee relationship despite legal changes to alter the basis of these ties. Local understandings of this relationship, often backed by the court, bent economic relationships to fit the expectations of responsibility and demands for justice.

Some scholars have argued for the transition from a moral economy to market-based exchanges over the course of the Qing period.[3] Yet, cases from late-nineteenth-century Ba County suggest the endurance of extra-economic social obligations. Rather than finding the erosion of social bonds in favor of cold market forces, these realms comingled as customary extra-economic obligations continued to shape economic exchanges.

Given the crucial shaping role that personal relationships played in these encounters, economic exchanges were perhaps less the acts of rational individuals and more the work of what some scholars have called "dividuals," persons who are "a composite of relationships that encompass other living humans as well as the world of spirits and ancestors."[4] Exchange, as well as gift giving, is central to the creation and maintenance of the dividual. Economic exchanges in Ba County can be seen as profoundly social acts that enmeshed dividuals, thereby binding them to the communities they constituted and constraining their actions. Moreover, many of these economic connections were built upon prior personal ties, particularly familial relations, further underlining the importance of the social in the economic. Market ties, in turn, helped to maintain local order. One of the ways these relations policed county norms was by disciplining community members.

As a key aspect of local justice making, market exchanges were often an opportunity to express and enforce norms. This is particularly clear in economic conflicts in the county, particularly in the violence and tension surrounding debt and land sales, and the relationship between employers and employees. Without trust and predictability, the terms and enforceability of debts and other economic transactions often became the subjects of dispute, local policing, and even violent conflict. While the state remained a periodic resource available for occasional and extraordinary oversight at the local level, highly commercialized Ba County continued to exhibit the subsistence ethic present in many peasant communities.

Moreover, economic conflicts make clear the processes of local justice, and reveal how economic pressures could manifest themselves first as disputes and then as violence. While some social theorists have stressed the natural emergence of order in communities, this process was often violent, particularly in enforcing norms and reducing uncertainty.[5] Indeed, violence was often a constituent element in non-state order, particularly where state authority was only occasional. The violence that surrounded these instances of economic conflict reveals justice in action: violence policed social roles and norms as well as economic exchanges.

Debt

What did indebtedness look like at the end of the Qing? Many of the debts were incurred as a result of small-scale loans, which were part of a larger repertoire of mutual-aid practices that peasants used to solve a variety of common problems. Many of these were based on kinship ties, but others were more organized, and they tended to focus on agricultural production, providing simple assistance such as collective labor and the use of tools or draft animals, and ritual occasions such as marriages or religion festivals.[6] Sometimes called "loan societies," these organizations pooled resources to fund routine expenses.[7]

Most of the debt cases from Ba County do not reference these organizations, but small, informal loans patched the same structural gaps that accompanied many transactions, such as purchasing land, wives, or coffins, and while debt took many forms in the county, small-scale loans seem to have had the highest potential for violence. This finding supports Philip Huang's argument that in Baodi county, outside Beijing, small, informal loans, often made between kin and others in close relationships solely on the basis of a verbal agreement, were the most likely to lead to conflict.[8]

These informal transactions, and their attendant violence, reveal the social relationships that formed the basis for many economic exchanges. In fact, many of these small loans were made among family members. The seemingly obvious ties that bound these individuals were central in small loans that did not use middlemen – familial bonds obviated the need for guarantors based on a presumption that trust could be secured by bloodlines. In this way, kinship ties, and other close relationships, produced extra-economic efficiencies as an "unintended by-product of action pursued by individuals seeking sociability, approval, and status."[9] Even when these agreements broke down and devolved into violence, thick social connections continued to underpin many debts.

In Ba County, debt was a seemingly endemic part of life, and a common source of violence, including suicide. For example, in the fourth month of 1891, Liu Mou Shi, aged 76 *sui*, a grandmother and widow, filed a plaint claiming her grandson, Liu Xuexing, aged 17 *sui,* had been driven to suicide by a gang of men pressing him to pay a debt.[10] She reported that Liu had been accused by Guo Heshang of owing 350 *wen* and that he had been pushing her grandson to repay it. Then, according to Mou Shi, one day behind the Yuantong temple, Guo and three other men seized Liu Xuexing and beat him. He was then held against his will in Li Laoqi's riverside teahouse while his attackers drank tea. At this point, her grandson became "desperate" [*qingji*] and ran and threw himself into the river and drowned. In this instance, a relatively small debt was the source of violence. Collection of this debt relied on informal processes of enforcement. Liu was beaten for failing to repay his debt. The initial burst of violence resulted in a more dramatic act, his suicide. Violence policed petty economic exchanges, and they often carried the threat of violence. Indeed, economic relationships sometimes required violence to impose contract compliance and conformity. Below the state's regular vision, this was contract enforcement. In these instances, violence played a dual role, with both instrumental and didactic aims.

The alarming power of debt is visible in other instances of violence as well. In a case from 1890, a petty clerk contrived a wild plan to exploit the death of his eight-*sui* son to escape from under the debt owed to his brother-in-law.[11] Mu Zaizhi, a county clerk, first reported to the court that his son had gone out after breakfast and had never returned. This prompted a frantic search that failed to yield any trace of the boy until the next day when the child's body was discovered in a stream. The boy's hands had been bound with rope, suggesting that he had been murdered. Mu claimed that his brother-in-law, Qu San the Southerner, held a grudge against him, and was the most likely suspect. As the facts trickled in, it became clear that Mu had staged his son's murder in order to repudiate a debt: Mu had borrowed 30 *liang* of silver from Qu's mother and had not returned it. Debt set into motion an elaborate and vicious scheme. Mu subsequently admitted that his son had accidently drowned in the river three days before he reported the case. But in this tragedy, Mu saw opportunity.

He had staged the crime by binding his dead son's hands, and then falsely accused Qu of having killed his boy. This was not the first time that Mu had attempted to escape his debt. He had previously bullied and detained Qu and members of his family, and had even tried to rip up the debt contract. Most egregiously, Mu and his nephew, Pockmarked Zhang Wu, had kidnapped and severely beaten Qu in an attempt to make him falsely confess to having murdered Mu's son. Zhang, Mu's nephew, admitted to his part in the beating, saying that even after being beaten with tree branches, Qu still would not perjure himself. In his own testimony, Qu described the ordeal that followed their initial argument over the outstanding debt:

> Mu Zaizhi then ordered me hung up and flogged. He wanted me to set up a contract [stating that I had borrowed from Mu] 120 *liang* of silver. Because I was unwilling, he again used private punishment to torture me, to force into confessing that I had drowned [Mu's son].[12]

Following these revelations, Qu described how he had been dragged before the magistrate to be formally accused of the murder. At that time, he was still so badly injured that he was unable to speak in court, prompting Mu to further obscure the truth by claiming that Qu was a mute who would not be able to testify. Qu reported that it took him three months to recover while in detention before he could make his case and assert his innocence. Beyond Mu's megalomaniacal sense of entitlement and outrageous impunity, this case illustrates the importance of community ties. As was true in this case, small loans were often made among family members. Moreover, Mu also enlisted a relative in his schemes to evade the debt. Networks for both economic exchange and interpersonal violence relied on close social connections, in this case family ties. Social ties animated all of these interactions. In this case, debt between family members led to outlandish scheming and violence, yet the centrality of preexisting social ties as the condition for loans is seen in other cases as well. Even where the scheming was less outsized, the social patterning of economic exchange is evident. This can be seen in a case from 1898, when Wu Zhou Shi reported the murder of her nine-*sui* adopted son, Wu Xisheng.[13]

In her testimony, Zhou Shi stated that a month before the crime she had returned to her parents' house. She had warned Wu to keep the door locked while she was away, but despite this, a neighbor's daughter reported that Gong Laifeng had broken into her home while she was gone. After breaking in, Gong stabbed Wu on the neck and in the head, fatally wounding the boy. This brief report describes the end of the conflict, but does not hint at its beginning or suggest Gong's motivation for such an assault. The same neighbors who originally informed Zhou Shi of her son's fate filled in some of the story with their courtroom testimony. They had heard Gong and Wu arguing over debts that Gong owed. He confirmed this, testifying:

> I am from Ba County. I am 21 *sui*. My father is dead, but my mother is still alive. I have no brothers. I am married to Li Shi, but we do not have any children. I am poor, many debts are pursuing me and weighing me down. Then, I borrowed money from my relative, Wu Zhou Shi, several times. Last month on the 26th, I walked over to their house to see if their house was locked. My relative, Wu Xisheng, lit some lights in the house. I smashed the lock on the door and went in. I grabbed some money, over 1000, [but] Xisheng was holding back some money. I was nervous; I was afraid I would be seen by someone. I was very anxious. I picked up a kitchen knife and cut him twice across the cheek. I was re-ally anxious, [so] I cut him again across the throat and then I let him go. I saw him fall to the floor. I went [farther] in and saw they had a sack of rice and 1800 *wen*. I carried it home. At home, I thought to myself that I had stabbed and hurt [him, but] I was afraid to report it; I wanted to run away. Later that night, [Wu Zhou Shi], along with community leaders, came and captured me.[14]

Gong must have known that Zhou Shi was away, and went to her house to rob her. He had not counted on Wu being at home.

When Wu lit a light in the house (perhaps in response to rustling outside), Gong escalated his transgression, smashing the lock and forcing his way in-side. Once inside and confronted by Wu, he was committed. The boy knew who he was. They argued, with neighbors close enough to overhear them. These circumstances make Gong's violence and desperation even more clear. He had very little chance of getting away with his offenses, yet instead of cutting his losses (and crimes), he escalated again and attacked Wu. In his own testimony, Gong repeatedly stated that he was very anxious. While this may have been a strategic attempt to portray his actions as something other than cold-blooded, this was perhaps also an accurate description of the palpable stress that drove him as well as the grim realization that each of his actions only further doomed him, highlighting something of a snow-ball effect in criminality. As things got out of hand, each act led to a greater transgression, with debt once again leading to violence.

Gong, harried by debts, resorted to successively more transgressive acts. He moved from breaking into the house, to theft, to assault, which became homicide (and perhaps not unpredictably so given the violence of the attack). His actions are more shocking given the seemingly close relationship that ex-isted between him and Zhou Shi. Her repeated loans (and, one must assume, Gong's repeated failure to pay her back) stress their ongoing relationship. Their kinship ties bound them with obligations of mutual aid, and Zhou Shi tried repeatedly to help her relative, thereby fulfilling social expectation. Be-yond simply market transactions, these loans were expression of social roles and responsibilities, and, by killing Wu, he pulled down the final support that the community offered him. There was a tension at the heart of these so-cial bonds that balanced the frequent use of kinship ties to secure small loans and these same loans' tendency to result in violence. Small loans could ena-ble survival, but they also invited a heightened potential for violence into the family. There were multiple and competing norms at work simultaneously in the family, and this put the family at the heart of local justice.

The tension within the family unit that animates this conflict led to acts of self-annihilation as well as interpersonal violence, and this other sort of violence is clear in a case from 1892. In testimony from the eighth month of that year, Tang Mingwan reported:

> In the second year of the reign of the Guangxi emperor, I was adopted by Tang Yihe along with my mother [who he took as his wife]. The adop-tion and the marriage went off without problem. Last fall, I, along with Chen Zongli, went out and conditionally purchased [*dian*] Wang Ji'an's land for 50 *liang* of silver. Last winter, my [adoptive] father died. Tang Mingdu and others came to the house and wanted to divide the [family] property, but they failed. They [then] counterfeited a fake contract, and falsely accused my father of borrowing 20 *liang* of silver from them. They brought the accusation to court and implicated us. The court run-ners came to the village and directed that I be detained.[15]

He further testified that his cousins and uncle had brought him and his mother to court to demand repayment. They were unable to repay the debt, and so his mother, Tang Zhou Shi, became "desperate" [*qingji*] and hanged herself. Tang Mingwan framed this violation of local norms as a dispute over family division, not as a matter of debt, and, in this attempt to get jus-tice, he garnered support from his maternal cousin, as well as his landlord.

By contrast, the Tang Mingwan's paternal cousins, Tang Mingdu and Tang Minghua (along with their father, Tang Linhe, although he played a secondary role in the case), initially presented the dispute primarily in terms of debt. They testified:

Last year, Tang Mingwan's father, Tang Yihe, contracted to borrow from me, Tang Mingdu, 80 *liang* of silver, and [from me], Tang Minghua, ten *liang* of silver. We asked for it back repeatedly but he would not give it to us. This previous winter, Yihe died.[16]

At this point, their call for justice stemmed from outstanding debts. However, they subsequently accused Zhao Shi and Tang Mingwan of plotting to take control of the family property and referred to Tang Mingwan as "Chen Jinshan's son," a tactic that stressed Tang's (more distant) status as an adopted son. Despite the widespread practice of adoption in the Qing, the cousins used Tang Mingwan's status to cast him as an interloper.

Community leaders testified that they had tried to mediate. They did not mention debts at all, instead returning to Tang Mingwan's characterization of the dispute as primarily stemming from the division of the family property.[17] The court, however, rejected this framing and described the conflict in terms of debt. Its summation of the dispute framed the case as follows:

Tang Zhao Shi's death was caused by hanging herself, and no one can be blamed. Tang Mingwan's father owed Tang Mingdu 80 *liang* of silver. According to Tang Linhe's testimony, because he [Mingwan] was bitterly poor he was unable to repay the debt. Every year, whatever profit he made, he without fail returned to pay down the principle. One can well perceive that Tang Mingwan's father's family, being so bitterly poor, had only a relative's, Wang Ji'an's, fields, which they had conditionally sold for 50 *liang* of silver. Other than that, they had no other property. We can already get the general idea [of the situation].[18]

The court ordered Tang Mingwan to repay to his cousin 2,000 *wen*, and, within ten years, a total of 20,000 *wen* to "dispose of the matter," although it is not clear how the court arrived at this number.

In this case, an economic dispute stood as a marker of social roles, and, in their appeal for justice, Tang's cousins attempted to assert that primacy of family roles and obligations, and so framed the conflict as an issue of family division. To do so, they marked Tang as standing outside the family – he was really Chen Jinshan's son after all. Both Tang and, ultimately, the court opposed this construction. While Tang also tried to frame the dispute as an issue of family relations and obligations, the magistrate rejected this interpretation as well. The court instead focused on Tang's poverty, and, in doing so, reshaped the social roles featured in the dispute, moving from a question of family division to one of family support. Imposing his own sense of justice, the magistrate ordered Tang to pay back a substantially lower amount than his cousins claimed. Tang's economic woes and his familial connection to his cousins took precedence over formal debt. As the state manufactured justice, economic concerns, in this case, would not be allowed to unravel deep social obligations.

Tang's family's attempts to construct a compelling framing of the conflict, a local truth, may not illuminate what in fact happened, but they did have to make sense – they had to be socially plausible, so he couldn't tell just any tale he wanted. In both the court's decision and the cousins' telling, relationships were at the center. Further, in making its decision, the court did not prioritize the economic relationship, just as in their defense the family stressed the social character of the conflict rather than the economic one. Debt cases, in particular, often demonstrate the centrality of preexisting social relationship within economic ones, as well as the role of regular violence to police norms.

Land sales

Land was also a major source of conflict in the county. Outstanding rents or other payments drove many disputes, and these economic exchanges remained, down to the late nineteenth century, a subject of ongoing contention and violence. While the increased commercialization of land over the course of the Ming and the Qing led to a progressively more vibrant market for land, the attendant complexity in the property regime could also be a source for conflict. In this system, rights to land use as well as actual ownership could be rented, sold, or "conditionally" sold, and land-use rights could also be resold to a third party.[19]

Conditional sales were perhaps the most common. In these transactions, peasants in need of cash could avoid permanently losing the land, frequently their only possession of real value, by conditionally selling it for less than the land's full value – conditional sale price was about 70 percent of the total value.[20] This sub-market price entitled the seller to recover his land if he repaid the buyer within a set period of time. These arrangements at least held out the possibility of recovery and reflected a deep-rooted aversion to the full alienability of land. However, conditional sale was frequently only the first transaction in a peasant's downward spiral. Indeed, in a largely agrarian society, a peasant who had to even conditionally sell his land was already hard up. And without land, it became even more difficult for peasants to raise the cash necessary to recover their property. Many never did. Finally, conditional sales also permitted a final outright sale of the land with payment of the final 30 percent or so of the land's value.

Conditional sales and their attendant delays in the transfer of cash invited subsequent haggling over fluctuations in the value of the land due to inflation or other factors. As land prices rose, sellers challenged buyers to pay the difference between the sales price and the current (now higher) value of the land. This process, called *zhaojia*, was laden with the potential for conflict. Instead of a single transaction, conditional land sales embedded buyer and seller in an evolving relationship that required the ongoing reassessment of the value of the land. Without clarity or trust, these sales were often the source of violence.[21] Studies of organized crime have pointed to similar conditions as sources of potential violence, often highlighting the need for local, and often violent, enforcement of contracts and debts, arguing that "if trust is scarce, and the state is not able or willing to protect property rights, it is sensible to expect a high demand for non-state, private protection."[22] These conditions do not automatically give rise to organized crime organization. Instead, a lack of trust creates this demand, which can be met – or not – in a variety of ways. Generally, the greatest potential for violence was in "unstable transactions in which trust is scarce and fragile."[23] Conditional land sales in Ba County exhibit a similar set of concerns. Given the economic uncertainty that marked these transactions, and the limited availability of the state, local forms of order developed that incorporated violence or the threat of violence. Locals policed their own economic exchanges to ensure compliance and a fragile sense of justice.[24]

A case from 1891 suggests the complexity of land transfers as well as the process of making local justice. In this case, Cen Bingnan had been beaten to death on his doorstep over a debt of 1,800 *wen*. The debt had been tied to the transfer of the land. Cen's accused killer, Wang Yutian, explained the origins of the clash:

> I am originally from Ba County. I am 30 *sui*. My father is dead. My mother is still alive and I have no older or younger brothers. I married a wife, Li Shi, [who] gave birth to one daughter. Ordinarily, I support myself with an opium bar that I opened... Wang Huanbi owes me 1800 cash, which he has not repaid. I have taken from him two copper ladles. Last year in the middle of the eighth month, my land was conditionally sold [*dian*] [by Wang] to Cen Bingnan to occupy and plow. He [Wang] called on Bingnan to honor [his] debt of 1800 cash.... I [later] received less than 1000 cash, the remaining 800 cash has not been made up. After that, I repeatedly demanded [payment]. Bingnan said that he wanted me to return the copper ladles before he would give me the cash. I returned the two ladles and he didn't even give me a little money. He and I argued, certainly. After that, Bingnan hid himself and didn't appear until this year on the third day of the second month.[25]

The debt obligation was transferred along with land use rights from the previous debtor to Cen. In this way, obligations piled up one on another such that multiple claims could exist to a single property, with each claimant taking a share of the product along the way. Cen, being new to the debt, perhaps did not feel its weight with the same intensity as Wang. Finally, according to Wang Yuitan, this already tense situation was brought to a boil by an assault on his mother:

> My mother ran into [Cen] on the street and said to him that we wanted the money. Shockingly, he was furiously harsh and unreasonable – beating and injuring my mother. Our neighbors worked to draw up a

mediated settlement up till the sixth day but could not resolve [it]. Then on the ninth, my mother demanded the money from him [again].... I returned home and heard that he had beaten my mother. I was over-come with emotion.[26]

According to Wang, this led him to track down Cen and beat him with a wooden staff. Wang admitted to hitting Cen repeatedly, but claimed that he had not intended to kill him.

In their testimony, the local authorities presented a slightly different ac-counting. While affirming the basic contours of the dispute and their role in attempting to mediate a settlement, they also described a conflict that Wang and his mother had had with a vendor about their failure to pay for rice they had purchased. Wang's mother was also beaten as a result of this altercation, and the anger and frustration from this dispute perhaps spilled over into Wang's conflict with Cen.[27] His mother had been beaten twice in public. After the second attack, by his own account, Wang flew into a rage and beat Cen to death. The public nature of the attacks undoubtedly com-pounded Wang's shame and rage.

At least part of the conflict in this case stemmed from complicated prac-tices of land use and rental. In Cen's case, the ongoing transfer of the land and rights to it created a complicated tangle of obligations and rights, which led to conflict. Individuals in Ba County could turn to the local state housed in the yamen, yet often this more distant authority was ignored in favor of the immediate power of local justice. Eschewing state institutions, locals turned to other arbiters.

In his study of a mafia syndicate in Sicily, Anton Blok writes: "People were dependent on kinsmen, friends, and powerful protectors for sheer physical survival. To right wrongs, settle conflicts, and to solve problems of various sorts, they could hardly turn to the police or to the courts."[28] While Ba County does not exactly mirror Sicily, both of these settings exhibit a high degree of uncertainty. In these situations, individuals tried to mini-mize their exposure to risk. Individuals who could not appeal to the court or the police to get what they were owed may have found that violence, or the threat of violence, limited individuals' willingness to default.

Moreover, the violent economic disputes make clear the uncertainty that existed as individuals disagreed over what constituted reasonable claims on social expectation. Even where communities recognized the right to *zhaojia*, when and how much was appropriate could still be matters of dispute. Con-sequently, within economic relationships, there were structural moments of uncertainty that produced competing claims and conflict. Everyday politics sought to resolve this tension, but violence could erupt when individual no-tions of justice were violated. In economic clashes, local justice making re-quired the assertion of socially meaningful claims to the reasonable use of recognized practices, such as *zhaojia*. The inherent tensions of this system were further heightened by the powerful extra-economic value land possessed.

Land had an emotional value in this primarily agrarian society. Land could be one's patrimony and a deep sense of filial duty and obligation might be attached to it, and it was also the foundation of one's status in the community. The landscape was imbued with multiple layers of ritual, spiritual, geomantic, economic, familial, and reputational significance. These complex social understandings of land and land ownership resisted full alienation and represent an intricate system of values and interests that reflected not only the way things were, but the way they should be as well, and were consequently an expression of local norms.[29] From this angle, a consideration of land conflicts lay bare competing understandings and reveal the ways that norms (or what can be considered the proper way of doing things) were not simply collective modes of solution but were instead frames through which people argued about social conflict. Reference to shared norms helped generate local truths to interpret, and possibly solve, disputes.

In many of these transactions, one party was on the way down both economically and socially. Land – or the lack of land – described who you were. Given this level of investment, there was often a profound emotional charge surrounding land sales. Additionally, the buyers of conditional sales "generally developed a strong proprietary sense over the land with the passing of years and years and came to take for granted his right to enjoy its use."[30] This strong proprietary sense was also expressed when conditional owners rented the land to others (sometimes back to the seller!) and even conditionally sold the land again, and in the demands made for supplementary payments after the fall alienation of rights to use the land. Challenges to this sense of ownership could also result in violent conflict. Given the many meanings of land and the many modes of alienability, violence was perhaps inevitable.

The complexity of land holding in the late-Qing period is further suggested by a case from 1900 in which the sale of burial grounds by one member of a lineage led to his violent disciplining and murder at the hands of his relatives.[31] Following this act of self-policing and private justice, the lineage attempted to cover their actions by bribing the woman they had just made a widow. In his testimony at court, Xiang Bingzhi presented the lineage's opening account of the dispute:

> The deceased, Xiang Bingchen, is my *tangxiong* [elder male paternal cousin]. Last year in the middle of the eleventh month he secretly conspired along with Xiang Shiqi, who was the instigator, to illicitly sell [*simai*] grave land on the burial hill to the Peng family. This year on the first day of the first month, a member of the lineage sought to put this in order. At Xiang Jiehong's house, they reprimanded him... On the third of that month, Bingchen, for some [unknown] reason, died.[32]

Xiang Bingzhi then accused Xiang Bingchen's widow, Zhang Shi, of having listened to rumors and of being misled into filing a complaint at court. To further stress the lineage's benevolence and innocence, Xiang Bingzhi noted that the lineage, because of the "bitterness" of widowhood and the presence of small children, had given Zhang Shi silver, and that there was a signed agreement testifying to this arrangement. In this document, Zhang Shi stated that her husband had indeed died of illness and that the lineage had given her 30 ounces of silver. Further, she pledged to drop matters and move on with her life. The agreement was signed with her name and mark, and was witnessed by 9 community leaders and 19 kinsmen.[33]

However, the lineage's official version of events was complicated by two factors. The first was the autopsy conducted on Xiang Bingchen's corpse. The resulting document squarely rejected the possibility that he had died from illness. After listing some general features of the corpse, the report noted: "it seems that there is an injury from being crushed with chunks of earth."[34] It also reported that there was blood dripping from both ears, both nostrils, and the mouth. The corpse also presented ligature marks and other clear evidence that Xiang Bingchen had been bound. After detailing a variety of other wounds, the report concluded that Xiang Bingchen had been buried alive and that the cause of death was asphyxiation.

The second factor troubling the lineage's account was the accusation by both Zhang Shi and one of Xiang Bingchen's cousins, Xiang Shiqi, that he had been buried alive by the lineage as punishment for selling off the burial grounds. In his testimony, Xiang Shiqi delivered his version of the events that had led to Xiang Bingchen's death:

> The deceased, Xiang Bingchen, is my *tangdi* [younger male paternal cousin]. Last year in the middle of the eleven month, I was going to help out Peng Duanmao by selling him a grave on grave land within my property. We negotiated a price but hadn't completed the transaction. Out of nowhere, this year on the first day of the first year, I along with my brother's son Xiang Fusheng went up to a gathering at the graves. We ran into Xiang Hexing, Xiang Yishun.... [and] they told us that Xiang Bingchen had illicitly sold nine large plots on the burial grounds. I responded that I had not sold [anything]. Xiang Hexing and the others did not permit [me to leave] and then bound me with fine linen and wanted to bury me alive.[35]

Xiang Shiqi then reported that he was only saved by his mother's intervention: she had pleaded with lineage members to spare her son's life. However, a relative then ordered two men to escort Xiang Shiqi home and lock him inside. The lineage then ordered Xiang Shiqi's nephew to go and get Xiang Bingchen or be buried alive. Xiang Shiqi testified that his nephew "fearing punishment, went to Jiangjin and brought Xiang Bingchen back."[36] He continued:

> On the third, I was again brought to the gravesite on the hill. Xiang Hexing and Xiang Yishun then said that Xiang Bingchen should not have illicitly sold grave land in the ancestral tombs. Bingchen replied that

he had not sold anything. Xiang Hexing and the others called Xiang Muchang, Xiang Dongshan, Leper [*laizi*] Xiang, Xiang Liumen to bind Bingchen two hands behind his back. They chose a hole and placed him in the grave, used rocks and mud to hold him down, [and then] carried water and poured it in. [He] died right away.[37]

Other lineage members eventually came forward and confirmed this account. Xiang Bingchen had been taught a lesson, and, equally importantly, he had demonstrated for his fellow kinsmen the penalty for failing to conform to the family's expectations. His murder was a message. It was a performance. And it was an assertion of family control of land rather than individual ownership. Lineage justice moved ahead of state justice.

Some individual land holdings were not fully alienable because they were invested with non-market value to the lineage. The violation of this communal claim on the property provoked the brutal murder of Xiang Bingchen. This was a demonstration of the superiority of the communal claim to the land over an individual's. The lineage did not come to court in order to argue that the land was not legally Xiang Bingchen's to sell. Instead, it pursued local justice, and asserted an immediate and violent collective claim to the land. This quarrel makes clear the enduring strength of non-market forces on property, as the land clearly had been imbued with significance beyond simple economic value. Lineage members did not bury Xiang Bingchen alive because they had not received shares from the sale. Instead, the land's ritual and spiritual meanings had eclipsed its other values, and put the land beyond Xiang Bingchen's individual rights.

The lineage violently affirmed this norm. Xiang Bingzhi testified that his cousin had attempted to "illicitly sell" the land, and, although this claim was made in court, I see this as less of a legal argument and more as an assertion of a local truth. In this case, the land was a collective good and not an individual one, and even before the case would ever enter court, the lineage had publicly asserted this understanding.[38] This case also returns to two themes from earlier in the chapter: the emotional weight of land and the uncertainty that could surround economic transactions. One scholar has argued that the two basic characteristics of property ownership in capitalist societies (the West and Japan specifically) were the "maximal alienability of property" and the "identification of property with the individual."[39] In Ba County, extra-legal significances constrained the full alienability of land. On occasions, land could be fully alienable, yet this outcome often stood in tension with competing claims and understandings of the land – there could be multiple norms at work and individuals had to assert (sometimes violently) their interpretation of the correct governing norm. These incidents could lead to conflict as individuals work to control the local truth of the situation, and perhaps the court's later understanding as well. This was the local process of justice making: arguing with norms to produce shared interpretations of events.

Employers, employees, and social obligations

During the late-Ming and early-Qing period, the legal treatment of many agricultural laborers had changed to make their legal status equal to that of their employer, yet male suicide cases from Ba County demonstrate that even at the very end of the dynasty, long-standing normative expectations of reciprocity and paternalism remained strong. This notion of local justice imposed an additional burden of support on employers, as the more powerful were made to care for the more vulnerable.

Pre-eighteenth-century legal practice had recognized a shift in the standing of employers and their employees when they were bound by a long-term contract. Such a contract legally changed the status of the laborer so that any violence against the employer would be punished as if the attack had occurred between superior and inferior members of the same household, resulting in a more severe punishment. Legally, the relationship moved from independent, contractual associations to an explicitly familial, and hierarchical, bond. This legal reasoning illustrates the unequal burden placed on the subordinate in such a relationship. The employee's burden, however, was mirrored in the customary obligations placed on employers to care for their employees. Despite the transformation of the legal regime, local practice (backed by the court) endured, and demanded extra-market responsibilities from employers, a form of locally imposed justice.

Most of these cases involve work in shops – a kind of work that bound the parties as apprentice and master, a special and legally recognized relationship. The Qing Code states: "In the case of everyone who strikes the master from whom he is receiving instruction add two degrees to [the penalty] for ordinary persons."[40] The code goes on to explain that this relationship does not only include teachers of the Confucian classics and their students, but that it also extended to "common persons who are studying arts or trades."[41] The two men, then, were bound in a legally recognized relationship that transcended simple economic ties to closely mirror family relations. In terms of relative legal status, the same logic applied to master/apprentice as to long-term employer/employee and master/servant relations. So, while compensation from employers to the families of deceased employees may have been a strategy to curry favor in court or to placate the deceased's relatives, these payments also suggest a social expectation of remuneration, and the court enforced this norm when it was asserted. Customary practice dictated how the more powerful person in a relationship should behave toward the subordinate member of that dyad. The original basis of the relationship might be economic (employment, tenancy, apprenticeship, money-lending), but there was a clear expectation of paternalistic obligation, especially when the weaker party had suffered misfortune.

For example, in the ninth month of 1894, a 32-*sui* man filed a plaint at court alleging that his elder brother, Qi Yangtai, had killed himself over the loss of 3,000 *wen* left as deposit on a conditional land purchase that his sometime business partner, Chen Gaofa, would not return.[42] In the plaint, as well as testimony given on the same day, the deceased's brother described a three-year-old business relationship that existed between his brother and Chen, and argued that the crumbling of this relationship was the impetus behind his brother's suicide. Specifically, he claimed that Chen's failure to return the deposit left Qi without the cash necessary to rent a new place to live. This cash-flow shortage, a clear marker of his dire circumstances, drove Qi to suicide.

In a counter-plaint, which Chen filed jointly with his brother (a member of the local security authority [*baozheng*]), Chen claimed to have already returned the money:

> In the eighth month, Qi Yangtai conditionally purchased [*dian*] a section of my good land. In the middle [of the land], there is a house with a tiled roof – whoever is renting the land from me lives there. The land is called Mandarin Orange Terrace. I take a deposit of 3000 *wen*, the annual rent is 600 *wen*. The *dian* contract is clear evidence [of this]. Last month on the 18th day, Yangtai returned the land, saying he had rented Liu's farm instead, so I refunded his 3000 *wen* deposit, all according to our contract. This month on the 20th day, he moved away and that was the end of it.[43]

Chen then professed ignorance of the causes behind Qi's death and, in his subsequent testimony, repeatedly stressed that the medical examiner had ruled it a simple suicide for which no one could be blamed. Chen further suggested that Qi's brother, who had brought the plaint to court, wanted a lavish funeral for his brother and that this was the true motive for his spurious accusation that Chen had provoked the suicide. Chen said he had already "helped" by giving the family the wood for Qi's coffin. Qi's neighbors, Wang Zhengshan and Liu Shaoyang, testified that Qi had received money from Chen, and that they had no idea why he killed himself. Despite the backing of community leaders, a lack of evidence, corroborating testimony, and an alternative theory of the plaintiff's motivation, Chen had still made a payment, in the form of the coffin, to Qi's family. Why did he do this? Chen played a dominant social role in their business relationship, and as a result he occupied a position something like employer. This understanding of the relationship between the two men framed Qi's brother's demands for payment. The complicated relationship that bound the two men imposed responsibilities on Chen beyond simple economic ones. Chen's donation of Qi's coffin was recognition of these obligations, even if it seemed insufficient to Qi's brother. The court's engagement in no-fault suicides suggests the weight of local expectations of justice. The court intervened beyond officially criminal matters to effect local settlements beyond the scope of the Code, often enforcing local claims to justice.

Numerous cases document the customary expectations that called on employers to fulfill extra-economic obligations to provide for employees and their families. For example, in the seventh month of 1896, a widow named He Bao Shi, aged 52 *sui*, filed a plaint alleging that her son, He Yinsheng, had killed himself after being beaten by his boss, Yu Qingyun. Four days later, the court heard testimony from all parties. Bao Shi reiterated her claim:

> My husband died many years ago. I had three sons in total. My eldest son has left home; my second son helps Li Ditang as a laborer. The deceased, He Yinsheng, is my third son. Last year he came to Chongqing to be Yu Qingyun's apprentice at his bakery. There were no problems; I never thought [it would come to this]. This month on the eighth, my second son, He Chun, called on Yinsheng to tell him to return home, but he didn't see him. Then on the ninth, I, along with my nephew He Yunting, went to see the situation at the shop. We asked Qingyun about my son, but he just hemmed and hawed, arousing our suspicions. We forced him to go to the local security head and explain. Then Qingyun started to talk and admitted that on the fifth, he had beaten my son and that afterward Yinsheng had taken opium and died. He had ordered my son's body to be privately buried so that I would not find out what had happened.[44]

Her nephew confirmed her story. More tellingly, community leaders described their attempts to settle the matter informally. Testifying at court, Bao Shi's landlord, Li Ditang (also her second son's boss), and three local security officers [*baozheng*] explained that they had attempted to broker a settlement. After hearing from Bao Shi, they had urged Yu to give her 10,000 *wen*, but Yu had said he was only willing to pay 5,000. Then, once the money had already been agreed on, Bao Shi had demanded a further 3,000 to pay her traveling expenses. At this point, negotiations had broken down, and Bao Shi brought the matter to court seeking justice. Yu framed events differently, testifying that He Yinsheng had had been involved in an argument, although he did not say with whom or what the cause was. Yu contended that this fight had led to He's suicide. Further, Yu reported that he had hired a doctor to treat He, but that they had been unable to save him.

Much of the remaining case record details the back-and-forth deliberation over payment, all carried out under community leaders' oversight. Finally, on the 24th, Bao Shi testified that she had received 10,000 *wen* from Yu, as had been first agreed upon, and was now satisfied. Community leaders and Yu confirmed this as well. In his judgment, the magistrate recorded that Yu had "voluntarily helped" with the funeral expenses. Given the heavy negotiations and the fact that Yu was detained for at least part of the trial, "voluntarily helped" is not accurate description. Rather, Yu had been compelled to fulfill normative expectations about an employer's responsibility to his employee. In this case, Yu seems to have played some role in his employee's death. However, local expectations of employers' responsibilities extended well beyond this. Indeed, employers who played no role in their employee's death still faced enduring social obligations and local demands for justice.

These calls for satisfaction are apparent in the hanging suicide of a barber, Yu Changshou. Yu's younger brother, Yu Xingfa, and his workmate brought the case to court in the fifth month of 1895. They claimed not to know why Yu Changshou had hanged himself, but asked his boss, surnamed Jia, to pay 8,000 *wen* in compensation because of Yu Changshou's long tenure as an employee (he had worked for Jia for 18 years). Given that Yu Changshou was only 24 at his death, he had worked for Jia nearly his entire life, beginning as a six-year-old apprentice. Jia agreed to pay. Long service had changed the nature of the relationship between employer and employee from a purely economic one to one that entangled both parties in a wider web of expectation and mutual responsibility.

The social obligations imposed on employers, particularly following explicitly no-fault suicide cases, are clear in a case from 1891. In the first month of that year, Chen Yuanxing, Chen Huanzhang, and Chen Runtang came to court following the suicide of their nephew, Chen Zhangsheng.[45] Chen Zhangsheng, whose parents were dead, had worked in Huang Yongshun's shop. The uncles claimed that their nephew had accused Huang of cheating him, and that the two had argued. This dispute, in their view, had led directly to Chen's suicide.

Huang, not surprisingly, had a different understanding, and he testified that he had employed Chen, but made no mention of any argument. He claimed not to know why Chen had eaten the opium that had killed him, other than that he had "encountered disaster" [*yuxie*]. He further testified that he had dutifully reported Chen's condition to community leaders, but was unable to save him. Huang calculated the remaining wage owed to Chen at 5,000 *wen* and agreed to pay it to his uncles, and further offered to pay the burial expenses as well.[46] The court accepted this offer, and again enforced compensation payment in a no-fault suicide, supporting the legal and customary obligations that the employer assumed. Huang continued to have responsibility for his employee even in death and paid his family. Their relationship could not be reduced to economic transactions. It was primarily social bond, not just an economic one.

The social connection between employer and employee was not easily jettisoned. In the following case, even the employee's stealing from his master did not relieve his employer from postmortem responsibilities. In his plaint from the 12th month of 1891, druggist Shen Changsheng reported that on the morning of the 15th day, just after breakfast, Peng Dong and his brother, Peng Xiang, had come to his medicine shop and shouted to Shen's wife that Peng Dong was suffering from stomach pains.[47] Peng Dong seemed in bad shape, and they offered him some tea, but within an hour he had collapsed on the floor. Peng Xiang demanded medicine and prevented Shen's wife from leaving. Finally, they called on the local security official to help. After questioning, it became clear that Peng Dong had argued with his boss, Liao Yufeng, at a different medicine shop where Peng was serving as an apprentice. He then had then eaten a fatal dose of opium. Later that night, Peng Dong died.

The same day that Shen submitted his plaint, the dead man's master, Liao, submitted his own plaint explaining that Peng Dong had become his apprentice nearly four years earlier. However, Liao said that the previous month he had discovered that Peng Dong had been stealing supplies, and that Peng had admitted to selling them to rival druggist Shen Changsheng. Consequently, Liao had fired Peng. Aside from that, Liao denied any knowledge of or responsibility for Peng Dong's suicide. Following this, the dead man's father, Peng Dongxuan (63 *sui*), filed a petition summarizing the case. In this document, he declared that his son had committed suicide of his own accord, and that it could not be blamed on anyone. This peacemaking petition was the result of a mediated settlement. As part of this process, the case file also contains the settlement agreement, dated to the same day that Peng Dongxuan had filed his petition, signed by Liao Yufeng, Peng Dongxuan, Peng Xiang, and Shen Changshang, and witnessed by 11 other men.[48] In this document, following the urging of the witnesses, Liao and Shen agreed to "help" the dead man's family by each providing one *liang* of silver for his burial expenses. In other words, even though Peng Dong had stolen from Liao and been fired, Liao was forced to provide compensation for his employee's suicide. Four years of service had inalterably changed the relationship between Liao and Peng, and even the latter's later transgression could not erase the former's obligations.[49]

This case adds important nuance to an understanding of employer responsibilities. Following this suicide, the employer still owed a debt to the family of his deceased employee. Thus, the obligation bound employer and employee's family, transcending any malfeasance on the part of the employee. This suggests a slightly different understanding of this obligation, and appears to mirror the obligation natal families claimed in cases of their married daughters' death.[50] In these instances of no-fault suicide, natal families often demanded compensation for their losses. Paired, these two forms of compensation speak to a web of expectation between families and those who now controlled their offspring's lives, employers and marital families alike. Families pressed for justice when these expectations were violated, and the local court played a vital role in resolving these disputes, enforcing local normative expectations that the powerful would help the weak under these circumstances. In instances where local justice appears to have broken down, locals could still call on the magistrate to enforce norms.

One such individual was Zeng Yuanfa, 62 *sui*, who found himself in grim circumstances following his son's death. In 1890, he filed the following plaint:

I rely on my son's, Zeng Mingtang's, physical labor for support. This year in the first month, Tan Sangao's people hired my son to work for his landlord Rao Zanting's family as a hired hand. They gave an annual wage of 160 *chuan*. I can prove this matter. Late on the 29th day of the fourth month, Sangao and his man Stonemason Liu carried my son [home] – by the time he entered the house, he was already dead. I summoned the community leaders and my neighbors to examine my son's body. His fingers were black. Zanting claimed he had died of cholera.[51]

Zeng then claimed that he had been pressured into accepting terms for the burial, although he conceded that it had been done properly. He also admitted that his son's employer had paid him his son's wages for a full year. But despite all this, Zeng remained unsatisfied.

This plaint was followed the next day by an account from community leaders. In this document, the authorities reported that Zeng's son was a long-term laborer [*changgong*], a status that in the past would have diminished his formal independence and increased his employer's responsibility for him. While this formal status had been slowly and unevenly replaced, community leaders continued to stress the son's status as a long-term worker to suggest the close, personal relationship with his employer and to explain his employer's seemingly generous compensation. This understanding of responsibility demonstrates the continuing local relevance of these connections despite formal transformations in the legal system. This relationship still had an important social meaning long after its legal basis had shifted. Breaking the (now informal) bond between employer and employee resulted in local claims for justice. The community leaders' account continued, saying Zeng's son had killed himself for unknown reasons and had died at home. Moreover, they noted that Zeng had been paid his son's wages as well as funeral expenses, and that he had signed a statement confirming the death as a no-fault suicide. However, despite the community's best efforts, Zeng had persisted in his "troublemaking."

Indeed, community leaders' involvement had begun immediately after the death and included drafting a document signed by Zeng in which he absolved the deceased's employer, Rao Wang Shi, of any wrongdoing or further responsibility. This document was attached to a plaint from Wang Shi, who also stated that Zeng's son had died at home and that his father had been paid his wages as well as funeral expenses. The signed agreement, which was witnessed by six men including the scribe, declared that Zeng's son "had encountered misfortune while returning home and killed himself by consuming poison."[52] The document also stated that Zeng's family was poor and consequently unable to provide for a proper funeral. As a result, the community would provide him with a year's worth of his son's salary for funeral expenses, and, from other documents, it is clear that the burden of paying this debt fell to Wang Shi's family.

However, despite the weight of the employer's account backed by the community leaders and his own signed agreement, Zeng continued his case at court by filing another plaint. In this document, he claimed that he had never received his son's wages. This was the crux of the case: a matter of money. Zeng's initial plaint did not carry a bold accusation of violence or other wrongdoing. Instead, it inserted uncertainty into the account and suggested the possibility of foul play. This muddying of the waters was sufficient to gain the court's attention.

The court's acceptance of the case was in part due to Zeng's desperate position. At the outset, Zeng made clear that he relied on his son's support to make ends meet; his son's death cast his own survival into doubt. Both he and the court looked to routine mechanisms of local support, in this case the employer' obligation to look after employees and their families, to safeguard his future. Zeng would no longer draw regular support from his son's labor, so he needed a large final payment to survive. The audacity of Zeng's accusation is reinforced by the vast asymmetry in the power relations between Zeng (the poor father of a tenant farmer) and the landlord family he challenged. Moreover, Zeng brought his case to court from a distance of nearly 25 miles. This boldness suggests both Zeng's desperation and the strength of local understandings of the burden that the powerful were supposed to bear.

In a final example of the extra-economic ties binding employer and employee, a case from 1890 suggests the perhaps outer limits of this obligation. Testifying at court, Yi Guangying, reported:

> The deceased, Yi Guangcai, is my younger brother.... Last month on the 25th day, Yi, while at home took money, 800 [*wen*], and loaded it into a pocket on the inside of his clothing. He then headed off to Tiaodeng Market to buy rice.[53]

Yi would never arrive at the market. On his way, he stumbled onto the property of Wan Xingyi. There, he was beaten so severely that he died of his injuries the following day.

The two men accused of this brutal attack, Zhang Yuanxing and Zhang Haiting, framed the attack as a case of mistaken identity. They testified:

> To make a living, we both assist at Wan Xingyi's charcoal factory as hired laborers. The factory had been robbed by thieves many times, and they had not been caught. Then, last month on the evening of the 25th, this Yi Guangcai, who lives nearby, came to the factory to steal charcoal. We caught him. I, Yuanxing, picked up a hoe and hit him twice on the head. I, Haiting, picked up a wooden cudgel and hit him several times on the back, arm and belly. We had no idea he would...fall to the ground, suffer all night and die from his injuries the next day.[54]

The court never heard from Wan Xingyi, the factory owner.[55] Wan's wealth and local power insulated him such that a simple homicide on his property could not compel his appearance in court. However, the court did hold Wan, and the other higher-ups in the factory, partially responsible for Yi's death. Moreover, the court took steps to limit the death's impact on Yi's family, particularly on his widow, Yi Zhang Shi.

After portioning blame, with the majority falling on Zhang, and ordering the faultless released and sent home, the court evaluated Zhang Shi's condition and acted to shield her from cruelties of her newfound widowhood:

> Yi Zhang Shi is truly bitterly poor and without ability to peacefully bury her husband. [We have] considered [the matter] and decided that Zeng Yuanyi and Qiu Zhushan [two landlords from Guangcai's village] shall, while in the city, give 5000 *wen* each [to Zhang Shi]. [Further, we] order a runner to take Xiong Chengsan to the village and to instruct factory boss Wan Xingyi to give Yi Zhang Shi 20000 [units not given, but one must assume *wen*] to pay the expenses for a peaceful burial and to show sympathy.[56]

This was a firm assertion of a shared norm: affirming the social value of the widow as well as the filial duty to support older family members. Moreover, the court found that Wan continued to have obligations to his employee's family, Zhang Shi, even after the blame for the murder was legally assigned to someone else. Although he was not directly responsible for the acts of violence that his workers engaged in, Wan was still called to account for the consequences of those actions. The state compelled Wan to financially assist the family of his convicted employee: "Yet, Zhang Yuanxing must [support] a family with two generations of old people without anyone to depend on or to lean on. Wan Xingyi every month will give 1,200 *wen* until the day [Zhang] is released from jail."[57] An employer's paternalistic duties to his employees and their families were not severed by acts of criminal violence. Indeed, as the court made clear, Zhang's family was now in a more precarious position, and in even more dire need of Wan's support.

Even criminal acts did not rend the social bonds between employer and employee. Justice called for Wan's support of Zhang Shi even as it simultaneously called for Zhang's imprisonment. There could be more to these relationships than simple economic bonds, and indeed the court recognized this. Yet, these other meanings had to be asserted through an appeal to a shared norm or value. There was often a contest of norms and values, questions of primacy and interpretation, that were at the root of justice making.

The social meaning of economic exchange

Social expectations and the market did not form discrete oppositional spheres. Instead, economic exchanges in these cases were largely built on preexisting personal connections, often familial, or social acts in which relationships were established, marked, and affirmed. Different exchanges have different meanings. The economic sociologist Vivana Zelizer contends that "instead of menacing alien intrusions, economic transactions repeatedly serve to create, define, sustain, and challenge our multiple intimate relations."[58] Economic exchanges were acts of community making and sustaining, and they contained within them social meaning. There was no choice between rational economic exchange and moral economy. The two were deeply entwined: economic exchange was a social act. More fundamentally, these social transactions built upon established relationships. The social world gave both shape and meaning to economic exchanges – they were products of local communities.

The constructive elements of these exchanges are even more important given the relative distance of the state. With the local space generated by the large size and population of the county, communities were the crucial site for generating economic norms and enforcing them, as well as processing them through existing norms and values. The severe limitations in the state's knowledge of local landholding patterns and other economic exchanges meant that agreements between locals took precedence over the state's authority. Local norms could break down and enter the court, yet there was a world of routine economic activity that never made its way to court, and the state never tried to be aware of it. Kentaro Matsubara contends that "land right in this property regime were secured in the first instance by agreement among private parties, be it through communal understanding or written land deeds."[59] Communal understandings shaped economic interactions. The economic regime was first constituted by local communities and only then – and only occasionally – taken from those local spaces to be adjudicated, again on the basis of local knowledge, by the state. While the state and local community came together to make both the property and tax systems, the process began with and was primarily shaped by local hands.

As discussed in Chapter 2, local violence fixed individuals within a community web, and constrained their actions. This urge to bind the economy to social norms can be found in conflicts in Chongqing, as well as in the surrounding countryside, which suggests that these practices were not simple rural holdouts but instead continued to endure in the heart of the region's economy. In many economic conflicts, multiple understandings of the same act were present. So, while the powerful often saw payments in these disputes as "gifts" (usually referring to them as "help"), many locals saw them as entitlements.[60] There was a debate over the appropriate meaning of social acts, and violations of these understandings led to demands for justice to reconcile competing claims. Individual assertions of emotional and other forms of attachment to economic resources did not automatically create a consensual social norm that was broadly accepted. Instead, shared community values provided a vocabulary for the assertion of justice claims, not a Rosetta Stone dictating conflict resolution. The meanings of these conflicts had to be fashioned – this was justice making.

Notes

1 For geomancy, see Brown, "The Veins of the Earth".
2 Granovetter, *Society and Economy*, 24.
3 Taisu Zhang has argued that rational economic processes, rather than "pre-commercial" morality, shaped land transactions in the late Qing and Republic, while also stressing the centrality of social arrangements, particularly kinship organization and generational hierarchy. Thomas Buoye dates this change even earlier, to the eighteenth century, and in his study of central-level homicide cases, he argues that extra-economic controls imposed by shared norms withered as land became fully alienable. Buoye writes: "Indigenously generated market forces were creating impersonal economic institutions that upset social harmony." Taisu Zhang, "Social Hierarchies and the Formation of Customary Property Law in Pre-industrial China and England," *The American Journal of Comparative Law* 62, no. 171 (Winter 2014): 199; and Thomas Buoye, *Markets, Manslaughter, and Moral Economy: Violent Disputes over Property Right in Eighteenth-Century China* (Cambridge: Cambridge University Press, 2000), 226.
4 Tuulíkkí Píetílä, *Gossip, Markets, and Gender: How Dialogue Constructs Moral Value in Post-socialist Kilimanjaro* (Madison: University of Wisconsin Press, 2007), 11. For further discussions of dividuals, see Marilyn Strathern, *The Gender of the Gift: Problems with Women and Problems with Society in Melanesia* (Berkeley: University of California Press, 1988) and Charles Piot, *Remotely Global: Village Modernity in West Africa* (Chicago: University of Chicago Press, 1999).
5 In Robert Ellickson's study of the emergence of non-state order in rural communities in northern California, he stresses that "...fear of physical retaliation is undoubtedly one of the major incentives for order...." Ellickson, *Order without Law*, 58.
6 For a fuller discussion of these sorts of organizations, see Ownby, *Brotherhoods and Secret Societies*, 29–54.
7 See Arthur Smith, *Village Life in China* (Edinburgh: Oliphant, Anderson & Ferrier, 1899), 152–160; and Hsiao, *Rural China*, 314–315.
8 Huang contrasts the casual nature of these petty loans with the greater formality of larger loans, which frequently included a middleman or guarantor. In his view, the informality of such transactions opened the door for misunderstanding and indeed violence. Huang, *Civil Justice*, 33.
9 Granovetter, *Society and Economy*, 24.
10 BXDA 7694. I discussed this case at greater length in regard to kidnapping in Chapter 2.
11 BXDA 7661.
12 Ibid.
13 BXDA 7919.
14 Ibid.
15 BXDA 7748.
16 Ibid.
17 For more on tension surrounding family division, see David Wakefield, *Fenjia: Household Division and Inheritance in Qing and Republican China* (Honolulu: University of Hawai'i Press, 1998).
18 BXDA 7748.
19 For a thorough discussion of land transactions, see Huang's *Civil Justice*, particularly 36–56.
20 Ibid., 36.
21 Taisu Zhang has documented the significant amount of conflict conditional sales generated in the late Qing and Republic, See Zhang, "Social Hierarchies and the Formation of Customary Property Law."

22 Federico Varese, *The Russian Mafia* (Oxford: Oxford University Press, 2001), 2.

23 Diego Gambetta, *The Sicilian Mafia: The Business of Private Protection* (Cambridge: Harvard University Press, 1993), 17.

24 The vast majority of these routine community policing efforts must have never ended up in court. Consequently, the legal record only hints at a vast reservoir of customary violent practices.

25 BXDA 7689.

26 Ibid.

27 The local authorities were able to resolve this conflict without troubling the court: Wang's mother was compensated with 200 cash.

28 Anton Blok, *The Mafia of a Sicilian Village 1860–1960: A Study of Violent Peasant Entrepreneurs* (New York: Harper and Row, 1975), 210.

29 The economic sociologist Mark Granovetter argues that a serious discussion of norms "requires us to take seriously that people may have some conception of how things are, ought to be, or must be that supplants, overrides, or at least modifies action that would otherwise follow from self-interest alone." Granovetter, *Society and Economy*, 26.

30 Huang, *Civil Justice*, 38.

31 BXDA 7966.

32 Ibid.

33 This document mirrors *zhaojia* agreements in which seller promised not to seek additional payments.

34 Ibid.

35 Ibid.

36 Ibid.

37 Ibid.

38 There is a linguistic parallel to the argument I am making. The "*si*" of *simai* here means "illicit" but elsewhere it can simply mean "private," as opposed to "collective" or "public," *gong*.

39 H. Franz Schurmann, "Traditional Property Concepts in China," *The Far Eastern Quarterly* 15, no. 4 (August 1954): 507.

40 *DLCY*, 311.00.

41 Ibid.

42 BXDA 7821.

43 Ibid.

44 BXDA 7878.

45 BXDA 7684.

46 Ibid.

47 BXDA 7726.

48 There are actually two copies of the mediation contract submitted to the court, one produced for each side.

49 Shen's motivation remains murkier. He never admitted to buying stolen goods from Peng, and there was no mention of this in any of the documents other than Liao's accusation. Still, local mediators' actions, as well as the court's, make clear the connection that they say as existing between the two men. This bond necessitated payment from Shen.

50 I discussed this phenomenon in Chapter 3.

51 BXDA 7658.

52 Ibid.

53 BXDA 7678.

54 Ibid.

55 The two Zhangs did report that the "factory head" brought Yuanxing to court.

56 Ibid.

57 Ibid.
58 Viviana Zelizer, *Economic Lives: How Culture Shapes the Economy* (Princeton: Princeton University Press, 2011), 167.
59 Kentaro Matsubara, "The Property Regime and the Dynamics of State Formation in Qing China," unpublished paper prepared for the International Conference on Chinese Law and History, Fudan University, Shanghai, July 2015.
60 Zelizer differentiates three types of payments and the relationships they imply – compensation, entitlement, and gift – and argues that

> money as compensation implies an equal exchange of values, and a certain distance, contingency, bargaining, and accountability among the parties. Money as an entitlement implies strong claims to power and autonomy by the recipient. Money as a gift implies subordination and arbitrariness.
>
> Zelizer, *Economic Lives*, 136

5   Conclusion
Life beyond the state

In my introductory class on Chinese civilization, I spent a lot of time detailing emperors' reigns, the organization of the bureaucracy, elite culture, and the workings of the imperial state. Indeed, for many people, China presents a classic example of empire. But what if all this misses the point? What if none of this mattered for most people in the late-Qing period? Perhaps I have been teaching all wrong, pulled in by the allure of the state's grandeur and archive. Of course I am overstating this irrelevance, but most Qing subjects would never meet a centrally appointed official; their religious and cultural practices would vary widely from orthodoxy, and their social practices reflected realities beyond the state's imagination. And when the state was confronted by locals with these behaviors, it was only after the fact, and the state often worked to reinforce local practices. So why do I spill so much ink and emit so much air on the state?

The local justice I sketched in this book suggests the deep realm of local community that dominated existence in the Qing. The relationships and the violence that could be found there mattered, and matters. Down to today, the richness of local life continues to plague the Chinese state. Current forms of local corruption bring us back to Bradly Reed's rich discussion of local "corruption." What if bribes and *guanxi* are enduring remnants of local life, monadnocks that attest to the state's lasting inability to permanently reshape local practice?

I have been frustrated by my ability to chart this local life, as the state's archive presents only partial glimpses into its full workings. Many of the legal cases held in the Ba County archive are incomplete. They are fragments. I often have not been able to tell you what happened in the end, or who was punished and how. I have lived with this frustration for years, and could hear it in the questions when I presented my work – "but what happened?" I now think this limitation offers an insight. The fragments of the archive reveal the illusory nature of state control. I do not mean that the state had no control. Indeed, the Qing state could be enormously powerful when it focused its attention on issues or individuals, but most of life was lived beneath the Qing state's awareness. The holes in the documents remind us of these voids in state power. The state's view was partial at best, and it, like me, read local life through this veil.

While the Qing local state worked with and occasionally shaped this local order, it was unable to fundamentally alter it. My study sits on the temporal edge of state collapse, as the 1911 revolution would end both the Qing and the Imperial system. Yet, the local order and authority outlived the Qing, although they would be severely tested and stained by successive waves of war and mass violence, as well as their attendant miseries such as famine, disease, and displacement. It fell to the emergent modern state, the People's Republic of China, to profoundly alter local life. Money, sex, and family, those important sites of local conflict and authority, were all violently re-made by the communist government.

Yet, as profound as these changes were, they were not total. Alterations in local life were consistently challenged, and money, sex, and family today re-main vital nodes of conflict and power in the PRC. The contemporary state's drive for a "harmonious society" [*hexie shehui*] underlines the absence of accord, and invokes the long history of Chinese states' desire for peaceful submission. Despite its vastly expanded tools of coercion and surveillance, the PRC's call for harmony mirrors the Qing state's Sacred Edict in its ongo-ing attempt to remake the local.[1] This book is a reminder of the limits to an earlier iteration of the PRC's project, and serves as a discordant reminder of the state's awkward embrace of local power.

This book has focused on locals, and sometimes on the ways in which they bent state power to their needs and desires. People acted on the state at least as much as the state acted on people. The state was pulled into life and made a local actor by Qing subjects themselves. Once there, the state contended with other forms of power in the local arena for legit-imacy and efficacy. Ba County's loose form of self-rule appears to be less a by-product of dynastic crisis than the predictable result of a non-modern state. Without the information or interest to consistently inter-vene in local affairs, the Qing left things to the locals to sort out, and they largely did so. While the limited timeframe of my study does not allow me to chart broad change across the period of Qing rule, the picture that emerges for late-Qing Ba County is one of a loosely working system. Local forms of authority in Ba County churned on despite the Qing's ap-parent deterioration. The system that existed beyond and below the state was highly resilient.

State ignorance

Much of this project has considered what happened beyond the edge of state's routine knowledge, and, in this way, this study has been an explo-ration of state ignorance. The Qing empire's population swelled over time, more than tripling the Ming's population and exceeding 400 million by the mid-nineteenth century, yet the number of local government officials (about

1,300 county-level magistrates and another 2,000 or so heading departments and sub-prefectures) remained basically static.[2] This meant that by 1900, the Ba County magistrate was responsible for a population of nearly one million individuals. Similarly, the Qing tax regime also slipped behind massive growth. During the Ming (1368–1644), Sichuan had been lightly taxed, due to its relatively small population, but this limited tax regime continued into the Qing, even as the population grew dramatically.[3] These features of the Qing state were mirrored in an official ideology that saw small government as a putative good, a view most succinctly expressed in notions of "benevolent government" [*renzheng*].[4]

The Qing state's limitations were not accidental then, but rather the outcome of strategic decisions. Thus, the state produced its own ignorance, creating "strategic unknowns," embracing forms of unknowing that absolved it from action.[5] For the Qing, like many states, ignorance was a strategy to limit cost and involvement in local particulars. As Robert Proctor has noted, ignorance is a matter of selection: "We look *here* rather than *there*... and the decision to focus on *this* is therefore invariably a choice to ignore *that*."[6] The Qing state focused on some projects while choosing to ignore others, creating oceans of routine ignorance where it did not deploy its energies.

Many historians have described early modern and modern states as profoundly interested in the acquisition of knowledge, and the creation of imperial knowledge has also been an important theme in Qing histories.[7] These are stories of transformation, where ignorance is progressively supplanted by knowledge, linking knowing to the linear progression of political power.[8] However, as the state focused on this project, it left other realms unknown, posing the question of where and when did the state wish to know.[9] There are specific seasons and geographies of ignorance. So, while many early modern and modern states were often aggressive acquirers of knowledge, there were also crucial processes of selection, and various forms of self-inflicted ignorance.

Much of the Qing countryside fell into this gulf of routine unknowing. This remained the case even as the Qing pushed deeper into many communities, particularly along the borders, where it abandoned "native official" [*tusi*] programs, which left local control largely in the hands of indigenous leaders, in favor of more invasive regimes headed by regular imperial bureaucrats [*gaitu guiliu*]. Despite this reorganization, massive amounts of land – even beyond the highlands – remained outside regular Qing knowing. Even in "state spaces," local knowledge remained weak.[10] Much of recent Qing historiography has focused on questions of borderlands and ethnic encounter, but a return to China proper reveals that this vast area was subject to a similar calculated balance between knowledge and ignorance – between direct state control and diffuse power that required local authority to maintain day-to-day control. Many of the nimble tools of governance deployed by the Qing in border encounters also served them well in China proper, or at least in Sichuan.

Indeed, this study suggests that there was no solid and stable Han Core that stood in contrast to highly flexible and differentiated peripheries. The Qing state faced ongoing limitations in all locales. While recognizing the different institutional structures that controlled China proper and the multi-ethnic edges, from a local perspective, the Qing state's project in the former Ming territories comes to much more closely resemble that on the borderlands. The Qing was riddled with *internal peripheries*, spaces where state presence was limited and irregular. These were places where the Qing turned a blind eye, exhibiting purposeful and strategic ignorance. In these communities, ignorance saved money and relieved the state of the burden of greater intervention. The production of ignorance was a choice, and the intrusive and unwelcome destruction of this crafted ignorance, often forced on the state by locals, compelled the state into action where it might rather have not expended its energies.

There is already an extensive and well-documented catalogue of some of these spaces, including swamps, marshes, islands, mountains, and administrative borderlands.[11] Yet the Qing's internal peripheries were larger still. Indeed, by the nineteenth century, the Qing state seems to have had a limited sense even of crucial information such as land ownership.[12] Most local communities across the empire fell outside the routine and everyday oversight of the state. Think of a map of the empire where locales overseen by routine state authority are represented by points of lights. I imagine these pinpoints of control as standing out against a night sky of looser, indirect control.

In this study, I have tried to push past the bright lights of state power to consider the dimmer workings of non-state authority. In these murkier spaces, the *ming'an* cases reveal the workings of a local system of justice, one that often relied on violence. Local forces of justice were dominant in Ba County, with the magistrate serving as an occasional and half-blind source of authority. He could be powerful, but he was always a late entrant to conflicts. Despite the challenges of finding source material documenting local, non-elite society, the vast bulk of life occurred here, and the state only visited occasionally.

Order beyond the state

Given the limited and selective role for the pre-modern Qing state, historians have examined local life, and the limits to the state's involvement in it. These studies demonstrate the emergence of local practices that bent the state to local needs, even drawing the state into formally illegal realms of actions, such as false accusations. Matthew Sommer has argued that in the face of the state's failure to project power, "people had to devise their own solutions and avoid official interference as best they could."[13] He sees the informal realm of illicit customary practice as highlighting the dysfunctional aspects of the Qing, an interpretation that challenges Philip Huang's vision of local authority as functioning, complementary part of the routine system of the control, which was overseen and dominated by the magistrate.[14] By contrast, my study of cases from Ba County argues that the informal realm was not part of the formal system or evidence of its dysfunction. Instead, I have argued that it was a manifestation of a different, undergirding local system. Sommer posits that such a local order would form as a shadow realm dominated by local thugs and proto-mafia. While these elements were certainly part of the local world of Ba County, they do not fully describe it. The late-Qing period is replete with denunciations of bandits and "local bullies and evil gentry" [*tuhao lieshen*], yet I am wary of too broad a denunciation, particularly on the basis of the state's archive.[15] For Ba County, Bradly Reed's dismantling of stereotyped visions of "yamen vermin" [*yadu*] further cautions against too dark an interpretation of local order. Reed has explored the expansive local administrative practices that led to the creeping creation of an informal but essential form of local administration. One magistrate's "vermin" was another man's essential yet illicit bureaucrat. I would suggest that people always devised their own solutions, including exploiting state authority, and that these local innovations do not represent a failure that emerged over the course of the Qing. Rather, this was a regular feature of the empire. Local systems of power, which produced justice when required, ran parallel to official systems, yet were the dominant form of authority in Ba County. Leaving behind state-ist analyses that focus on the success or failure of the Qing state, enduring forms of local power take center stage.

Local authority was neither black nor white. It could empower local toughs, but so too could it find a modicum of justice for deceased relatives. It could enforce a subsistence ethic as well as exploit the weak. The local system's inherent *grey-ness* mirrors more formal systems for rendering justice. The Qing legal system frequently reinforced normative patterns of authority, even as it could occasionally be used to overturn those same powers. Orthodox Confucianism disciplined and subjected even as it could provide a moral lash to strike for better treatment. That the local justice system could be violent, often reinforced normative patterns of domination, and tended to fail in the production of some form of objective justice cannot be used to denounce it as none of the systems available at the time were free of such problems.

Local power was not an idyll beyond the state's reach, and my attempt to view local life from the state's archive finds a key role for violence in ordering local life. Ba County had a culture of violence.[16] This culture is best seen in the small moments and as a local tool for maintaining local community. Violence seems to have coalesced around vital points of contact and conflict – money, sex, and family – and throws into relief the often brutish workings of local order. Moreover, beyond the instrumental role that bloodletting played in local life, violent acts and their consequences open a view on the social life of emotion in the late-Qing period.

These may not be unfiltered emotion, but they are, at least, the performance of a shared cultural lexicon. As William Reddy notes, "conflict cannot be important, unless the culture teaches individuals how to engage in conflict."[17] Shared cultural scripts of outrage, anger, sadness, and loss serve to round out the too-often flat depictions of the Chinese past. In the end, legal cases do not grant unmediated access to interiority, but they do suggest an emotional, and perhaps moral, repertoire. In this process, sturdy cultural bedrocks, such as Confucianism, could be deployed in an array of unanticipated ways that place these heuristic black boxes alongside state power as tools to navigate local worlds.

Moving from orthodoxy to practice, individual needs, wants, and strategies to achieve them are fleetingly clear. Competing norms had to be articulated and asserted – this was how justice was made – and in this process local truths could become legal truths. Understanding justice making in this way makes clear the many shaping hands that molded this process, and the collective efforts that went into it. Justice did not flow from the court out into communities. Local gentry did not determine outcomes. Non-elites were ever-present. All of the groups worked in dynamic coordination and contention to make justice.

My kaleidoscopic approach to this subject has focused on the various actors (individual and collective), the multiple venues, and protracted lifespans of dispute at the end of the Qing. Throughout all of these modes, I have stressed ongoing attempts to construct and control the narrative of the conflict and its meaning. The making and remaking of truth in these disputes was a central feature of disputing, and these struggles reveal the powerful layering of authority in the late-Qing period. The truth was not known – it had to be constructed out of the norms and values available to interpret events. Many hands fashioned truths in a process that was pliable and resilient. While some voices carried more weight than others in this process, it was an open system that allowed, and occasionally favored, insurgent interpretations of events that cut against dominant power structures. In the main, however, this system, dependent on shared social norms to build meaning, tended to favor the already powerful.

Ba County in the 1890s exposes key aspects of the Qing in twilight. In particular, legal records from the county demonstrate that violence was an important and regular tool used to defend and construct the county's communities. David Robinson argued that, during the Ming at least, "illicit force was as much a part of local order as it was a threat to that order."[18] In a similar vein, everyday violence in Ba did not seem to signal the breakdown of order, but was itself a force of local order, and a central component in the making of local justice. My study exposes different patterns of quotidian violence that continued to shape life at the very end of the Qing.

The dead bodies found in the *ming'an* files attest to the relationship between violence and local justice. Fundamentally, access to justice was predicated on community ties, including familial and economic bonds. This was true in both acts of purely local justice and justice made in court. In this way, justice was a limited and valuable resource in the late-Qing period. It was not (and never is) available to everyone. You had to merit justice.

Notes

1 All 16 of the Edict's maxims stress the importance of harmony, and just as the PRC's call for a harmonious society is supposed to invoke historical antecedents, so too was the Qing's Edict built on earlier examples, perhaps most notably the Ming founder's Six Maxims, which also call for harmony.
2 By officials, I mean centrally appointed, degree-holding officials, rather than local *yamen* staff, whose numbers did grow.
3 By 1728, Sichuan had 3.4 times the total taxable land that the province had in the Ming Wanli era (1563–1620), but its tax rate was only 40 percent that of the Wanli period. Di Wang, *Kuachu fengbi di shjie: Changjiang shangyou quyu shehui ya jiu, 1644–1911* [Striding Out of a Closed World: Research on Society in the Upper Yangzi Macroregion, 1644–1911] (Beijing: Zhonghua shuju, 2001), 422. A concise history of the development of Sichuan's tax regime can be found in Xiaowei Zheng, *The Politics of Rights and the 1911 Revolution in China* (Stanford: Stanford University Press, 2018), 30–34.
4 While *renzheng* is an expressly Confucian norm, a strong interest in small government is found in other strains of Chinese thoughts as well, such as Laozi's well-worn comment in the *Daodejing* that "governing a large state is like boiling a small fish" because a small fish can fall apart with too much fiddling. Beliefs in "nonaction" [*wuwei*] could also advocate for small government. See Lao Tzu, *Tao Te Ching*, trans. D.C. Lau (New York: Penguin Books, 1963), 67. For more of the organization of local government, see Ch'ü, *Local Government in China under the Ch'ing* (Stanford: Stanford University Press, 1963).
5 I borrow this term from Linsey McGoey. See Linsey McGoey, "Strategic Unknowns: Towards a Sociology of Ignorance," *Economy and Society* 41, no. 1 (2012): 1–16.
6 Robert Proctor, "Agnotology: A Missing Term to Describe the Cultural Production of Ignorance (and Its Study)," in *Agnotology: The Making and Unmaking of Ignorance*, eds. Robert N. Proctor and Londa Schiebinger (Stanford: Stanford University Press, 2008), 6 (emphasis in original).
7 For a leading example of this scholarship, see Christopher A. Bayly, *Empire and Information: Intelligence Gathering and Social Communication in India, 1780–1870* (Cambridge: Cambridge University Press, 1999).
8 For example, Matthew Mosca describes a broad process of Qing knowing in his study of the empire's ignorance regarding India and its efforts to build knowledge to counter the growing British threat. His work highlights the process of the Qing's choosing to know, and of deciding to expend energy to know. Matthew Mosca, *From Frontier Policy to Foreign Policy: The Question of India and the Transformation of Geopolitics in Qing China* (Stanford: Stanford University Press, 2013), 305–309.
9 For more on state ignorances, see Shannon Sullivan and Nancy Tuana, eds., *Race and the Epistemologies of Ignorance* (Albany: State University of New York Press, 2007).
10 In thinking about "state spaces," I follow James Scott, as laid out in *The Art of Not Being Governed: An Anarchist History of Upland Southeast Asia* (New Haven: Yale University Press, 2009), 40–63. Scott develops this idea mainly in contrast to his primary interest, *nonstate spaces*. These two areas are primarily defined by the land's "agro-ecology" and its potential as a site for appropriation

(manpower, grain, etc.) by an interested state. Indeed, Scott's chapter on state spaces is subtitled: "zones of governance and appropriation" I deploy this term slightly more baldly to suggest spaces where state presence and power were thick.

11 For histories of some of these regions, see Perry, *Rebels and Revolutionaries in North China*; Rowe, *Crimson Rain*; Robert Antony, *Like Floss on the Floating Sea: The World of Pirates and Seafarers in Late Imperial South China* (Berkeley: China Research Monograph, 2003); and Scott, *The Art of Not Being Governed*.

12 For examples of this process, see Matsubara, "Land Registration and Local Society in Qing China"; John Shepard, *Statecraft and Political Economy on the Taiwan Frontier, 1600–1800* (Stanford: Stanford University Press, 1993); Isett, *State, Peasant, and Merchant.*

13 Sommer has made clear the importance of "illicit customary practices," such as wife-selling and polyandry, in the Qing, and his "perspective from the margins" has reconceptualized marriage and the family, as well as the realms of sex and work, for the Qing. Sommer, *Polyandry and Wife-Selling*, 381.

14 Huang, *Civil Justice*, 110–137.

15 I am reminded of Barend ter Haar's counsel against relying on the state's labels and "pseudo-autonyms" to understand those outside formal authority, cautioning me against a general denunciation of this local order. ter Haar, 13–15, 196–246.

16 In contrast to Philip Kuhn's argument that violence emerged as a sustaining force in the mid-nineteenth century, William Rowe stresses an earlier and enduring "local culture that was persistently and systematically violent" in Hubei Province. Rowe compiles a series of bloody episodes to examine one county's "culture of violence." He ties this violence to the county's "small-place consciousness," central-local tensions, and local patterns of dominance and resistance, as well as to a broader cultural context that celebrated violence. Philip Kuhn, *Rebellion and Its Enemies in Late Imperial China: Militarization and Social Structure, 1796–1864* (Cambridge: Harvard University Press, 1970); Rowe, *Crimson Rain*, 326, 322–325.

17 William Reddy, *The Navigation of Feeling: A Framework for the History of Emotions* (Cambridge: Cambridge University Press, 2001), 47.

18 David Robinson, *Bandits, Eunuchs and the Son of Heaven* (Honolulu: University of Hawai'i Press, 2001), 167.

Appendix

Most of this book has focused on narratives of individual cases, but in this appendix I broadly profile two types of interpersonal violence, suicide and homicide, and put the county in a broader comparative perspective.

Suicide

There were 64 legal cases concerning suicides, 33 were committed by men and 26 by women, a perhaps surprising division given contemporary China's unique predominance of female suicides and the existing scholarship's focus on female deaths.[1] In terms of age, 19 of the dead could be considered "young," 6 "old," with 2 somewhere in the middle, and 32 unknown.[2] And of these dead of "unknown" age, 11 were women – 10 of whom were already married at the time of death. Overall, 25 of the dead were married, 6 single (with one engaged), and 4 widows. For the remaining 24, their marital status was unclear. Of these 24, a total of 23 were men. From these numbers, it is clear that women who killed themselves tended to be married, which is perhaps not surprising, given the near ubiquity of marriage among Qing women.

To push the numbers a little harder, it seems that many of the men whose marital status was unclear from the records were in fact unmarried (or at least away from home), given the absence of their spouse in the legal record. So, it appears that married women and single men killed themselves. While these trends generally conform to expectation, they do reveal an interesting structural tension within normative gender roles. Women who killed themselves were more explicitly fixed in society. They were following expectation in inhabiting these roles. Indeed, most female suicides occurred within normal social roles, suggesting a tension within this role itself. These women were married, for better or worse, while their male counterparts exhibit a greater variety of social attachments. These men's deaths suggest a point of structural weakness in young males' transition to full commoner status, or one of the "good people" [liangmin], and thus positions of normative masculinity.

The occupations of these dead were only occasionally recorded. Given the time and the place, we can assume that many of these individuals were agricultural workers. In fact, one might suggest that farming formed a default occupation, and that perhaps jobs were only noted when they failed to conform to this presumption. Recorded occupations included laborer, apprentice in a "handicraft" shop, tailor, barber, shopkeeper, bucket maker, cotton worker, baker, medicine shop assistant, and so forth. This reads as a litany of regular working people. Perhaps not surprisingly, women were never presented as having "occupations," despite their integral contributions to the family economy.[3]

The data show that most people killed themselves at home, with only three deaths occurring in public or away from home. Interestingly, the city and surrounding countryside seem to be equally represented on the rolls of suicides.[4] Historians of Europe have largely debunked the notion of cities as particularly violent places.[5] However, while about one in four residents of Ba County lived in the city, half the suicides occurred there. There was a nearly perfect balance between the city and the countryside, with 25 cases occurring in the villages and 26 in the city.[6]

Historians of Europe have also thoroughly challenged the assumption that urbanization axiomatically brings isolation and anonymity, and therefore crime. Clive Emsley argues that "urbanization did not destroy the ability of groups bound by work, ethnic, religious or other ties, from existing as communities; nor did it leave the new urban dweller as an isolated individual among a society of strangers."[7] One sees a similar situation in England. Industrialization and urbanization changed communities, "but the experience was not so shattering that people, especially poor immigrants spreading to cities or sprawling open villages, ceased to live in, and to perceive themselves as part of, communities."[8] Here, parallels with experiences in China come quickly to mind. Qing urban dwellers, rather than finding themselves lost and alone in their new settings, were usually bound up in a web of native-place and work relations that constituted well-developed sub-communities within the city. These ties were the key to urban survival; as much research has shown, one's fate in the city was intimately tied to the exploitation of these communalistic ties.[9] Lingering in the background of many anti-urban understandings is a notion of an ideal rural community, but "violence was always just as prevalent, and often more so, in the countryside as it was in the city, and big cities were no more violent than smaller ones."[10] The Qing countryside was a frequent site of violence. I strongly suspect that both a reporting bias that favored the city and the informal modes of dispute resolution away from state centers further diminished crime reports from many rural areas. Combined, these two trends suggest that the equilibrium between rural and urban violence found in my samples masks a reserve of rural violence.

The data further indicate no strong seasonal bias. Spring saw the most suicides with 19 deaths (10 women and 9 men), followed by summer with

15 (8 women and 7 men), winter with 13 cases (11 men and 2 women), and autumn with 12 (6 women and 6 men).[11] Also, the cases exhibit no annual pattern over my (brief) timeframe.[12] The method of suicide shows a much clearer bias.

Consuming lethal amounts of opium was the method of choice in 39 of the cases, followed by 12 hangings, 4 cut throats, 2 drownings, 1 leap off a cliff, and 1 case of arsenic poisoning.[13] Opium was a common cash crop and widely available to those who decided on suicide. Interestingly, one finds no correlation between gender and method of suicide.[14] However, one does see a strong gender bias in the alleged reasons and circumstances of the suicide. Of our sample, 19 cases can be broadly classified as "family related," and all of the dead in this group are women. Another 25 cases can be seen as stemming from economic troubles, and 23 of the dead in this category are men.[15] These divisions are crude and elide the artificiality of the separation between family units and economic units, but this gendered difference is mirrored in the existing scholarship, which exhibits an almost exclusive focus on female suicide.

Homicide

There were 90 "homicide" cases in the files.[16] From this, I subtract cases of false accusation in which it was clear that no murder took place, of which there were 17. Subtracting only the more glaring examples of false accusation leaves 73 homicide cases for the decade under study. Of these, 39 were animated by economic conflicts, particularly disputes over debts and land transfers. Economic conflict as a source of violence is not surprising. However, although these cases may have hinged on an economic dispute, additional motivating factors comingled with financial imperatives. In the case of land transfers, land held important non-economic value as well in this predominately agrarian society. Land was seen as one's patrimony and afforded individuals a degree of respect as a full member of the community. This sense of reputation could also be present in other "economic" conflicts as well. Heuristic shorthand should not obscure multi-causality or simple contingency at work in these clashes.

Twenty-two homicides were committed in the wake of some other, smaller crime or offence. In these cases, murder was a response to an affront. The precipitating challenges could be petty, such as name calling, or they could be grave, such as rape. In other cases, the perpetrator of the initial crime also committed the resulting homicides. For example, a thief might be caught red-handed and kill his witness. Crime often exhibited a snowball effect, generating its own momentum and wilding out of control.

In addition to economic- and criminally related homicides, a third category of murder was family related. In a large number of cases, the conflict can loosely be described as family related. This is a broad and rather nebulous rubric, but these cases are held together by the central role that family members played either in the acts of violence or in bringing them to court. Consider a case in which an uncle claims his niece was murdered by her husband,[17] or one in which a man beats his brother to death over outstanding debts.[18] In these cases, violence and conflict occurred within the family, illustrating the tensions within this foundational unit.

Gender, another essential building block of local society, is also an instructive lens through which to view these crimes. In 12 cases, women were involved in violence. There are two cases in which the murderer was female and seven cases in which the victim was female. In the remaining cases, violence against women (rape or beatings) played an important role in the conflict that led to murder. In all other cases, the main actors in the homicide (victim or killer) were male.

The relative absence of violence against women in the record reflects, in part, the enormous degree to which such violence was routinized. The Qing Code permitted wife beating as long it was not excessive: "As for the husband striking the wife, if he does not break [her bones], there is no punishment."[19] The Code further stipulated that even if a husband did fracture his wife's bones while beating her, his punishment should be reduced two degrees from that for an assault by a non-relative. On the other hand, the Code increased punishment for wives who assaulted their husbands. Moreover, the Code allowed for the murder of adulterous wives and their lovers: "Whenever a wife or concubine commits adultery with another, and (her own husband) catches the adulterous wife and the adulterer at the place [in the very act] of adultery and immediately kills [both of] them, there is no punishment."[20] If the husband did not kill his wife, she was still to be punished with 90 strokes of the bamboo for fornication. While structural inequality not only erased many forms of violence against women from the social category of criminal violence, these figures sketch an unsurprising profile of individuals likely to be involved in homicidal violence: working-age males. These men were likely to engage in violence (1) to solve economic disputes, (2) to resolve family conflicts, or (3) in the wake of other transgressions.

Moreover, the extant records, when they are clear on the matter, suggest a method of choice. Beatings (both with and without weapons) were the most common method of murder. In 23 cases, the victim was clearly beaten to death. In 11 cases, stabbing was the cause of death. Two individuals were buried alive. There was also one poisoning and one drowning. The predominance of beatings as the cause of death suggests that many of these fatalities were brawls that got out of hand rather than premeditated homicides.

Finally, Ba County can be viewed from a comparative perspective. Legal records suggest a rough homicide rate of 8.1 per 100,000 persons.[21] By comparison, in 2004, the People's Republic of China had a reported homicide rate of 2.2 per 100,000 persons.[22] Ukraine, Kyrgyzstan, and Thailand, also in 2004, all had comparable homicide rates as Ba County.[23] How does late-nineteenth-century Ba County compare with its contemporaries? Rome had a similar homicide rate of around eight from 1890 to 1910.[24] From 1855 to 1905, France had a homicide rate of 0.8/100,000,[25] while the UK in 1870 had a homicide rate of somewhere between 1.5[26] and 2.[27] At that time, Corsica had the highest murder rate in Europe at 14/100,000.[28] Japan in 1900 had a homicide rate of 1.3.[29] Finally, the United States reported in its Vital Statistics a rate of 1.2,[30] although some scholars had estimated its actual homicide rate as high as nearly 8.0.[31] In this light, Ba County seems to have been a fairly violent place by global standards, but not outrageously so.

Notes

1 Several of these 64 cases did not in fact contain suicides. In these instances, the "suicides" were subsequently determined to have been deaths by other causes, such as disease. This accounts for differences between the total 64 cases and the 59 I describe in greater detail. For a discussion of suicide in contemporary China, see Michael R. Phillips, Huaqing Liu, and Yanping Zhang, "Suicide and Social Change in China," *Culture, Medicine and Psychiatry* 23, no. 1 (March 1999): 25–50. I discuss scholarship on female suicide in Chapter 2.

2 I did not attempt to approximate age from the deceased's life circumstances. If the age was not immediately clear, I designated it as "unknown."

3 In *China's Motor*, Hill Gates discusses in detail women's contribution to household incomes and their exclusion from our understandings of productive work. A false dichotomy is frequently drawn between the family and the economy. In most instances, these units overlapped. Hill Gates, *China's Motor: A Thousand Years of Petty Capitalism* (Ithaca: Cornell University Press, 1996).

4 There is probably an element of reporting bias in favor of the city, but the extent of this distortion in unclear.

5 For the debate about Europe, Eric Johnson has grouped the major proponents of violent city theory into five categories. First, the "Conservative Political Argument" was promulgated by conservative forces within the modernizing societies which attacked these processes in defense of their own interests, which were frequently based in the countryside. Second, the "Marxist Argument" shares this negative view of cities by seeing them as the main site for bourgeoisie capitalism and it associated with miseries. Third, the "Classical Sociological Argument" blames the shift from community to society that it associated with urbanization. Fourth, the "American Sociological Argument" adds empirical data to the Classical Argument while basing its conclusions on the highly particularistic American experience as the basis for its normative claims. Finally, the "Recent European Historical-Cultural Argument," represented by Foucault among others, which is generally opposed to the modernization process. Eric A. Johnson, *Urbanization and Crime: Germany, 1871–1914* (Cambridge: Cambridge University Press, 1995), 8–12.

6 There were eight cases in which the location was not clear.

7 Clive Emsley, *Crime and Society in England, 1750–1900* (London: Longman, 1987), 86.

8 Ibid., 97.

9 See Bryna Goodman's *Native Place, City and Nation: Regional Networks and Identities in Shanghai, 1853–1937* (Berkeley: University of California Press, 1995), Elizabeth Perry, *Shanghai on Strike: The Politics of Chinese Labor* (Stanford: Stanford University Press, 1993); and Gail Hershatter, *Workers of Tianjin, 1900–1949* (Stanford: Stanford University Press, 1986) for further elaboration of these ties.

10 Johnson, *Urbanization and Crime*, 234.

11 Winter is defined as months 12, 1, and 2 in the lunar calendar; spring is months 3, 4, and 5; summer is months 6, 7, and 8; and fall is months 9, 10, and 11. I use this system rather than the traditional ritual markings of the seasons in order to better capture the agricultural realities and imperatives of Sichuan.

12 Suicide cases per year: year 15 of the reign of the Guangxu Emperor had 5 cases; year 16 had 12 cases; year 17 had 6; year 18 had 3; year 19 had 7; year 20 had 10; year 21 had 4; year 22 had 5; year 23 had 0; year 24 had 2; and year 25 also had 2.

13 The strong predominance of opium as the killer of choice is echoed in contemporary China's heavy favoring of chemical pesticides as method of suicide, suggesting an interesting arc in China's history from opium to chemical pesticides.

14 Female suicides: 20 opium, four hangings, one cut throat, and one drowning. Male suicide: 19 opium, eight hangings, three cut throats, one drowning, one leap off a cliff, and one use of arsenic.

15 There are five cases where the reasons are not clear, and the remaining ten cases are a motley assortment of suicides following fights, thefts, and other transgressions.

16 These cases do not exist as a separate subset in the archival file; rather they have been labeled as such by me.

17 BXDA 7752.

18 BXDA 7862.

19 *DLCY*, 315.00.

20 Ibid., 285.00.

21 73 homicides for an estimated population of 917,765.

22 *The Guardian*, "Global Homicide: Murder Rates around the World|News|Guardian. co.uk", October 13, 2009, http://www.guardian.co.uk/news/datablog/2009/oct/13/homicide-rates-country-murder-data.

23 Ibid.

24 Ibid.

25 Pieter Spierenburg, *A History of Murder: Personal Violence in Europe from the Middle Ages to the Present* (Cambridge: Polity, 2008), 168.

26 Randolph Roth, *American Homicide* (Cambridge: Belknap Press, 2009).

27 Spierenburg, *A History of Murder*, 168.

28 Ibid.

29 Japan. *Nihon Tokei Nenkan* [Japan Statistical Yearbook] (Tokyo: Nihon Tokei Kyokai: Mainichi Shinbunsha, 1949).

30 United States. Bureau of the Census, *Vital Statistics Rates in the U.S., 1900–1940 Sixteenth Census of the U.S. : 1940/* (Washington: U.S. G.P.O., 1943).

31 Roth, *American Homicide*, 4.

Character list

baojia 保甲
baozheng 保證
changgong 長工
chong 沖
chuan 串
chuan 釧
chujia 出家
cun 寸
Da Qing lü li 大清律例
dai lümaoi 戴綠帽
dan 石
diao 弔
dou 斗
fan 煩
fang 坊
fen 墳
fen 分
gaitu guiliu 改土歸流
gan xue lao 乾血癆
gong 公
hexie shehui 和諧社會
hongchuan 紅船
jia 家
jiansuo 姦所
jianghu 江湖
jianzheng 監正
jiaohua 教化
jin 斤
juan 卷
kouan qian 口岸錢
la 臘
laizi 癩子

laoyao 老幺
li 例
liang 兩
lü 律
ming'an 命案
mu 畝
nan 難
neishan 內山
panjie 盤詰
paoge 袍哥
pi 痞
qing 清
qingji 情急
ruyi 如意
shendan 審單
si 私
siya 私押
simai 私賣
songgun 訟棍
songshi 訟師
sui 歲
tangdi 堂弟
tangxiong 堂兄
tian 田
tu 土
tubao 土堡
tusi 土司
waishan 外山
wen 文
wugao 誣告
wugu 無故
wuwei 無為

wuxing 五刑

wuzuo 仵作

xiaojia 小甲

xian 縣

xiangyue 鄉約

xigu 細故

xishi 細事

yadu 衙蠹

yamen 衙門

yanguan 煙館

yaoque 要缺

yi 義

yuxie 遇邪

zhaojia 找價

zhuo jian 捉姦

zuzheng 族証

References

Cases from the *Baxian Dang'an* [Ba County Archive, Sichuan Provincial Archive, Chengdu] are identified by case number. For example. BXDA 7693.

Allee, Mark A. "The Status of Contracts in Nineteenth-Century Chinese Court." In *Contracts and Property in Early Modern China*, edited by Madeline Zelin, Jonathan K. Ocko, and Robert Gardella. Stanford: Stanford University Press, 2004.

Asen, Daniel. *Death in Beijing: Murder and Forensic Science in Republican China.* Cambridge: Cambridge University Press, 2016.

Baxian zhi minguo [Ba County Gazetteer, Republican Period, 1939]. Reprinted in *Zhongguo Difang Zhi Jicheng: Sichuan Fu Xian Zhi Ji* [Compendium of China's Local Gazetteers: Volume Containing the Gazetteers from Sichuan's Prefectures and Counties]. Chengdu: Ba Shu shushe, 1992.

Bayly, Christopher A. *Empire and Information: Intelligence Gathering and Social Communication in India, 1780–1870.* Cambridge: Cambridge University Press, 1996.

Benton, Lauren. *A Search for Sovereignty: Law and Geography in European Empires, 1400–1900.* Cambridge: Cambridge University Press, 2009.

Blok, Anton. *Honour and Violence.* Cambridge: Polity, 2001.

———. *The Mafia of a Sicilian Village 1860–1960: A Study of Violent Peasant Entrepreneurs.* New York: Harper and Row, 1975.

Bodde, Derek and Clarence Morris. *Law in Imperial China: Exemplified by 190 Ch'ing Dynasty Cases (Translated from the Hsing-an Hui-lan), With Historical, Social, and Juridical Commentaries.* Cambridge: Harvard University Press, 1967.

Bossen, Laurel and Hill Gates, *Bound Feet, Young Hands: Tracking the Demise of Footbinding in Village China.* Stanford: Stanford University Press, 2017.

Bossler, Beverly. "'A Daughter is a Daughter All Her Life:' Affinal Relations and Women's Networks in Song and Late Imperial China." *Late Imperial China* 21, no. 1 (June 2000): 77–106.

Brown, Tristan G. "The Veins of the Earth: Property, Environment, and Cosmology in Nanbu County, 1865–1942." PhD diss., Columbia University, 2017.

Buoye, Thomas. *Manslaughter, Markets, and Moral Economy: Violent Disputes over Property Right in Eighteenth-Century China* (Cambridge: Cambridge University Press, 2000).

———. "Murderous Intent Arose: Bureaucratization and Benevolence in Eighteenth-Century Qing Homicide Reports." *Late Imperial China* 16, no. 2 (December 1995): 72–74.

Chabrowski, Igor Iwo. *Singing on the River: Sichuan Boatmen and Their Work Songs, 1880s–1930s*. Leiden: Brill, 2015.

Chang, Chung-li. *The Chinese Gentry*. Seattle: University of Washington Press, 1955.

Chen, Li. "Legal Specialists and Judicial Administration in Late Imperial China, 1651–1911." *Late Imperial China* 33, no. 1 (2012): 1–54.

Ch'ü, T'ung-Tzu [Qu, Tongzu]. *Law and Society in Traditional China*. Paris: Mouton, 1961.

———. *Local Government in China Under the Ch'ing*. Stanford: Stanford University Press, 1962.

Conley, Carolyn. "The Agreeable Recreation of Fighting." *Journal of Social History* 33, no. 1 (1999): 57–72.

Davis, Natalie Zemon. *Fiction in the Archives: Pardon Tales and Their Tellers in Sixteenth-Century France*. Stanford: Stanford University Press, 1987.

———. *Society and Culture in Early Modern France: Eight Essays*. Stanford: Stanford University Press, 1975.

Diamant, Neil, Stanley Lubman, and Kevin O'Brian. *Engaging the Law in China: State, Society, and Possibilities for Justice*. Stanford: Stanford University Press, 2005.

Duara, Prasenjit. *Culture, Power, and the State: Rural North China, 1900–1942*. Stanford: Stanford University Press, 1988.

Durkheim, Emile. *The Elementary Forms of Religious Life*. New York: Free Press, 1995.

Dykstra, Maura. "Complicated Matters: Commercial Dispute Resolution in Qing Chongqing from 1750 to 1911". PhD diss., UCLA, 2014.

Ellickson, Robert. *Order Without Law: How Neighbors Settle Disputes*. Cambridge: Harvard University Press, 1994.

Emsley, Clive. *Crime and Society in England, 1750–1900*. London: Longman, 1987.

Entenmann, Robert Eric. "Migration and Settlement in Sichuan, 1644–1796." PhD diss., Harvard University, 1982.

Esherick, Joseph W. *The Origins of the Boxer Uprising*. Berkeley: University of California Press, 1987.

Faure, Bernard. *The Red Thread: Buddhist Approaches to Sexuality*, expanded and revised edition. Princeton: Princeton University Press, 1998.

Faure, David. *Emperor and Ancestor: State and Lineage in South China*. Stanford: Stanford University Press, 2004.

Gambetta, Diego. *The Sicilian Mafia: The Business of Private Protection*. Cambridge: Harvard University Press, 1996.

Gates, Hill. *China's Motor: A Thousand Years of Petty Capitalism*. Ithaca: Cornell University Press, 1996.

Goodman, Bryna. *Native Place, City and Nation: Regional Networks and Identities in Shanghai, 1853–1937*. Berkeley: University of California Press, 1995.

Granovetter, Mark. *Society and Economy: Framework and Principles*. Cambridge: The Belknap Press of Harvard University Press, 2017.

The Guardian. "Global Homicide: Murder Rates around the World." October 13, 2009, http://www.guardian.co.uk/news/datablog/2009/oct/13/homicide-rates-country murder-data.

Harley, J. Brian and David Woodward. *The History of Cartography, Volume 2, Book 2: Cartography in the Traditional East and Southeast Asian Societies*. Chicago: University Of Chicago Press, 1995.

He, Yaozu. *Chongqing yaolan* (Chongqing) 1945.

Hershatter, Gail. *The Workers of Tianjin, 1900–1949*. Berkeley: University of California Press, 1985.

Ho, Ping-ti [He, Bingdi]. *The Ladder of Success in Imperial China: Aspects of Social Mobility, 1868–1911*. New York: Columbia University Press, 1962.

Hostetler, Laura. *Qing Colonial Enterprise: Ethnography and Cartography in Early Modern China*. Chicago: University of Chicago Press, 2001.

Hsiao, Kung-chuan [Xiao, Gongquan]. *Rural China: Imperial Control in the Nineteenth Century*. Seattle: University of Washington, 1960.

Huang, Liuhong. *A Complete Book Concerning Happiness and Benevolence: A Manual for Local Magistrates in Seventeenth-Century China*. Tucson: University of Arizona Press, 1984.

———. *Fukkei zensho*. Tokyo: Kyūko Shoin, 1973.

Huang, Philip. "Centralized Minimalism: Semiformal Governance by Quasi Officials and Dispute Resolution in China." *Modern China* 34, no. 1 (2008): 24–25.

———. *Civil Justice in China: Representation and Practice in the Qing*. Stanford: Stanford University Press, 1996.

———. "Public Sphere/Civil Society in China?: The Third Realm Between State and Society." *Modern China* 19, no. 2, Symposium: "Public Sphere/Civil Society in China" Paradigmatic Issues in Chinese Studies (April 1993), 216–240.

Isett, Christopher M. *State, Peasant, and Merchant in Qing Manchuria, 1644–1862*. Stanford: Stanford University Press, 2006.

Imperial Maritime Customs. *Imperial Maritime Customs, I. Statistical Series: No. 6. Decennial Reports on the Trade, Industries, etc. of the Ports Open to Foreign Commerce, and on Conditions and the Development of the Treaty Port Provinces, 1882–1891*.

Japan. *Nihon tokei nenkan* [Japan Statistical Yearbook]. Tokyo: Nihon Tokei Kyokai: Mainichi Shinbunsha, 1949.

Javers, Quinn. "The Logic of Lies: False Accusation and Legal Culture in Late Imperial Sichuan." *Late Imperial China* 35, no. 2 (December 2014): 27–55.

Johnson, David. *Spectacle and Sacrifice: The Ritual Foundations of Village Life in North China*. Cambridge: Harvard University Asia Center, 2010.

Johnson, Eric A. *Urbanization and Crime: Germany, 1871–1914*. Cambridge: Cambridge University Press, 1995.

Johnson, Walter. *Soul by Soul: Life Inside the Antebellum Slave Market*. Cambridge: Harvard University Press, 1999.

Karasawa, Yasuhiko. "Between Oral and Written Cultures: Buddhist Monks in Qing Legal Plaints." In *Writing and Law in Late Imperial China*, edited by Robert E. Hegel and Katherine N. Carlitz, 64–80. Seattle: University of Washington Press, 2007.

Karasawa, Yasuhiko, Matthew Harvey Sommer, and Bradly Ward Reed. "Qing County Archives in Sichuan: An Update from the Field." *Late Imperial China* 26, no. 2 (2005): 114–128.

Kerkvliet, Benedict. "Everyday Politics in Peasant Societies (and ours)." *The Journal of Peasant Studies* 36, no. 1 (2009): 227–243.

Katz, Paul. *Divine Justice: Religion and the Development of Chinese Legal Culture*. New York: Routledge, 2009.

Kertzer, David I. *Ritual, Politics, and Power*. New Haven: Yale University Press, 1989.

Kivelson, Valerie. *Cartographies of Tsardom: The Land and Its Meanings in Seventeenth-century Russia*. Ithaca: Cornell University Press, 2006.

Kuhn, Philip A. *Rebellion and Its Enemies in Late Imperial China: Militarization and Social Structure, 1796–1864*. Cambridge: Harvard University Press, 1980.

———. *Soulstealers: The Chinese Sorcery scare of 1768*. Cambridge: Harvard University Press, 1990.

Laozi. *Dao De Jing*. Translated by D.C. Lau. Baltimore: Penguin Books, 1963.

Li, Xiaoxiong. *Poppies and Politics in China: Sichuan Province, 1840s to 1940s*. Newark: University of Delaware Press, 2009.

Liang, Linxia. *Delivering Justice in Qing China: Civil Trials in the Magistrate's Court*. Oxford: Oxford University Press, 2007.

Lu, Hanchao. *Beyond the Neon Lights: Everyday Shanghai in the Early Twentieth Century*. Berkeley: University of California Press, 1999.

Lu, Weijing. *True to Her Word: The Faithful Maiden Cult in Late Imperial China*. Stanford: Stanford University Press, 2008.

Ma, Xiaobin and Liu Jun. "*Sichuan Qingdai dang'an pingshu*" (Qing Archives in Sichuan). In *Sichuan Qingdai dang'an yanjiu* (The Study of Qing Archives in Sichuan), edited by Li Shigen. Chengdu: Xinan jiaotong daxue, 2004.

Macauley, Melissa. *Social Power and Legal Culture: Litigation Masters in Late Imperial China*. Stanford: Stanford University Press, 1998.

Mann, Susan. "Grooming a Daughter for Marriage: Brides and Wives in the Mid-Qing Period." In *Chinese Femininities, Chinese Masculinities*, edited by Susan Brownwell and Jeffrey Wasserstrom. Berkeley: University of California Press, 2002.

———. *Precious Records: Women in China's Long Eighteenth Century*. Stanford: Stanford University Press, 1997.

Matsubara, Kentaro. "Land Registration and Local Society in Qing China: Taxation and Property Rights in Mid-Nineteenth Century Guangdong," *The International Journal of Asian Studies* 8, no. 2 (2011): 163–187.

———. "The Property Regime and the Dynamics of State Formation in Qing China.'" Unpublished paper prepared for the International Conference on Chinese Law and History, Fudan University, Shanghai, July 2015.

McGoey, Linsey. "Strategic Unknowns: Towards a Sociology of Ignorance," *Economy and Society* 41, no. 1 (February 2012): 1–16.

McIsaac, Mary Lee. "The Limits of Chinese Nationalism: Workers in Wartime Chongqing, 1937–1945." PhD diss., Yale University, 1994.

Mencius. *Mencius*. Translated by D.C. Lau, Harmondsworth: Penguin, 1970.

Menegon, Eugenio. *Ancestors, Virgins, and Friars: Christianity as a Local Religion in Late Imperial China*. Cambridge: Harvard University Asia Center, 2009.

Merry, Sally Engle. *Getting Justice and Getting Even: Legal Consciousness among Working-Class Americans*. Chicago: University of Chicago Press, 1990.

Menegon, Eugenio. *Ancestors, Virgins, and Friars: Christianity as a Local Religion in Late Imperial China*. Cambridge: Harvard University Press, 2010.

Meyer-Fong, Tobie. *What Remains: Coming to Terms with Civil War in 19th Century China*. Stanford: Stanford University Press, 2013.

Migdal, Joel. *State in Society: Studying How States and Societies Transform and Constitute One Another*. New York: Cambridge University Press, 2001.

Mnookin, Robert H. and Lewis Kornhauser. "Bargaining in the Shadow of the Law: The Case of Divorce," *The Yale Law Journal* 88, no. 5 (April 1, 1979): 950–997.

Mol, Annemarie. *The Body Multiple: Ontology in Medical Practice*. Durham: Duke University Press, 2007.

Mosca, Matthew. *From Frontier Policy to Foreign Policy: The Question of India and the Transformation of Geopolitics in Qing China*. Stanford: Stanford University Press, 2013.

Muir, Edward. *Ritual in Early Modern Europe*. Cambridge: Cambridge University Press, 2005.

Naquin, Susan. "Funerals in North China." In *Death Ritual in Late Imperial and Modern China*, edited by James L. Watson and Evelyn Sakakida Rawski, 37–70. Berkeley: University of California Press, 1988.

———. *Millenarian rebellion in China: The Eight Trigrams Uprising of 1813*. New Haven: Yale University Press, 1992.

Neeb, Gunter R. *Blood Stasis: China's Classical Concept in Modern Medicine*. London: Churchill Livingstone, 2006.

O'Brian, Kevin. *Rightful Resistance in Rural China*. Cambridge: Cambridge University Press, 2006.

Ownby, David. *Brotherhoods and Secret Societies in Early and Mid-Qing China: The Formation of a Tradition*. Stanford: Stanford University Press, 1996.

Perry, Elizabeth J. *Rebels and Revolutionaries in North China, 1845–1945*. Stanford: Stanford University Press, 1983.

———. *Shanghai on Strike: The Politics of Chinese Labor*. Stanford: Stanford University Press, 1993.

Phillips, Michael. R., Huaqing Liu, and Yanping. Zhang. "Suicide and Social Change in China." *Culture, Medicine and Psychiatry* 23, no. 1 (March 1999): 25–50.

Pietilä, Tuulikki. *Gossip, Markets, and Gender: How Dialogue Constructs Value and Post-Socialist Kilimanjaro*. Madison: University of Wisconsin Press, 2007.

Piot, Charles. *Remotely Global: Village Modernity in West Africa*. Chicago: University of Chicago Press, 1999.

Pomeranz, Kenneth. *The Making of a Hinterland: State, Society, and Economy in Inland North China, 1853–1937*. Berkeley: University of California Press, 1993.

Proctor, Robert N. "Agnotology: A Missing Term to Describe the Cultural Production of Ignorance (and Its Study)." In *Agnotology: The Making and Unmaking of Ignorance*, edited by Robert N. Proctor and Londa Schiebinger, 1–36. Stanford: Stanford University Press, 2008.

Rawls, John, *A Theory of Justice*, revised edition. Cambridge: The Belknap Press of Harvard University Press, 1999.

Reddy, William. *The Navigation of Feeling: A Framework for the History of Emotions* Cambridge: Cambridge University Press, 2001.

Redfield, Robert. "Primitive Law." In *Law and Warfare: Studies in the Anthropology of Conflict*, edited by Paul Bohannan. New York: The Natural History Press, 1967.

Reed, Bradly. "Bureaucracy and Judicial Truth in Qing Dynasty Homicide Cases." *Late Imperial China* 39, no. 1 (2018): 67–105.

———. *Talons and Teeth: County Clerks and Runners in the Qing Dynasty*. Stanford: Stanford University Press, 2000.

Rieder, Jonathan. "The Social Organization of Vengeance." In Donald J. Black, ed. *Toward a General Theory of Social Control*. New York: Academic Press, 1984.

Robinson, David. *Bandits, Eunuchs and the Son of Heaven*. Honolulu: University of Hawai'i Press, 2001.

Ropp, Paul, ed. *Passionate Women: Female Suicide in Late Imperial China*. Leiden: Brill, 2011.

Roth, Randolph. *American Homicide*. Cambridge: Belknap Press of Harvard University Press, 2009.

Rowe, William. *Crimson Rain: Seven Centuries of Violence in a Chinese County*. Stanford: Stanford University Press, 2006.

———. *Hankow: Commerce and Society in a Chinese City, 1796–1889*. Stanford: Stanford University Press, 1984.

Sang, Tze-lan. *The Emerging Lesbian: Female Same-Sex Desire in Modern China*. Chicago: University of Chicago Press, 2003.

Schurmann, H. Franz. "Traditional Property Concepts in China." *The Far Eastern Quarterly* 15, no. 4 (August 1956): 507–516.

Scott, James C. *Against the Grain: A Deep History of the Earliest States*. New Haven: Yale University Press, 2017.

———.*The Art of Not Being Governed: An Anarchist History of Upland Southeast Asia*. New Haven: Yale University Press, 2009.

———. *Domination and the Arts of Resistance: Hidden Transcripts*. New Haven: Yale University Press, 1990.

———. *Weapons of the Weak: Everyday Forms of Peasant Resistance*. New Haven: Yale University Press, 1985.

Service, Grace. *Golden Inches: The China Memoir of Grace Service*. Berkeley: University of California Press, 1989.

Shepard, John Robert. *Statecraft and Political Economy on the Taiwan Frontier, 1600–1800*. Stanford: Stanford University Press, 1993.

Skinner, William, G. "Introduction: Urban Development in Imperial China." In *The City in Imperial China*, edited by G. William Skinner, 3–33. Stanford: Stanford University Press, 1977.

Smail, Daniel Lord. *The Consumption of Justice: Emotions, Publicity, and Legal Culture in Marseille, 1264–1423*. Ithaca: Cornell University Press, 2003.

Smith, Arthur Henderson. *Village life in China*. Boston: Little, Brown, 1970.

Sommer, Matthew H. "The Gendered Body in the Qing Courtroom." *Journal of the History of Sexuality* 22, no. 2 (May 2013): 281–311.

———. "Making Sex Work: Polyandry as a Survival Strategy in Qing Dynasty China." In *Gender in Motion: Division of Labor and Cultural Change in Late Imperial and Modern China*, edited by Bryna Goodman and Wendy Larson. Lanham: Roman and Littlefield, 2005.

———. *Polyandry and Wife-selling in Qing Dynasty China: Survival Strategies and Judicial Interventions*. Berkeley: University of California Press, 2015.

———. *Sex, Law and Society in Late Imperial China*. Stanford: Stanford University, 2000.

Song, Ci. *The Washing Away of Wrongs: Forensic Medicine in Thirteenth-Century China*. Translated by Brian McKnight. Ann Arbor: Center for Chinese Studies, University of Michigan, 1981.

———. *Xi Yuan Ji Lu: 5 Juan* [Collected Writings on the Washing Away of Wrongs]. Beijing: Falü chubanshe, 1958.

Spence, Jonathan D. *Treason by the Book*. New York: Viking, 2001.

Spencer, J. E. "Changing Chungking: The Rebuilding of an Old China City." *Geographical Review* 29, no. 1 (1939).

Spierenburg, Pieter. *A History of Murder: Personal Violence in Europe from the Middle Ages to the Present*. Cambridge: Polity, 2008.

Stapleton, Kristin. *Civilizing Chengdu: Chinese Urban Reform, 195–1937.* Cambridge: Harvard University Asia Center, 2000.

Strathern Marilyn. *The Gender of the Gift: Problems with Women and Problems with Society in Melanesia.* Berkeley: University of California Press, 1988.

Sullivan, Shannon and Nancy Tuana, eds. *Race and the Epistemologies of Ignorance.* Albany: State University of New York Press, 2007.

Szonyi, Michael. *The Art of Being Governed.* Princeton: Princeton University Press, 2017.

———. *Practicing Kinship: Lineage and Descent in Late Imperial China.* Stanford: Stanford University Press, 2002

Teng, Emma. *Taiwan's Imagined Geography: Chinese Colonial Travel Writing and Pictures, 1683–1895.* Cambridge: Harvard University Asia Center, 2004.

ter Harr, Barend J. *Telling Stories: Witchcraft and Scapegoating in Chinese History.* Leiden: Brill, 2006.

———. *White Lotus Teachings in Chinese Religious History.* Leiden: Brill, 1992.

Theiss, Janet M. *Disgraceful Matters the Politics of Chastity in Eighteenth-Century China.* Berkeley: University of California Press, 2004.

Thompson, E. P. "History and Anthropology." In *Making History: Writings on History and Culture.* New York: New Press, 1994.

———. "Rough Music." In *Customs in Common: Studies in Popular Culture.* London: Merlin Press, 2009.

Thongchakul Winichakul. *Siam Mapped: A History of the Geo-Body of a Nation.* Honolulu: University of Hawaii Press, 1997.

United States. *Bureau of the Census, Vital Statistics Rates in the U.S., 1900–1940 Sixteenth Census of the U.S.: 1940.* Washington: U.S. G.P.O., 1943.

———. *Dispatches from the US Consulate in Chungking, 1896–1906.*

Varese, Federico. *The Russian Mafia: Private Protection in a New Market Economy.* New York: Oxford University Press, 2005.

Wakefield, David. *Fenjia: Household Division and Inheritance in Qing and Republican China.* Honolulu: University of Hawaii Press, 1998.

Walter, Ann Beth. *Getting an Heir: Adoption and the Construction of Kinship in Late Imperial China.* Honolulu: University of Hawaii Press, 1990.

Wang, Di. "Chengshi renkou yu chengshi jingji, shehui zuzhi" [Urban population and the city's economic and social organization]. In *Chongqing Chengshi Yanjiu* [Studies of the Urban History of Chongqing], edited by Wei Yingtao (Chengdu: Sichuan Daxue chubanshe, 1989).

———. *Kuachu fengbi di shjie: Changjiang shangyou quyu shehui ya jiu, 1644–1911* [Striding Out of a Closed World: Research on Society in the Upper Yangzi Macroregion, 1644–1911]. Beijing: Zhonghua shuju, 2001.

———. *Street Culture in Chengdu: Public Space, Urban Commoners and Local Politics, 1870–1930.* Stanford: Stanford University, 2003.

———. *The Teahouse: Small Business, Everyday Culture, and Public Politics in Chengdu, 1900–1950.* Stanford: Stanford University Press, 2008.

———. *Violence and Order on the Chengdu Plain.* Stanford: Stanford University Press, 2018.

Watson, James L. "The Structure of Chinese Funerary Rites." In *Death Ritual in Late Imperial and Modern China,* edited by James L. Watson and Evelyn Sakakida Rawski, 3–19. Berkeley: University of California Press, 1988.

Watt, John R. *The District Magistrate in Late Imperial China.* New York: Columbia University Press, 1972.

Wei, Yingtao, *Jindai Chongqing chengshi shi* [*Modern urban history of Chongqing*]. Chengdu: Sichuan daxue chubanshe, 1991.

Will, Pierre-Etienne. "Developing Forensic Knowledge through Cases in the Qing Dynasty." In *Thinking with Cases: Specialist Knowledge in Chinese Cultural History,* edited by Charlotte Furth, Judith T. Zeitlin, and Ping-chen Hsiung, 62–100. Honolulu: University of Hawai'i Press, 2007.

Wolf, Arthur P. *Sexual Attraction and Childhood Association: A Chinese Brief for Edward Westermarck.* Stanford: Stanford University Press, 1995.

Wolf, Arthur P. and Chieh-shan Huang. *Marriage and adoption in China, 1845–1945.* Stanford: Stanford University Press, 1980.

Wolf, Margery. *Women and the Family in Rural Taiwan.* Stanford: Stanford University Press, 1972.

Wyman, Judith. "Opium and the State in Late-Qing Sichuan," In *Opium Regimes: China, Britain, and Japan, 1839–1952,* edited by Timothy Brook and Bob Tadashi Wakabayashi Berkeley: University of California Press, 2000.

Xing'an Hui Lan san bian [Three Volumes of the Conspectus of Penal Cases]. Beijing: Beijing guji chubanshe, 2004.

Xue, Xiaoxun. *Trial of Modernity: Judicial Reform in Early Twentieth-Century China, 1901–1937.* Stanford: Stanford University Press, 2008.

Xue, Yunsheng. *Du Li Cun Yi* [Lingering Doubts after Reading the Substatutes], edited and punctuated by Huang Jingjia. Taibei: Chinese Materials and Research Aids Service Center, 1970.

Zelin, Madeline. "The Rights of tenants in Mid-Qing Sichuan: A Study of Land-Related Lawsuits in the Baxian Archives." *The Journal of Asian Studies* 45, no. 3 (May, 1996): 499–526.

Zelizer, Viviana A. *Economic Lives: How Culture Shapes the Economy.* Princeton: Princeton University Press, 2011.

Zhang, Taisu. "Social Hierarchies and the Formation of Customary Property Law in Pre-industrial China and England." *The American Journal of Comparative Law* 62, no. 171 (Winter 2014): 231–253.

Zhang, Ting. "Marketing Legal Information: Commercial Publications of the Great Qing Code, 1644–1911." In *Chinese Law: Knowledge, Practice, and Transformation, 1530s to 1950s,* edited by Li Chen and Madeline Zelin, 231–253. Leiden: Brill, 2015.

Zheng, Xiaowei. *The Politics of Rights and the 1911 Revolution in China.* Stanford: Stanford University Press, 2018.

Zhou, Xun. *Shuhai congtan* [Comments on the World of Sichuan]. Taipei: Wenhai chubanshe, 1966.

Index

Note: page numbers followed by 'n' refer to endnotes.